Bringing Back the Child

Bringing Back the Child:
Language Development
after Extreme Deprivation
(Children and Childhoods 4)

By

Lisa J. Brown and Peter E. Jones

With a Foreword by Joy Stackhouse

CAMBRIDGE
SCHOLARS
P U B L I S H I N G

Bringing Back the Child:
Language Development after Extreme Deprivation
(Children and Childhoods 4),

by Lisa J. Brown and Peter E. Jones

This book first published 2014

Cambridge Scholars Publishing

12 Back Chapman Street, Newcastle upon Tyne, NE6 2XX, UK

British Library Cataloguing in Publication Data
A catalogue record for this book is available from the British Library

ISBN (10): 1-4438-5972-9, ISBN (13): 978-1-4438-5972-1

Lisa would like to dedicate this book to the memory of her mother,
Pauline Jane Brown, née Allen.

TABLE OF CONTENTS

ACKNOWLEDGEMENTS

We would like to warmly thank Joy Stackhouse for invaluable help and support in guiding the doctoral study to successful completion and for writing her present Foreword to the book. We would also like to express our appreciation of the help and support of other members of staff of the Department of Human Communication Sciences of the University of Sheffield, in particular Mick Perkins and Patty Cowell.

We are particularly grateful to Tom Klee of the Department of Communication Disorders, Canterbury University, New Zealand, who was the external examiner for the doctoral thesis, for his continued support and encouragement of this research project.

We would like to express our gratitude to John Locke, who initiated the doctoral research project on which this book is based and who led it and contributed to it during the first two years.

At Sheffield Hallam University we would like to thank the Humanities Research Centre, and Head of Centre, Chris Hopkins, for financial support for the preparation of the manuscript.

Thanks also go to Sarah Streater and Hemendra N.S. Headworth for their belief in and help with the book project over the years.

Most of all, we would like to acknowledge our profound indebtedness to the real Serena, Gabrielle and Ingrid and to their families who opened up their homes, gave so generously of their time to the lead researcher, Lisa Brown, and told their stories so candidly.

LIST OF FIGURES

LIST OF TABLES

TRANSCRIPTION CONVENTIONS
FOR CONVERSATIONAL DATA

{ }	Non-verbal activity
( )	Inaudible or unclear material
[[	Overlapping speech
__	Emphasis on syllables or words
_	Possible grammatical omission.
= =	Utterances that are latched with no gap (on either side of the = symbol).
:	Elongation of sound
hh	Audible exhalation of breath.
-	Sound cut-off or false start (e.g., "I thi-").
(.)	Micropause mid-turn
(2)	Length of pause in seconds mid-turn.
?	Question intonation.
.	Statement intonation.
{pause:}	Marks a break in the conversation or pause between turns and includes information about the context as in *{pause: A. is licking her lolly}*

FOREWORD

This longitudinal study of three Romanian orphans adopted at ages 7, 6 and nearly 4 years following extreme deprivation is an essential read for anyone interested in language development and the relationship between language and cognition in children. The children were 10, 11 and 13 years old at the beginning of a two year data collection period and so the study is unusual in providing detailed qualitative linguistic analyses of a less well researched older age range in parallel with standardized measures of language and cognition. As a result it is possible to examine the strengths and limitations of different perspectives on children with significant language delays, and the data raises questions about the nature of language "delay" versus "disorder" in such children. It is also unusual to have so much contextual information about the children's lives – both past and in particular subsequent adoptive home life - which allows the role of positive as well as negative environmental factors to be considered.

Three clear questions are addressed in this book. The first focuses on how language develops in older children and includes analysis of conversation data. The second examines the notion of critical periods in development and specifically focuses on grammar. The third questions the existence of cognitive "modularity" and leads to a search for dissociations between linguistic and non-linguistic abilities. In short this is a fascinating and provocative theoretical study of children's language development in unique circumstances and it should fuel further academic debate.

However, this book not only tackles conflicting theories and demonstrates a range of linguistic analyses. There are also some important messages for practitioners involved in identifying language delay in children from impoverished backgrounds. The limitations of standardized tests with norms derived from suppositions of what are "typical" children are highlighted in this study and fit with current concerns that such measures may not capture the true language abilities of children from areas of less extreme but still significant social disadvantage. Perhaps above all the reader will come away with a sense of hope for children with severe language delay and renewed energy to continue to support children's language development well beyond the early years. This final message may be helpful for speech and language therapists, teachers, and other professionals involved in securing funding to provide services for children with speech, language and communication needs, as well as reassuring for parents and carers.

Joy Stackhouse

Professor of Human Communication Sciences
University of Sheffield, UK.
March 2014

BRINGING BACK THE CHILD: INTRODUCTION

1. Aims and scope of the book

This book gives a detailed account of the acquired linguistic competence of three Romanian orphan girls, Serena, Gabrielle and Ingrid, as they will be known here, who were adopted by British families after surviving prolonged global deprivation during their early years.[1] Serena was 7 years old, Gabrielle was 6 and Ingrid was nearly 4 when their new lives began. In bringing the girls back from the institutions where they languished for years, the girls' parents had given them back their childhood. Upon entering their homes, the girls were no longer mere "charges" requiring minimal routine maintenance but could, at last, *be children* - daughters of parents, sisters of siblings - with an identity to make and a future to forge. Here we will describe what the girls experienced in the orphanages and what happened to them when they were rescued. While our primary focus is on the language of the three girls, we will try to view their linguistic skills in the context of their overall development post-adoption.

Over the last 15 years, a substantial research literature has built up regarding the development of formerly institutionalized internationally adopted children, with a few studies focussing specifically on language (Chapter 1). However, our study of Serena, Gabrielle and Ingrid differs in key respects from this body of research.

Firstly, we are not directly concerned with issues of diagnostic assessment and therapeutic intervention, although we hope our findings may be of interest to clinicians and educationalists as well as to those working with internationally adopted children more specifically. Rather, our main

---

[1] We use the term "global deprivation" to refer to living conditions which prevent or severely restrict *all* aspects of children's development. The term "deprivation" is more apt than "isolation" since the girls were not kept on their own, although both ability and opportunity for interaction were minimal. The term "neglect" is perhaps a better fit for the girls' circumstances although the "neglect" in question was the scheduled "care package" of the relevant institutions.

intention is to provide a detailed, longitudinal case study account of each of the girls, documenting their progress in transcending the awful privations of their early lives. Such a study is, we believe, of general interest for the insights it affords into human development in exceptional circumstances. Secondly, we are interested in drawing out the implications of the girls' linguistic abilities for our general understanding of language. To that end, we will discuss their linguistic and communicative proficiencies in the light of current theoretical perspectives on language and language acquisition, paying particular attention to the relevance of the "Critical Period Hypothesis" for language (Chapter 1). Thirdly, in contrast with virtually all other studies of the language development of internationally adopted children, we have employed *both* qualitative *and* quantitative methodologies (Chapters 2-7) to allow as rich a view of the girls' linguistic competence as possible. This, then, is the first and only study, to our knowledge, which has drawn on the insights of Conversation Analysis in order to explore naturalistic conversational skills in severely deprived children (Chapter 3). And it is the only study to critically explore the differences between the qualities of naturalistic speech and the picture of language competence which results from the use of standardized test procedures (Chapter 6). Indeed, the range of methods adopted affords, we believe, the most detailed and systematic qualitative study of linguistic ability in globally deprived children since Susan Curtiss's original study of Genie (Curtiss, 1977). Finally, this study is unusual in that it is entirely devoted to the experiences and acquired competencies of the *older* adopted child and may therefore contribute in some small way to addressing the "gaping hole" (Scott, Roberts and Glennen, 2011) in our understanding of the post-adoption progress of older children.

2. Background to the research

This book is based on the doctoral thesis of one of the co-authors, Lisa Brown (Brown, 2003).[2] The research participants were drawn from the population of children adopted from Romanian childcare institutions with an early history of global deprivation. The adoptive parents of the research

---

[2] The doctoral research was conducted at the University of Sheffield. The original supervisory team comprised John Locke, then of the University of Sheffield, as Director of Studies with second co-author, Peter Jones, of Sheffield Hallam University, as First Supervisor. John Locke left the team in 2000 to be replaced by Joy Stackhouse of the University of Sheffield in 2001. Some of the data from the doctoral project has been previously presented and discussed in Brown (2006), Brown and Jones (2008), Brown, Locke and Jones (1999) and Brown et al. (1998).

participants were contacted through the Parent Network for the Post-institutionalized Child (PNPIC UK) in 1997. Parents who expressed an interest in participating were asked for brief biographical details of their adopted child or children. Preference was given to children who had spent longer than 3 years in a Romanian institution and who, to the parents' knowledge, did not have a history of neonatal trauma or a known genetic disorder. Because data were to be analysed qualitatively, only a small sample was required. Ultimately, six children (three who had clearly acquired some spoken language and three who had not) were initially selected as suitable for the study and their parents invited to participate in the research.[3] During the course of the study, it was decided to concentrate on Serena, Gabrielle, and Ingrid since their spoken language abilities were sufficiently advanced to allow the key research questions about linguistic development to be addressed.

Basic biographical details for Serena, Gabrielle, and Ingrid along with key dates for the research study are summarised in Table 1. A full account of the girls' early life histories and experiences after adoption will be given in Chapter 2.

Table 1 Biographical details and key dates[4]

	Serena	**Gabrielle**	**Ingrid**
Date Entered Adoptive Home	August 1994	October 1991	August 1991
Age at Adoption	7;5	6;3	3;10
Age at Data Collection Start	11;3	13;1	10;8
Time since Adoption	3;10	6;10	6;10
Age at Data Collection End	13;2	14;10	12;7
Time since Adoption	5;9	8;7	8;5

---

[3] For further details of the life histories and development post-adoption of all six children see Brown (2003).

[4] Participants' ages will be expressed throughout as "years; months". Thus 11;3 means 11 years and 3 months of age.

3. Conduct of the research

To begin with, parents were interviewed in order to obtain an accurate description of the girls' backgrounds and their lives in institutions. Reports, observations and assessments completed by health care professionals and schools together with parental reports and testimony were then examined in order to gain a detailed account of each child's history since adoption. Family contacts and personal visits were conducted by Lisa Brown with the permission of the parents at pre-arranged times. All meetings with the children involved informal interactions with them or direct observations of their behaviour during everyday activity, familiar routines or assessment tasks and were recorded on audio or videotape for later transcription and analysis. Data were collected in this manner at regular intervals for 2 years. All in all, an immense amount of data on the girls' behaviour and abilities was collected of which only a small selection is presented here. But it is to be hoped that readers will "hear" the girls, albeit at some distance, in the transcribed materials and will be able to come to their own judgements as to the levels of linguistic and communicative expertise on display.

The girls' linguistic, communicative and non-linguistic cognitive abilities were examined by close analysis of their naturalistic behaviours as well as by standardized tests. In addition, we compared the performances of Serena, Gabrielle and Ingrid on specific standardized tests of nonverbal cognition with those of younger, typically developing children between the ages of 3;6 and 8;0 (Chapter 7). While this procedure has no strictly scientific rationale, it was useful and interesting to see what similarities and differences could be observed between the test responses of Serena, Gabrielle and Ingrid and those of a group of flesh-and-blood younger children of varying ages.

4. Content of the book

The book is organized as follows:

Chapter 1, *Beginnings*: *life before and after* adoption: an account of the girls' early histories and their lives and development after adoption.

Chapter 2, *Language development after extreme global deprivation*: a review of literature on child development post-deprivation with a discussion of theoretical models of language and language acquisition, followed by a statement of research questions to be addressed by subsequent chapters.

Chapter 3, *Life in conversation: talk in everyday settings*: a detailed examination of the girls' everyday conversational skills informed by Conversation Analysis.

Chapter 4, *Putting language to the test*: a presentation and discussion of the girls' results on a series of standardized language tests.

Chapter 5, *Words and word formation: the acquisition of morphology*: an analysis and discussion of morphological structures and morphosyntactic processes in the girls' spontaneous speech.

Chapter 6, *Speaking in sentences: the acquisition of syntax*: an analysis and discussion of syntactic structures in the girls' spontaneous speech.

Chapter 7, *Thinking without words: putting nonverbal cognition to the test*: presentation and discussion of the girls' results on standardized tests of nonverbal intelligence.

Chapter 8, *Bringing back the child: conclusions and implications*: a summary of the findings of previous chapters in relation to the research questions and a consideration of the implications of these findings for theory and for future research.

CHAPTER ONE

LANGUAGE DEVELOPMENT AFTER EXTREME GLOBAL DEPRIVATION

1.1 Introduction

The fate of children abandoned or isolated during their first years of life has held a fascination for many cultures since the most ancient times. What potential for learning and for language learning in particular will such children retain? What will be their prospects in life upon re-entering society? Traditional interest in this topic has usually centred on so-called "feral children", left in the wild to fend for themselves or occasionally, at least according to legend, to be raised by friendly animals. In the late 20th century, scientific attention turned to the developmental progress of infants deprived of everyday social contact for prolonged periods, most famously Genie, the "modern day wild child" (Curtiss, 1977). Such cases then became a central focus of debate in linguistics, psycholinguistics and psychology over the relative contributions of "nature" and "nurture" in the acquisition of a first language. The process by which children learn language and the character of the linguistic knowledge thereby attained have become some of the most widely studied and hotly contested questions in the history of western science.

In this chapter, we set the scene for our later discussion of the linguistic abilities of Serena, Gabrielle and Ingrid by giving an overview of previous studies of the development of socially deprived and neglected children, including Romanian orphans, followed by a brief account of the theoretical debates on language and language acquisition relevant to the interpretation of the linguistic material to be presented.

1.2 Development after social deprivation

1.2.1 "Feral children"

Throughout history, there have been many reports of "feral" children, sometimes with accounts of attempts to rehabilitate them into civilised society (for reviews and discussion see Malson, 1972; McNeil, Polloway and Smith, 1984; Candland 1993; Comrie, 2000; Hoff, 2001). Perhaps the best known case is that of Victor of Aveyron, as documented by Itard, the 18th century French psychologist who took charge of Victor (Lane, 1976). There is also the intriguing case of Kaspar Hauser who mysteriously entered Copenhagen society in 1828 with little or no speech, having been socially isolated for the first seventeen years of his life (Clarke and Clarke, 1976, 2000; Simon, 1979). In addition there have been occasional reports of infants and young children reared by wild animals, such as that of the "wolf girls", Amala and Kamala of Midnapore, allegedly discovered at the respective ages of 2 and 7 huddling in a den with a family of wolves (Singh and Zingg, 1939; Benzzaquen, 2001). Fujinaga et al. (1990) reported on the 1972 discovery in Japan of two animal-like children aged 5 and 6 who had been forced to live in an outside shed since infancy. Even more recently, the cases of Oxana Malaya in the Ukraine and "Alex the Dog Boy" in Chile (in 2001) (*Feral Child, 2014*) came to light, both children having allegedly spent their early years living with, and learning from, dogs, although there is little factual corroboration of these stories.

The linguistic outcomes in such cases, when reported, are usually very poor. Victor and the "wolf girls" apparently never learned to speak, despite many hours of careful tuition, while, at the other extreme, Kaspar Hauser regaled polite Copenhagen society in articulate language, kept poetic company with the aristocracy and even wrote his memoirs (Nicole, 1979). However, cases of "feral children" have been dismissed as scientifically irrelevant by scholars such as Bettelheim (1959) who argue that these children were suffering from learning difficulties, autism or emotional disturbances and had only recently been deposited by their parents in wild and remote countryside on account of these problems (Clarke and Clarke, 1976, 2000).

1.2.2 Global deprivation in childhood

1.2.2.1   Deprivation in the family home

Reliably documented reports of cases of childhood isolation and its aftermaths are discussed by Skuse (1984a, 1984b), Clarke and Clarke (2000) and Koluchova (1972; 1976; 1979, 1991) of which the most well known are those of the "Koluchova twins", Isabelle, Alice and Beth, Louise, Anna, Mary and Genie.

The Koluchova twins were discovered in 1967 at the age of 7 after 5 and a half years in almost complete isolation (Koluchova, 1991). The boys' speech was limited to a few words and they communicated using gestures and imitation. They could barely walk and fine motor coordination and play were severely compromised. Their developmental level was considered to be similar to 3-year old children and they were given a very poor prognosis. The twins' progress was followed over the next 22 years using observation and psychometric tests. The twins were placed with a sympathetic foster family where they showed "an immense acceleration in development" (Clarke and Clarke, 1976, p.30) and their speech developed rapidly. At age 11, their expressive language was "quite normal both in form and content (Koluchova, 1991, p.24). At 18, the boys' IQs of 114 and 112 were within the range that would be considered typical for their age. 12 years later, aged 30, the twins had IQs above the national average, were married and had professional careers. The twins' cases are considered by Koluchova (1991, p. 27) to have "already proved the possibility of recovery from psychic deprivation and its durability."

Isabelle (Mason, 1942) was discovered at 6;6 after having been imprisoned since infancy in a darkened room with her mother who was unable to hear and speak (Clarke and Clarke, 1976, p.41). When rescued, Isabelle could not walk or talk but used non-verbal gestures and showed curiosity about her surroundings (Mason, 1942). Her performance on an unspecified psychological test was equivalent to that of a 3 year old. Isabelle was observed for 2 years and her language development recorded in diaries. According to Mason, Isabelle's language acquisition at 6;6 proceeded like that of a 1-2 year old child, though at a more rapid rate. At 8, Isabelle had a vocabulary of around 2000 words and had also learned to speak in full sentences, ask questions, sing and tell stories. She was also reported to be of "normal intelligence" (Skuse, 1984b, p.557). Clarke and Clarke state:

"The case is sufficiently well documented to make it clear that one child showed substantial recovery to normality from a level of severe retardation. Moreover, deprivation of language experience during the normal period of development of this function did not prove to be critical" (1976, p.29).

Twins Alice and Beth (Douglas and Sutton, 1978) were discovered at 4;11. Their development was assessed using standardized tests until at least 6;4 when their level of language was nearly age appropriate on the Reynell Developmental Language Scale, while their verbal and performance IQs were within the normal range.

Louise (Skuse, 1984a) was discovered at 3;6 and her development was documented until 14;5, at which time a school report described her expressive and receptive language as age appropriate (Skuse, 1984b).

These cases report considerable, if not complete, recovery of language learning ability after experiencing global deprivation until 3;6 and beyond. As Skuse (1984b, p.557) contends, once the children's environments improved for the better, language developed rapidly and they "reached virtually age-appropriate levels within a few years."

However, these positive reports are counter-balanced by accounts of relatively poor post-deprivation outcomes for Anna (Davis, 1940, 1947), Genie (Curtiss, 1981, 1988a, 1988b) and Mary (Skuse, 1984a), none of whom exhibited the rapid developmental catch-up of the previous cases and whose linguistic progress was reported to be minimal at best, although this has been disputed in the case of Genie which deserves special attention.

1.2.2.2   The Genie case

By far the most well known case involving a globally deprived child is that of Genie (Curtiss, 1977). The "Genie case" has been treated to numerous re-tellings in academic and popular literature and media to the point where a particular, and arguably flawed, interpretation of the case has become part of linguistic and psycholinguistic mythology.[1]

---

[1] The movie *Mockingbird Don't Sing* (2001, Dorian Films) is a lightly fictionalized account of the Genie case which ends with the on-screen announcement: "Katie's [i.e., Genie's] inability to master a language proved the legitimacy of the Critical Period Hypothesis".

The basic background facts are familiar to anyone with any acquaintance with the topic of language acquisition. Genie was discovered in 1970 at the age of 13;7. She was extremely neglected from infancy to adolescence, permanently restrained and beaten by her father if she tried to speak. Having reached adolescence without any appreciable linguistic ability, Genie was considered ideal material for an investigation of language development after prolonged isolation and, more particularly, as a test case for Lenneberg's Critical Period Hypothesis (see below), although Lenneberg himself , consistent with his expressed views on the scientific intractability of "feral children" cases (1967, pp. 141-142), "declined to participate, saying no definite conclusions could be drawn because the level of trauma associated with Genie's confinement and her father's beatings would be impossible to discern" (*Genie (feral child)*, 2013).

The case was further muddied from the outset by suggestions that Genie showed signs of neurological impairment which may have affected her linguistic development. Nevertheless, it has been argued, that, quite categorical evaluations of her linguistic progress and potential have been made by the principal linguistic researcher in the case. A picture has been repeatedly painted of a girl who was intellectually agile but whose language development was restricted to short and random combinations of uninflected content words as a consequence of passing Lenneberg's critical period deadline. However, as Jones (1995) argues, this picture is misleading and quite inaccurate on many points of detail if the account of Genie's progress in Curtiss's original study of Genie (1977) is to be accepted.

Via a detailed and systematic comparison of the data and analysis presented in Curtiss (1977), which Jones refers to as "the (1977) account)", with the accounts given by Curtiss in later publications ("the post-(1977) account"), Jones argues that the progress in Genie's language development reported in the former is underplayed without explanation or appears to have been misrepresented in the latter. A few examples will serve to illustrate Jones's point.

The post-(1977) account has it that Genie was unable to learn grammar and, consequently, that her language was "syntactically primitive and undeveloped" (Curtiss, Fromkin and Krashen, 1978, p. 29) while her "lexical and propositional semantic abilities" were "good" and "nonlinguistic cognitive function" was "relatively normal" (Curtiss, 1988b in Jones, 1977, p. 274). Genie was, in other words, a striking confirmation of a revised, "modularized" version of Lenneberg's Critical Period Hypothesis with "dissociations" both within language and between language and non-linguistic cognition (see below). It is this post-(1977) interpretation of Genie's linguistic development that has become the fundamental "fact" of the Genie case as presented in most scholarly accounts (see, for example, Foster-Cohen, 1999). However, the original (1977) account tells a different story – *with the same data*. While noting that "Genie's language is far from normal" (1977: 204), Curtiss "paints a picture of unusual, but steady, uninterrupted, and unfinished development in both morphology and syntax in Genie's speech" (Jones, 1995, p. 264) over the 4-5 years of her study. Curtiss carefully charts significant milestones in Genie's growing linguistic competence, from 2-word utterances in July 1971 and 3-word utterances with "all basic constituents" in November 1971, to "internal negatives" at the end of 1974 and embedded sentences ("now definitely acquired") in 1975 (Jones, 1995, pp. 264-265). While describing Genie's speech as still "largely telegraphic" (Curtiss, 1977, p. 193) at the end of the study, Curtiss cautions against superficial judgements about Genie's underlying linguistic competence:

> "in contrast to normal children, Genie's utterances continued to appear 'telegraphic', even long after exceptional utterances revealed that she had acquired much of the morphological machinery omitted from these 'telegraphic' strings" (1977, pp. 196-197).

The most glaring discrepancies between (1977) and post-(1977) accounts are in the area of syntax. The post-(1977) account has it that "much of the grammar remained unacquired" (Curtiss, 1988b, p. 98). To illustrate her claim, Curtiss cites 11 of Genie's utterances (undated and without communicative context) which demonstrate, amongst other things, "the inconsistent and ungrammatical order of subject, verb object" and "the omission of obligatory constituents" (p. 98). The (1977) account, on the other hand, has it that:

> "Genie's utterances, like those of normal children acquiring English, follow strict word order: Modifier-Noun, Possessor-Possessed, Subject-Verb-Object, Preposition-Noun Phrase. There are exceptions to S-V-O order, but as with data on normal children … such order reversals are rare" (Curtiss, 1977, p. 193).

Furthermore, the "obligatory constituents" allegedly "missing" from Genie's utterances are confidently listed amongst Genie's linguistic acquisitions in Curtiss (1977) (Jones, 1995, p. 276).

Contrary to the later assertions of the post-(1977) account, the (1977) account, therefore, appears to demonstrate that "Genie was able to acquire the morphology and syntax of English and was still in the process of acquiring it when she was 18 years old" (Jones, 1995, p. 278).

Jones finds a simple explanation for the interpretative about-face in the circumstances of Genie's life as reported for the first time in Rymer (1993). Genie, whose linguistic development was still continuing at the time (Jones, 1995, pp. 264-265), was removed from the care of a family (the Riglers) in June 1975 and was placed in a series of temporary foster homes where she suffered ill-treatment:

> "Genie's reaction to the regime was to regress, seemingly intentionally, shedding by degrees the skills in comportment and communication that she had developed over the previous several years" (Rymer, 1993, p.155).

In other words, Genie's failure to maintain her linguistic progress was, in part at least, a response to the traumatic events which she experienced from the summer of 1975, a vital context which is missing from the post-(1977) account. The Genie case, then, actually tells us nothing about what Genie might have been capable of in different circumstances.

After nearly 20 years since its publication, Jones (1995) remains the only independent review of the linguistic evidence in the Genie case, despite the unprecedented attention that the case has attracted and its theoretical importance.

1.2.3 Institutionalized deprivation

1.2.3.1   Childcare institutions

Children are also known to have suffered social deprivation, to various degrees, within childcare institutions, as longitudinal studies by Spitz (1945, 1946), Goldfarb (1943, 1945, 1947, 1955), Goldfarb and Klopper (1944), Skeels (1937, 1945, 1965, 1966), Skeels and Harms (1948) and Skodak and Skeels (1947, 1949) have shown. Goldfarb found that the effects of early institutionalization were both pervasive and long lasting, affecting motor ability, social relatedness, personality, non-verbal intellect and language:

"There is cumulative evidence that an extensive period of deprivation of babies in an infant institution is profoundly detrimental to their psychological growth. There is also evidence that the pernicious effects of the early experience persist even in the face of careful placement in selected foster homes" (Goldfarb, 1945, p.32).

However, an opposing view is offered by Skeels (1966) whose longitudinal observations suggest that some children raised in orphanages, whose circumstances change for the better, can enjoy a wholly positive development as adults. Skeels concluded that the negative effects of institutionalization could be overcome with a move to a stimulating home environment. The positive effects of intervention and remediation within an orphanage setting have also been noted by Flint (1978), Provence and Lipton (1962), Dennis (1973) Batchelor, (1999) and Singh (2001) and particularly emphasised by Clarke and Clarke (2000).

1.2.3.2   Internationally adopted children

The Romanian legacy
In 1989, with the fall of the Romanian dictator Nicolai Ceaucescu, the world was exposed to Romania's previously hidden secrets. The most tragic of these was the appalling degradation that many thousands of children were found to have suffered in state-run child care institutions (Chapter 2). These children existed in unprecedented conditions of social deprivation and squalor in which few or no attempts were made to encourage their development on any level. Many of these children were subsequently internationally adopted and their progress monitored and assessed. The mass scale of international adoptions of Romanian orphans combined with the severity of deprivation to which they had been exposed provided "an invaluable 'natural experiment'" (Rutter et al., 2010, pp. 5-6) in which the effects of extreme global deprivation on subsequent development could be studied.

Published work to date on the development of children adopted from Romanian orphanages includes a substantial body of research which, taken together, provides a comprehensive overview of the profound developmental, behavioural and medical consequences of extreme deprivation (e.g., Macvei, 1986; Ames and Carter, 1992; Johnson et al., 1992; McMullan and Fisher, 1992; Rosenberg, Pajer and Rancurello, 1992; Kaler and Freeman, 1994; Chisholm, 1998, 2000; Handleyderry et al., 1995; Morrison, Ames and Chisholm, 1995; Johnson, 2000; Carlson, 1997; Carlson and Felton, 2000; O'Connor et al., 2000; O'Connor and Rutter,

2000; Rutter, Kreppner and O'Connor, 2001; Croft et al., 2001; Chugani et al., 2001; Gunnar et al., 2001; Thompson, 2001; Groza and Ryan, 2002; Wilson, 2003; Merz and McCall, 2010; Rutter et al., 2010).

A substantial body of research on the development of Romanian orphans, indeed on internationally adopted children generally, has been built up by Michael Rutter and colleagues of the English and Romanian Adoptees (ERA) Study which began in the early 1990s (Rutter, et al., 2010). 144 "institution-reared" children and 21 children "from a very deprived background" up to the age of 42 months were selected from the 324 children who were adopted by UK-resident families between February 1990 and September 1992 (Rutter, Sonuga-Barke and Castle, 2010, p. 7). Children were assessed at the age of 4, then at 6, 11, and most recently at 15 (p.13). The study employed "systematic, standardized measurements of key behavioral patterns that seem to be specific to institutional deprivation" (pp. 1-2).

On adoption, the children presented an extremely poor picture: "Even the oldest children were, to all intents and purposes, nonverbal in the Romanian language at the time of U.K. entry" (p.15). Furthermore, *all* aspects of cognitive development seemed to be equally affected by this institutional deprivation (Beckett et al., 2010, pp.125-142). However, most children began to quickly make the most of their new surroundings. In terms of physical development: "By age 6 years, there had been virtually complete catch-up in the children's weight and height as judged by U.K. population norms" (Rutter et al., 2010, p.13). There was also a "major catch-up in psychological functioning in the first few years after adoption" although "cognitive deficits and other sequelae were still evident in a substantial minority of the children at ages 4, 6, and 11" (p. 13).

A major finding was the existence of a significant difference in outcomes between children adopted before and after the age of 6 months (Rutter and Sonuga-Barke, 2010). As Kreppner et al. (2007, p. 942) note:

> "it seems that apparently full recovery usually occurs when the deprivation did not persist beyond the age of 6 months. What was surprising was the marked stepwise increase in the rate of multiple impairments for children whose institutional deprivation lasted for the first 6 months and beyond".

A number of possible explanations for this finding were considered, including "biological programming" and "neural damage" as a result of the experience of deprivation itself ("how the environment gets under the skin") (p. 943), with no definitive conclusion: "Although it would be premature to draw conclusions about the mechanisms involved, it is justified to conclude that some form of biological change is likely" (p. 943). However, the researchers are quick to qualify their remarks about the implications of the 6-month dividing line:

> "Both biological programming and neural damage hypotheses are often interpreted as meaning that the effects are both universal and immutable. Our findings do not support that view" (p. 943).

A second major finding "at all ages" was "heterogeneity in outcome" (Rutter, Sonuga-Barke and Castle, 2010, p. 14). As the authors put it: "even with the children who had the most prolonged experience of institutional care, there were some who at age 11 showed no indication of abnormal functioning on any of the domains that we assessed" (p. 14). On the other hand: "there was a substantial proportion of children who showed impairments in multiple domains of functioning" (p.14). This "marked heterogeneity of effects" has been found in all such research (Rutter and Sonuga-Barke, 2010, p. 225) although the reasons for it are not clear. In examining possible factors, the research team found "one moderating effect" in "the presence of the minimal language skill of imitating speech" (Rutter, Sonuga-Barke and Castle, 2010, p. 15). This skill was "associated with significantly higher verbal and nonverbal IQs at age 11" (pp. 15-16) possibly as a result of its representing "some kind of cognitive reserve that operated only with respect to cognitive outcomes" (p. 16). Similarly, Beckett et al. (2010, p. 138) argue that "minimal language skills at the time of leaving institutional care were associated with superior cognitive performance at the age of 15 but not with better psychosocial outcomes". This finding is important, they claim because "it implies that the minimal language skills did not constitute an index of the severity of institutional deprivation" and, therefore, "the minimal language skills needed to be viewed as some kind of index of cognitive capacity". However, they concede that "neither the underlying mechanisms nor the meaning of capacity in this context are at all clear" (p. 138).

The ERA Study team also latterly focused on the possible existence of unique "deprivation-specific psychological patterns (DSPs)", concluding that there was "good evidence that institutional deprivation does truly cause DSPs" which "constitute rather unusual patterns in contrast to the broad run of emotional disturbance and disruptive behaviour" (Rutter and Sonuga-Barke, 2010, pp. 226-227).

The significance of the 6-month dividing line was queried by Clarke and Clarke (2000) who saw the findings as offering a possible challenge to their "wedge model" of human development (see section 1.3.1.2). While accepting that "those babies rescued before the age of six months made, on average, spectacular gains in development by age four, maintained at age six" (p. 97), they emphasise that "children adopted after the age of six months also made massive average gains, though not as great, from an initially lower level" (p. 97). They comment:

> "the difference between before and after six months must have reflected lengthier institutional privation, suggesting a sensitive (but not critical) period in their lives. But this sensitive period was not universal; some children did well or very well cognitively, even though adopted after (and sometimes long after) six months" (pp. 97-98).

Despite its undoubted importance, the study by Rutter and colleagues does not place any special emphasis on language and gives no detailed qualitative information about individuals' post-adoption linguistic progress. There is also very little specifically on older adopted children (beyond the age of 4). In fact, studies devoted specifically to the language development of adopted (post-institutionalized) Romanian children are thin on the ground. An early exception is Hess and Thompson (1996) although this study is very brief and contains no observational or qualitative material. The authors track the progress of "functional verbal and nonverbal communication over a six-month period" (p. 945) in a 4;6 year old Romanian child who had been adopted 2 years previously. According to the tests used, the child's communicative gestures and use/knowledge of "semantic roles" (e.g., agent, action) increased during the study and relative to published data were "comparable to those of the normative group at the same stage of development but at a much younger age" (Hess and Thompson, 1996, p. 945).

Other internationally adopted children
Romanian adoptees join a much larger group of internationally adopted (IA) children. Indeed, almost 200,000 children were adopted into the U.S. alone between 2000 and 2009 (Snedeker, Geren and Shafto, 2012), most of them infants or toddlers but including thousands of older children as well. There is a substantial and growing body of research examining the development of these children although, once more, there are few studies focussing specifically on language (Glennen, 2008), and hardly any which use qualitative methods alongside or instead of quantitative methods and standardized tests. However, there are a number of important studies and

reviews, some attempting to comprehend the overall picture of language development in internationally adopted children (Meacham, 2006; Glennen, 2007a; Scott, Roberts and Glennen, 2011), some aiming to focus on particular aspects of linguistic competence (Geren, Snedeker and Ax, 2005; Desmarais et al., 2012).

While early deprivation is a common factor in adopted children from Eastern Europe and China, non-Romanian children, as a rule, have not suffered the extremes of global deprivation seen in the Romanian cases. In particular, non-Romanian children usually have at least some acquired competence in their native language(s) prior to adoption. The first issue surrounding the study of language development in IA children, therefore, is that of their status as language learners. In English speaking adoptive homes, for example, should they be considered to be developing as bilingual speakers (their birth language plus English), as second language learners (with English as second language), or as monolingual speakers (with English as first language)? Gindis (2005) criticises the tendency, especially pronounced in school settings, to consider IA children as bilingual when they are more realistically "monolingual upon arrival (they know only one language, for example, Romanian), and after several months they are monolingual again, only this time in English" (p. 298). The unique position of IA children whose "native" language skills are relatively undeveloped prior to adoption has led other researchers to speak of "a second first-language acquisition pattern" (Scott, Roberts and Glennen, 2011; cf Guitiérrez-Clennan, 1999; Schiff-Meyers, 1992).

Some studies have concentrated on giving a broad overview of language development in the population of IA children. Meacham (2006), drawing on other studies, argues that "the language of typical IA children catches up with their non-adopted peers by ages 3-4 years and continues to develop at a normal rate throughout their school-age years" (p. 75). Meacham also claims that "recent research suggests that age at time of adoption and length of exposure to English are significant contributors to language learning progress for IA children" (p. 75).[2] Meacham is particularly concerned with the problem of developing meaningful assessment criteria for the language progress of IA children. How are practitioners or child care professionals to know whether an adopted child is doing well linguistically or not? She argues that standardized tests of

---

[2] However, the "recent research" referred to is Glennen and Masters (2002) which Glennen herself has distanced herself from in later work (see below).

language "are not appropriate for use with IA children" since "IA children do not match the national group to which they are being compared within standardized assessments" (2006, p. 77). Instead, she recommends "a criterion-referenced assessment or a developmental checklist, which can be effectively used to set developmentally appropriate goals for the child, to guide parents in stimulating sequential progression of specific skills, and to monitor overall progress" (p. 77).

Schoenbrodt, Carran and Preis (2007) studied the language abilities of 48 children adopted into the US from East European orphanages over a 3 year period using a standardized language test. The children, aged 3-16 years, had already acquired a first language to some degree in the countries of origin. The researchers found that "these children were able to follow the same language development patterns as non-adopted peers" while "overall language development continues to lag behind in all areas" (p. 67). In particular, they noted longer-lasting problems, possibly linked to cultural background, in areas of pragmatic understanding of utterances. Furthermore, the "variables of age at adoption and previous health problems showed no effects in this study" (p. 67).

Glennen (2007a) studied 27 children adopted into the US from Eastern Europe between 11 and 23 months of age using standardized assessment tools. She reports that "1 year after adoption, these internationally adopted children made rapid progress in English language development" (p. 544). While "[a]uditory comprehension and articulation abilities were well within normal limits", "English expressive language abilities were still in the process of emerging to chronological age expectations" (p. 544). She notes that "poor language abilities were rare" with the "majority of children" having "normally developing language by age 2 (78%), with many testing above average when using norms for monolingual children speaking English" (p. 545). Glennen notes that "length of exposure to the language" (p. 544) is an obvious factor in "any language learning process" and reports that "all of the expressive language scores were slightly but not significantly correlated with length of exposure to English ... indicating that a small part of the variability in expressive language abilities was due to this factor". However, she also reports that "[r]eceptive language abilities ... did not correlate with time home ... indicating that this area of language as tested by the P[reschool] L[anguage] S[cale] –A[uditory] C[omprehension] had fully emerged and was no longer influenced by length of exposure". Furthermore, she notes that "age of adoption was not a factor in any initial assessment or age 2 outcomes", as contrasted with "length of exposure to English", although this may be due to "the narrow range of adoption ages for the children in this study" (p. 544).

Glennen also draws attention to the problem of how to assess children's linguistic progress:

"Language assessment is a challenge during the period when the birth language is undergoing attrition and the adopted language is emerging. Because of the language transition, measures based on standard American English cannot be used to assess newly adopted children. Likewise due to attrition, language measures based on the birth language are not valid either. One solution is to develop 'local norms' for internationally adopted children while they are in the process of English language learning" (p. 531).

Such "local norms" are "peer-based standards developed for specific linguistic, cultural, geographical, or disability groups, among others. Children are then compared with the local norm group instead of the standard norm population" (p. 531).

Glennen (2007b) is one of the few published studies to focus on the older adopted child, albeit as second language learner. She concludes:

"Older internationally adopted children undergo the same changes in language and culture as younger adopted infants and toddlers. The key difference is that younger children have several years to develop English before beginning school. In contrast, most older adopted children have to begin school soon after arriving home. They are presented with the complex task of learning academic skills in a language they don't initially speak or understand" (p. 106).

Glennen (2008) notes the paucity of studies devoted specifically to language development in IA children. Taking issue with her own previous research (e.g., Glennen, 2002), she counters a number of "myths" about adoptees' language development. She argues that an extremely pessimistic picture of children's linguistic prospects is in circulation bolstered by a deterministic perspective on the role of the child's early deprived experience on subsequent development. In opposition to this position, she affirms:

"The majority of internationally adopted children have rapid language learning that begins within a few days of arriving home. After one year home, children adopted under the age of 24 months develop English language comprehension, production, and articulation abilities that are well within normal limits using standard norms".

She concedes that less is known "about children adopted at older ages, but preliminary data indicate equally rapid rates of language learning". She notes:

"Within one year of adoption, most children adopted as 2-year-olds score within normal limits on English language tests of comprehension and expression. Children adopted as 3- and 4-year-olds also score within normal limits on English language comprehension measures after one year, but take more time to develop expressive language abilities fully in English".

In terms of the role and effect of any first language on the child's subsequent learning of English she argues that "the first language has no inhibitory or facilitory effect on learning a new language or its phonology" and reports research according to which "children adopted from China learned vocabulary in patterns typical for children who spoke English". In the case of older adopted children, however, she argues that they "do show signs of interference and facilitation between the birth and adoptive languages. However, it is unknown whether they follow the same pattern as bilingual children or if they transition differently from one language to another".

Glennen also considers whether the child's age at adoption is a significant factor in their subsequent linguistic progress. She notes that: "Parent-reported data on children adopted at 3-6 years of age from Eastern Europe found that after five years home, 57% of girls and 82% of boys were diagnosed with communication disorders" and that one research study found that "children adopted from Colombia at older ages were more likely to have poor academic language abilities at school age than children adopted at younger ages". However, what this means, and the reasons for it, can be disputed:

"It is clear that children adopted at older ages are more susceptible to risk factors that impede speech and language development; more longitudinal data will help determine whether those risk factors cause a temporary gap in speech and language development or indicate a real difference in language abilities".

Once more, a complicating factor is the difficulty in assessing the language of older children: "The spoken language abilities of older children can't be validly assessed because there is no proficient language".

Snedeker, Geren and Shafto (2007) studied second-language learning by 27 children adopted from China between 2;7 and 5;6 over an 18-month period. At regular intervals, parents of the adopted children were asked to complete the MacArthur-Bates Communicative Inventory 2 (a parent report measure of early expressive language) and to provide a recording of linguistic interaction with their child. The children were not "nonverbal" but had "already started to learn one language" (p. 80) and had, therefore, "presumably ... already acquired any possible cognitive and maturational prerequisites for early language development" (p. 85). The study found that "[t]he internationally adopted pre-schoolers went through the same shifts in early language development as typically developing infants" (pp.84-5). In particular "they initially learned a disproportionate number of nouns, developing a more balanced lexicon over time" and "initially produced utterances that lacked inflectional morphemes and closed-class words, which were gradually added as vocabulary grew"(p. 85). The authors argue that this similarity in acquisition patterns between young second language learners and monolingual infants suggests that "these features of early language production are due to the nature of the learning problem rather than the limitations of infant learners" (p. 85), a thesis which is explored at more length in Snedeker, Geren and Shafto (2012) in relation to vocabulary development. The authors argue for "Contingent-Acquisition Hypotheses" on which "the emergence of new abilities is driven by the child's growing knowledge of the language" as opposed to "Developmental Hypotheses" on which such emergence is attributed to "changes in the learner that are independent of her experience with a given language" (2012, p. 40). The authors explain that this theoretical distinction "is orthogonal to the nativist/empiricist and domain-specific/domain-general dichotomies that typically organize theoretical discussions of language development" (2012, p. 41).

Scott, Roberts and Glennen (2011) have provided an important meta-analysis of data on language development from a large range of studies of different kinds. Their analysis reveals that "children who are internationally adopted present with great variability in their language outcomes" (p. 1164) and that there is "no 'unified adoption language profile'" in IA cases (p. 1167). They acknowledge that an "unresolved issue in the literature … is the nature of the relationship between age at the time of adoption and long-term language outcomes" (p. 1154). They note that some researchers "have found that children who are younger at the age of adoption have better language outcomes than children who were adopted at older ages" while "other researchers have not always found this to be the case" (p. 1154). Their own analysis "revealed a slight trend favouring better language outcomes for children who were adopted at the age of 1 year or younger" (p. 1166). However, they also offer a caution: "one must bear in mind that the reported age-at-adoption ranges were 'artificially' created, and, as such *we are not suggesting that this analysis uncovered a sensitive period for language development*" (p. 1166, our emphasis). The authors also draw attention to the "different" pattern of language learning for children as they get older and face the demands of school and "higher metalinguistic skills necessary for school-age language tasks" (p. 1164).

Furthermore, they point to a difference in the results of language assessments depending on the methods of assessment, noting that "poorer language outcomes" are found with "norm-referenced instruments ... than in studies that used survey instruments" (p. 1164). In addition, they identify "age at the time of testing" as a "variable of interest" which "not only subsumes the amount of exposure to the new language that the child has experienced, but it also may reflect the changing nature of language skills over time" (p. 1154). As a consequence they argue that "these findings strongly support earlier recommendations of using multiple sources of information, employing good evidence-based instruments, and exploring the use of local norms" (p. 1166).

Finally, the authors report "a gaping hole in our current understanding of the language development of internationally adopted children who are adopted at older ages" and conclude that "there is an urgent need to examine the language acquisition of children who are adopted at older ages" (p. 1166).

Desmarais et al. (2012) is a study of sentence comprehension in 23 internationally adopted, post-institutionalized (PI) children with an average age at adoption of 27.2 months, using standardized tests of sentence comprehension and spatial memory. The main finding was as follows:

> "PI children have more difficulty with comprehension of decontextualized sentences and spatial working memory than do peers who live with their birth families. This is in line with previous suggestions that everyday

language is preserved, whereas school-related language is impaired, in PI children" (p. 52).

Geren, Snedeker and Ax (2005) studied aspects of the lexical and syntactic development of 14 children adopted from China between the ages of 2;7 and 5;1.The researchers used a number of methods including parental reports and analysis of spontaneous speech samples in order to calculate Mean Length of Utterance (MLU) values (see Chapter 5). The authors concluded:

"The IA preschool children in our study showed rapid lexical and syntactic development during the first year after they arrived in the United States. These children went through many of the stages that we see in first language acquisition, albeit at a faster pace ... After about a year, the children in our study had lexical knowledge and syntactic abilities that surpassed those of the typical 30-month-old child. Yet they still appeared to have a long way to go before they would catch up with their monolingual peers" (pp. 51-52).

1.3 Theoretical perspectives on language acquisition

The current field of academic research in language and language acquisition is conflicted, with no overall consensus amongst scholars on the most fundamental questions to do with what language is or how it is learned (for recent reviews see Bavin, 2009; Ambridge and Lieven, 2011). Here we give a brief overview of the main lines of theoretical debate.

1.3.1 Nativism

1.3.1.1   Nativist linguistic theory

A new conception of language introduced by the "Chomskyan revolution" in the 1960s (Chomsky, 1957, 1965) had dramatic consequences not only for linguistics but also for the development and direction of the cognitive sciences overall. This inspired intense and prolonged programmes of international research dedicated to the study of child language acquisition. Chomsky argued that humans have a species-specific predisposition for language, an innate language faculty, initially referred to as a Language Acquisition Device (LAD), which was assumed to have a dedicated, although unspecified, neurological basis. In support of this view, he appealed to the rapidity and universality of language acquisition despite the variability, in quantity and quality, of language input, and to the syntactic complexity, as he saw it, of the linguistic structures so acquired, arguing that children must already have implicit knowledge of grammatical principles to be able to identify and learn such structures in such short order. These principles belonged to Universal Grammar (UG), a core component of the innate LAD. However, Chomsky's linguistic nativism was only part of a broader biological- determinist perspective on the human mind, to include not only principles of grammatical form but also word meanings (including scientific and mathematical concepts), scientific enquiry, artistic creativity and morality (Jones, 2003, p. 92).

In a context in which behaviourist learning theory, based on processes of imitation and reinforcement/inhibition, reigned supreme (Chomsky, 1959), nativists found useful ammunition for their position in the "over-regularizations" observable in children's speech, that is, the application of regular inflections to irregular verb and noun stems as in "taked" and "mans". Such unforced grammatical "errors" suggest that children have inferred and are applying *rules*, rather than merely repeating what they hear from adults. Rule-based creativity of this kind became the centre-piece of the nativist case and, as we shall show, has figured prominently in theoretical controversies over the language acquisition process.

An attempt to put some neurological flesh on Chomsky's biological determinist thesis was made by Eric Lenneberg (1964, 1967, 1968) whose theory followed on from the work of Penfield and Roberts (1959). Lenneberg's contribution to the nativist paradigm was his concept of a critical period for language, the Critical Period Hypothesis, that is, the idea that there is a species-specific time window for the unimpaired acquisition of language.

Chomsky's own theoretical system continued to change, and perhaps the most significant innovation was the adoption of a "modular" approach to linguistic structure (Chomsky, 1981) in the context of a general theory of mind and later elaborated by Fodor (1983). In brief, Chomsky argued that language as commonly understood was actually a product of the integrated action of a number of distinct and independent linguistic-cognitive systems or "modules of grammar" (1981, p. 135), each responsible for a particular sub-domain such as lexical meaning, morphology, syntax, or phonology. Some of these areas, like word meaning and reference, would have close connections with more general cognitive processes, while the syntax system and its associated acquisition mechanism would run more or less independently of other influences either outside the language faculty or within the language system itself.

Clearly, modularity carries significant implications for learning theory generally. If cognitive activity is underpinned by modular brain mechanisms, then it would follow that different cognitive abilities or levels of processing could be selectively impaired whilst other systems operate smoothly. In other words, modularity theory would predict the possibility of varied patterns of cognitive impairment including so-called "dissociations" (e.g., Bellugi et al., 1993) between different cognitive systems or sub-systems. Such "dissociations" could occur within the language system itself with, say, a child able to learn words but not grammar (Locke, 1997; Bates and Goodman, 1997), or between different cognitive systems if, for example, linguistic modules are spared but those for spatial cognition are impaired (Bellugi et al., 1993 in relation to Williams syndrome), or vice versa. A further implication is that each linguistic (or cognitive) module might have its own critical period for activation and operation, an idea examined in more detail below. Evidence in support of modularity has been presented in a number of single case and small group studies of developmentally compromised participants. These studies involve participants with Turner's syndrome (Yamada and Curtiss, 1981), children with Down syndrome (Rondal, 1995), children with Williams syndrome (Bellugi et al., 2001), children with hydrocephalus (O'Connor and Hermelin, 1991), children with specific language impairment (SLI) (van der Lely, Rosen and McClelland, 1998) and participants with impairments of unknown aetiology (Curtiss and Yamada, 1981; Yamada, 1990).

1.3.1.2 "Critical period" concepts

Concepts of "critical" or "sensitive" periods in development are common to a number of disciplines, including ethology (Sanchez, Ladd and Plotsky, 2001; Boccia and Pedersen, 2001), psychology, particularly attachment theory (Bowlby, 1951), and linguistics of the nativist variety (e.g., Lenneberg, 1967; Chomsky, 1965; Pinker, 1994). Bateson (1979) notes the variability in terminology and conception across different disciplines but points out that the common idea is that "an individual's characteristics can be more strongly influenced by a given event at one stage of development than at other stages" (p.470). The concept, has, however, always been controversial, particularly in its application to human social behaviour and there have always been clear and coherent alternatives to the idea that experiences (or the lack of them) during early infancy or childhood exert a deterministic effect on subsequent development. Clarke and Clarke, for example, have insisted "that the whole of the life path is important, including the early years" (2000, p. 19). Instead of a critical period concept, Clarke and Clarke have argued for a "wedge model" with "the thick end representing early potential responsiveness to change, tailing off to the thin end much later in life" (p. 19).

A critical period for first language acquisition[3] was proposed by Penfield and Roberts (1959) and then taken up by Lenneberg (1967) on the basis of his observation of recovery patterns in children with aphasia due to brain injury sustained at various ages. Lenneberg claimed that there was an increasing left-hemisphere specialization for language from early childhood which was complete by the onset of puberty, giving a critical period for language development between 2 years and puberty.

While the concept of a critical period for language was widely accepted, often uncritically, some researchers registered disagreement about both the timing of lateralization and even its relevance to the language acquisition process. Some scholars suggested lateralization was complete at 2 years of age (Kinsbourne and Smith, 1974), others at 5 or 6 (Krashen and Harshman, 1972; Krashen, 1973; Locke, 1992a, 1992b, 1997). Still others have suggested that brain maturation and, therefore, the lateralization of language to the left hemisphere, is present at birth (Wada and Davis 1977; Stromswold, 1995). While yet others, such as Deacon (1999), argue that lateralization is actually a red herring and has no real bearing on the major arguments surrounding language acquisition. Advocates of the critical period concept also differ on the relevance and precise role of early linguistic experience for subsequent language development as well as on the temporal parameters of the period itself. Thus, Johnson and Newport (1996), for example, distinguish between "the exercise hypothesis" and the "maturational hypothesis", only the former taking early linguistic experience as decisive to the workings of the LAD. Attempts at conceptual refinement of the critical/sensitive period idea have also been made by Moltz (1973), Oyama (1979) and Colombo (1982). Scovel (1988), while in agreement with the time frame of Lenneberg's model, proposes to

---

[3] Discussion of the application of the sensitive/critical period concept to second language learning can be found in Flege, (1999), Oyama (1976), Snow and Hoefnagel-Hohle (1978), Patkowski (1980), Genesee (1981), Chiang and Costello (1983), Wuillemin, Richardson and Lynch (1994), Johnson and Newport (1989, 1991), Ioup et al. (1994), Obler and Hannigan (1996).

restrict its scope to speech rather than language on the grounds that "a critical period is defensible only for phonological learning" (p.59).

Lenneberg's classic statement of the critical period model was also subsequently modified by other researchers, including Pinker (1984, 1989, 1994) and Locke (1997, 1999a, 1999b), in response to the emergence of Chomsky's modular perspective on the organization of the language faculty and Fodor's (1983) book, 'Modularity of Mind' claiming many of the processes involved in language were assumed by specialised brain 'modules'. Pinker appealed specifically to children's capacity to "over-generalize" structures such as the regular past tense:

> "Focusing on a single rule of grammar, we find evidence for a system that is modular, independent of real-world meaning, nonassociative (unaffected by frequency and similarity), sensitive to abstract formal distinctions (for example, root versus derived, noun versus verb), more sophisticated than the kinds of 'rules' that are explicitly taught, developing on a schedule not timed by environmental input, organized by principles that could not have been learned, possibly with a distinct neural substrate and genetic basis" (1999, p. 482).

Pinker (1999) further argues that this modular ability to generalise rules has a fixed developmental schedule restricted to the first 4 years of life:

> "I suspected that at least some of the timing of language development, including the past tense rule, is controlled by a maturational clock. Children may begin to acquire a rule at a certain age for the same reason they grow hair or teeth or breasts at certain ages" (p. 203).

Locke's developmental neurolinguistic theory (1994a, 1997) is perhaps the most elaborate and time-restrictive of critical period concepts. Locke presents a picture of "species typical" language development happening in four critically timed over-lapping phases, each requiring an "allocation" of dedicated neural resources (Locke, 1994a, p.608):

1. Vocal learning (gestation to about 1 year): the infant is oriented to the caregiver's face and picks up basic vocal characteristics during social interaction;
2. Utterance acquisition (beginning around 5 months): the child begins to acquire under-analysed linguistic material in the form of formulaic utterances by using social cognition mechanisms located in the right hemisphere. The child learns to associate prosody (sounds/rhythm)

with certain words or phrases but cannot generate these prosodic patterns yet.

3. Analysis and computation (20-37 months): previously stored utterances are "decomposed" into component parts - segments and syllables (p.609). This process helps the child to discover the structural rules and regularities in language and is thereby responsible for the discovery (and acquisition) of grammar.

4. Integration and elaboration (3+ years): the child learns to integrate and elaborate the functions accomplished via the previous phases, using linguistic resources in both cerebral hemispheres.

Locke proposes that there is a critical period for the development of grammar, rather than for language per se, which starts within the first few months of life and may end around 5 or 6 years (Locke, 1997). The crucial event is the activation of a left-hemisphere mechanism referred to as the Grammatical Analysis Module (GAM) (Locke, 1995) between 20 and 37 months within the third phase ("Integration and elaboration") of language acquisition (Locke, 1997). GAM activation is "something that happens only once in the life of each individual" (1997, p. 304). The most conspicuous evidence that GAM is turned on is the child's over-application of regular rules to irregular lexical stems between 20 and 37 months of age (Locke, 1994a, 1997) giving forms such as "comed", "childs" and "gooder". These "errors" may actually come later than the child's initial production of the "correct" forms, "came", "children" and "better". Locke (1994b) explains:

> "These lapses signal that the children instead of merely reproducing what they have heard, are now 'computing' words from word elements. Although it might seem that the children are regressing, they are really just surging happily forward. They have discovered and are applying the same rules the rest of us use to form the past tense or the plural" (p. 444).

Locke argues that language acquisition after the GAM critical period will involve using *right* hemisphere resources which are not specialized for language. In such cases, grammatical processes are likely to be permanently impaired while the ability to learn vocabulary, for example, could remain relatively intact, resulting in "dissociations" between lexis and grammar. Reported cases of children who were late in their vocabulary learning (phase 2) and, subsequently, exhibited "impairments" in inflectional morphology are taken as supporting evidence (Locke, 1997; Smith-Lock, 1993). In order to falsify the theory, then, one would "require evidence from a range of naturalistic behaviours and experimental tasks to indicate that analytical and computational capabilities are present' after the hypothetical GAM critical period deadline and "that utterance analyses are taking place in the vicinity of the left perisylvian area" (Locke, 1997, p. 309). We return to the predictions of Locke's neurolinguistic theory in Chapter 5.

1.3.1.3 Critical period concepts: empirical evidence

In addition to considerable theoretical debate around the critical period concept, there is also a substantial research literature devoted to the empirical testing of particular versions of the hypothesis for a range of linguistic phenomena.

Neville, Mills and Lawson (1992) present evidence suggesting that semantic and grammatical aspects of language develop independently of each other and have different sensitive periods. Ruben (1997) and Ruben and Schwartz (1999) argue that components of language have different developmental time frames with phonology developing until the 12th month of infancy, syntax until the age of 4 years and semantics until the age of 15 or 16 years. Kuhl, Williams and Lacerda (1992) found that infants' phonetic perception was altered within the first 6 months of life after exposure to a particular language. Eimas (1985) showed that the ability to perceive speech sounds involving phonetic contrasts is present in neonates, but suggested that this perceptual sensitivity declines within the first few months of life "through exposure to a restricted environment" (p.40). Several studies have also examined possible critical period effects on the acquisition of sign language by deaf and hearing-impaired people (see Emmorey, 2001, for a broad overview). Fitch, Williams and Etienne (1982) and Serbetcioglu (2001) argue that reduction of auditory stimuli during an early time period can hinder a hearing impaired child's capacity to acquire a fully developed communication system. Marcotte and Morere (1990) found evidence of a "developmental critical period" in their investigation of cerebral lateralization in a varied sample including normal, hearing and congenitally deaf participants. Mayberry (1993) concluded that there was evidence for a modality-independent critical period for language on the grounds that the later the age that sign language was acquired, the less proficiency that was ultimately attained. Mayberry's (1993) opinion is echoed to some extent by Newport (1990, 1991) who argues that there is a linear decline in language performance that starts in childhood and plateaus in adulthood. Finally, critical periods have also been invoked for the transmission of tactile information in populations of deaf, hearing impaired and blind children (Richardson and Wuillemin, 1981). However, arguably, very few of these studies have a genuine bearing on the concept of a critical period for language. Many are concerned with *speech* phenomena rather than with the (medium-independent) capacity for *language* on which the nativist case rests, and evidence of declining ability to attain native-like fluency is not in itself evidence of narrowly defined innate capacities (Clarke and Clarke, 2000). Furthermore, while such studies may appear to lend some empirical weight to the critical period concept for first language acquisition, there is also a significant body of empirical research making the opposing argument, to be reviewed in section 1.4.4.

1.3.2 Alternatives to nativism

1.3.2.1   Anti-nativist theory

Despite their influence on linguistics, psychology and allied disciplines, the nativism paradigm and modularity concept were challenged, with growing insistence, by scholars who could not accept nativist doctrine in itself or the sharp separation imposed by Chomsky and Fodor between linguistic abilities and the contexts of social interaction in which those abilities were developed and exercised.[4] Here we outline some key points on the anti-nativist theoretical spectrum, referred to by Ambridge and Lieven as "the constructivist, emergentist, socio-pragmatic, functionalist, usage-based approach" (2011, p. 1).

Bates and MacWhinney (1979) and Bates and Goodman (1997) argued that language is primarily a learned ability and that pragmatic factors underlie the process of language acquisition. Language is seen as an outgrowth of high-level cognitive principles acquired by observation of and participation with the environment with social and communicative functions of language as the basis for structural properties of language, including syntax. On this view, there is no specific neurological device responsible for language; learning of linguistic forms only requires repeated exposure in meaningful contexts with knowledge of grammatical consistencies the result of pattern-recognition activity in the brain.

---

[4] In addition to linguistic criticism of nativist theory, objections were also raised to Chomsky's self-professed Cartesianism which was regarded by many scholars as incompatible with the findings and methods of modern science (see Jones, 2003).

The view that interaction with the social environment significantly influences and shapes language development is also found in a variety of social-interactive approaches to language acquisition (Snow, 1972, 1977; Dore, 1974; Bruner, 1974, 1975a,b, 1977; Nelson, 1996; Bates, 1979). Scholars of this persuasion have appealed to the firmly anti-nativist ("cultural-historical") perspective on linguistic and cognitive development proposed by Vygotsky (1962). Others have found a firm theoretical foundation for a social perspective on language structure and use in the Systemic Functional Grammar of Halliday (1978). In this context, Bruner's theoretical evolution is particularly significant. Bruner was initially a strong advocate of Chomskyan nativism in principle although he recognised that a Language Acquisition Device (LAD) could only work if rooted in a rich soil of interpersonal interaction and communication, which he dubbed the "Language Acquisition Support System" (LASS) (Bruner, 1977). However, Bruner subsequently parted company with nativism, partly under the influence of Vygotsky, abandoning his LASS in favour of a more thorough-going social interactionist position (see Bakhurst and Shanker, 2001).

Amongst all those approaches which attribute the major role in language acquisition to social and cultural factors, the contribution of Michael Tomasello (1999, 2003) perhaps stands out as the most developed and the most substantial, weaving a range of fundamental topics in theoretical linguistics, language acquisition and animal communication into a coherent and empirically based alternative to nativism. Tomasello, himself influenced by Vygotsky's conception of language as a cultural tool (see also Everett, 2012), has challenged nativist theory both on the more technical aspects of linguistic analysis as well as the learning processes involved in language acquisition. Most importantly, he has helped to rescue the processes of imitation and analogical modelling from behaviourist theorising and given them their due as creative and intelligent processes involved not only in language but in other fundamental social practices. Consequently, Tomasello (2003) suggests that language is constructed by the child on the basis of general cognitive mechanisms and is inextricably linked with other abilities such as the child's capacity to understand other people as intentional agents and to relate to them as such. Rather than being the result of some language instinct, grammar begins to emerge as the child speaker creates linguistic combinations out of the recurring patterns of verbal symbols which s/he hears in the surrounding world as the expression of particular communicative intentions. When language is considered to be interwoven with other cognitive domains and the external socio-cultural milieu in this way, the very idea of a critical period for language (or for any aspect of grammar) is rendered incoherent.

The current theoretical spectrum of views on language and communication also includes more radical positions which would not give house room in principle to a LAD or critical period concept but would also take exception to the rather conventional conception of language and language structure which still remains at the heart of Tomasello's "usage-based" account (cf. Taylor and Shanker, 2003). For example, Conversation Analysis (CA) (Sacks, Schegloff and Jefferson, 1974), an original outgrowth of Garfinkel's "ethno-methodological" orientation in sociology, has consistently resisted any attempt to theorise linguistic communication as an independent system of forms, meanings and structures and has grounded its own analyses of language use in the observable conduct of speakers themselves. A very detailed picture has emerged of language as a flexible toolkit of specialised communicative resources designed for the cooperative construction and interpretation of utterances in context. It then becomes possible to understand such fundamental constructs as the clause or sentence in terms of their role in the interactive composition of turns at talk (Sacks, Schegloff and Jefferson, 1974). Thus, utterance structure is a profoundly *interactional* matter, a property of the communicative processes taking place in real time between speakers, rather than the outward expression of some inner mental state. CA is now also increasingly used as an exploratory methodology in the study of speech and language disorders, affording new insights into both the linguistic and communicative difficulties as well as the creative communicative strategies of, for example, patients who have aphasia (Whitworth, Perkins and Lesser, 1997).

While the proponents of CA have, by and large, restricted themselves to the study of linguistic communication, other theorists have turned to the links between linguistic activity and other types of activity of which, in particular contexts, language is a part. Thus, Clark's theory of "joint action" (Clark, 1996) offers a powerful account of those ways in which language, in combination with nonverbal signals, serves as a "coordination device" within episodes of collaborative activity. Indeed, as Clark shows, conversation itself is "joint action", subject to the same organizational and interactional principles as are evident in nonverbal, practical collaboration. This notion of "coordination" has enormous implications for understanding language and communication in general, including the basic processes of language acquisition (see Clark, 2009; Raczaszek-Leonardi and Cowley,

2012). Furthermore, insights from CA and from studies of coordination are now being merged into a powerful inter-disciplinary focus on communicative interaction as the very foundation of human sociality (Levinson, 2006).

More radical still is the "integrationist" approach to language and communication developed by Roy Harris and colleagues from the early 1980s (Harris, 1981, 1996). The hallmark of integrationism is its refusal to conceive of language as an isolated or impersonal system independent of other aspects of the intelligent conduct of individuals in particular contexts. From this perspective, most branches of modern linguistic thinking represent a monumental misconception about the nature of language which is deeply ingrained in western philosophical and linguistic traditions. As Harris puts it (1996, pp. 17-18):

> "Any initial academic strategy which, for theoretical purposes, treats communication processes or communication systems as segregated, self-contained structures, and assumes that each must be analysed exclusively 'in its own terms', without any reference whatsoever to neighbouring processes or systems, is not merely methodologically flawed but promotes an utterly misleading view of the matters it purports to deal with."

By contrast, the integrationist "invites us to focus first on the human capacity for creating and developing signs appropriate to the many different situations in which human beings find themselves" (1996, p. 12). On this view, language is not a stable, internal psychological construct, but a social activity, something we *do* as people. Language is not a "fixed code", nor is it rule governed, but is dynamic, unique to the individual, and context specific (Harris, 1996). There are, consequently, no pre-existing or universal standards against which linguistic knowledge or usage can be judged or measured as "correct", "normal" or "appropriate", contrary to traditional linguistic assumptions and, more particularly, to the underlying rationale for conventional language description and assessment.

This brief survey, we hope, is enough to show how much the theoretical landscape in language and linguistics has altered since the times when generative grammar and its nativist credo dominated the intellectual landscape. Against this surging tide of work dedicated to understanding language as a creative activity of active, social individuals, the nativist school with its emphasis on seeing language as a internal "mental" or, rather, biological, phenomenon has begun to look questionable indeed.

On the specific issue of the relationship between language and other aspects of cognition there are, similarly, rival theoretical perspectives to the nativist modularity position which we now briefly survey.

1.3.2.2 Alternatives to modularity

The view that language arises on the basis of a more fundamental set of human dispositions for perceiving and thinking is generally referred to as the Cognition (or Cognitive) Hypothesis (Bloom, 1970, 1973; Cromer, 1974, 1988) with roots in the earlier and extremely influential work of Piaget (1926, 1954). The strong form of this hypothesis asserts that particular cognitive attainments are both essential and sufficient for language development. Bowerman (1973, 1974), for example, argues for such cognitive prerequisites as the capacity to use symbols to signify events and objects that may not be perceptually salient, the ability to follow temporal and spatial order and the ability to categorize and form hierarchical relationships (see also Yamada, 1990). Furthermore, children's linguistic abilities will be consistent with their intellectual level and, consequently, "dissociations" between language and other cognitive capacities should not occur (Miller, 1981). A weaker form of the hypothesis holds that cognitive abilities are at least necessary but not sufficient for language learning. This view accepts that there may be specifically linguistic skills in addition to general cognitive structures and capacities that may account for language acquisition (Cromer, 1976). On this version the prediction would be that language development can never be in advance of cognitive development generally, although it could lag behind (Miller, 1981).

The view that linguistic and non-linguistic cognitive abilities are strongly associated is referred to as the Correlational Hypothesis (Brown, 1973; Bates et al., 1977; Miller, 1981). The hypothesis is that there are common underlying mechanisms or principles that govern the developmental sequences in both the linguistic and general cognitive domains (Yamada, 1990). It is these underlying mechanisms or principles that are seen as a requirement for language and may be manifested in such processes as classification, categorization, extraction or abduction of rules and the construction of hierarchies (Yamada, 1990; Maratsos and Chalkley, 1980). Maratsos and Chalkley (1980) also suggest that the learning of syntactic and morphological categories is similar to learning in other spheres such as concept formation and the learning of social/pragmatic roles. The hypothesis also states that the linguistic expressions of these shared governing principles are just as likely to develop first as non-linguistic expressions are: "The Correlational Hypothesis is consistent with some, but not frequent, variation between language and cognitive levels in *either* direction" (Miller, 1981, p.5).

Some theorists (e.g., Karmiloff-Smith, 1998) reject the "nature" versus "nurture" debate as based on a false dichotomy, arguing that human development is influenced by both nature (prespecification) and nurture (experience) while rejecting the nativist conception of the role of prespecified structures in the developmental process. The "Neuroconstructivist" position, developed by Karmiloff-Smith and others (Karmiloff-Smith, 1998, 1999; Thomas and Karmiloff-Smith, 2002; Elsabbagh and Karmiloff-Smith, 2006) suggests that highly specialized abilities, such as are involved in linguistic communication, are not innately prefigured in the form of a "domain specific" mechanism but instead take off from a more general "domain relevant" mechanism. This latter mechanism starts out "as somewhat more relevant to one kind of input over others, but it is usable – albeit in a less efficient way – for other types of processing" (Karmiloff-Smith, 1998, p. 390). Thus, specific skills are formed as a function of gradual specialization occurring in and through the developmental process itself rather than directly given at the outset: repeatedly using a domain relevant mechanism to process a specific sort of input leads it to become domain specific "as a result of its developmental history" (p. 390). Conversely, a small impairment in a "domain relevant" mechanism early on can have significant cascading effects as development continues which subtly change the direction of developmental pathways with implications for eventual outcomes (Karmiloff-Smith, 1998; Thomas and Karmiloff-Smith, 2002). It is also highly unlikely, on the assumptions of this model, that there will be highly specific, "clean cut" disorders or impairments (Karmiloff-Smith, 1998) and researchers are encouraged to look beyond the obvious to consider other possibly related symptoms. For example, what might look like a specific problem with vocabulary learning or morphology might have to do with "lower-level" and more fundamental problems with attention or hearing. Furthermore, Karmiloff-Smith (1998) goes on to challenge the conventional wisdom that "typical" and "atypical" development of particular skills (e.g., language) should be ascribed to the working of the same cognitive (and neural) mechanisms. To Thomas and Karmiloff-Smith (2002) such a view is entrenched in a "static" model of adult neuropsychology which is inappropriate for capturing the dynamic nature of development. Accordingly, Karmiloff-Smith (2001) has argued against nativist claims for within-language and inter-cognitive "dissociations" in the case of children who have Williams syndrome. Bates and Goodman (1997), on the basis of close analysis of lexical and syntactic aspects of utterance production, have also dismissed arguments for "dissociations" in children with Down syndrome as well as children with Williams syndrome.

Opposition to nativist views of language has also been fuelled by criticism of the critical period concept on theoretical and empirical grounds.

1.3.2.3 Critical period concepts: evidence against

Krashen (1972) and Krashen and Harshman (1972) argued against Lenneberg's (1967) hypothesis that language lateralization is completed by puberty, claiming that language function is lateralized to the left hemisphere as early as 5 years and that this is primarily influenced by the linguistic environment rather than maturational factors. They also suggest that language-learning constraints *after* puberty are more likely to be caused by cognitive maturity than biological factors per se.

Alajouanine and Lhermitte (1965) were unable to demonstrate any critical period effect in their study of 37 children who sustained brain injury within the age range of 18 months to about 11 years. Chapman et al. (1998) compared the linguistic production of a group of 47 participants with Down syndrome (DS), aged 5 to 20 years, with that of a group of 47 control children aged 2-6 years, and concluded that there was "no evidence of a critical period for language ending at adolescence, nor of a 'syntactic ceiling' at MLUs corresponding to simple sentences for the DS group" (p. 861). St. James-Roberts (1981) re-evaluated data on post hemispherectomy patients whose brain damage occurred at infancy, childhood and adulthood and found no evidence to support Lenneberg's main contentions. Similarly, Boatman et al. (1999), who examined the post left hemispherectomy language recovery patterns of 6 children aged 7-14 years, found no evidence for critical period effects. A similar conclusion is reached by Vargha-Khadem et al. (1997) in their study of Alex, a boy with Sturge-Weber Syndrome causing damage to the left hemisphere. Vargha-Khadem, et al. conclude:

> "Alex's achievements appear to challenge the widely held view that early childhood is a particularly critical period for acquisition of speech and language or any of their selective aspects, including phonology, grammar, prosody and semantics" (p. 159).

1.4 Language development after extreme global deprivation: conclusion and research questions

The language development of children with early histories of global extreme deprivation has always been, and remains, an issue of universal interest as well as lively theoretical controversy. Documented cases show that children can recover, often completely, from prolonged adversity in their early years although developmental outcomes are highly variable between individual cases. Recent studies of the development of post-institutionalized internationally adopted children, including Romanian orphans, tend to paint an optimistic general picture of the psychological, linguistic and social prospects of adoptees at whatever age they are adopted. While no evidence at all has emerged from this body of research which would clearly support the "critical period" concept for language, most studies have concentrated on very young children or older children who "are well within the critical or sensitive period for learning language" (Snedeker, Geren and Shafto, 2012, p. 40). There is certainly evidence from the largest such study (Rutter et al., 2010) of a "sensitive period" for overall development up to the age of 6 months, although the findings on which this proposal is based are open to interpretation and their relevance to the critical period concept for language specifically is questionable. In general, very little is known about the linguistic progress of older adopted children. There are also very few detailed, qualitative accounts of the progress of particular children, most studies mainly relying on quantitative methodologies or standardized tests with their acknowledged limitations.

The understanding of language acquisition in the case of globally deprived children clearly raises a host of fundamental theoretical questions relating to the relative contributions of "nature" and "nurture" in language learning and cognitive development more generally. Modern interest in these issues was amplified by the advent of Chomsky's linguistic nativism in the 1960s, with its associated concept of a critical period for language, and the later turn to a "modular" view of language and cognition. However, the theoretical climate has now decisively shifted: anti-nativist views, foregrounding the cultural, communicative and interactional foundations of linguistic and cognitive development are now in the ascendant. By the same token, the Critical Period Hypothesis, one of the most important and influential proposals in linguistics and psycholinguistics of the last half century, is now not only theoretically contested but has been shown to be questionable on empirical grounds.

This, then, is the evolving theoretical context in which we offer our study of the language of Serena, Gabrielle and Ingrid and to which we hope to contribute. More specifically, we aim to frame the presentation and discussion of data around the following three research questions:

Question 1

What progress have these children made overall in terms of their linguistic, communicative, cognitive and social development from backgrounds marked by extreme global deprivation during the first years of their lives?

Question 2

Does the linguistic development of these children provide evidence of a "critical period" for language generally or for "grammar" more specifically?

Question 3

Do these three cases provide evidence of cognitive "modularity" in the shape of "dissociations" between linguistic and non-linguistic competencies or between different aspects of linguistic competence?

We will investigate these issues with a "mixed methods" approach, that is, using a range of both quantitative and qualitative analytical methodologies in order to build up as rich and detailed an account as we can of the linguistic, social and psychological proficiencies of the three girls against the backdrop of their overall progress post-adoption.

CHAPTER TWO

BEGINNINGS:
LIFE BEFORE AND AFTER ADOPTION

2. 1 Introduction

In this chapter we try to give as accurate and complete a picture as possible of the living conditions and personal development of Serena, Gabrielle, and Ingrid from their days in orphanages to their adoption by UK families and their new lives in their new homes.

Since the three girls spent their earliest years in the state orphanage system of Romania, we will begin with an overview of these institutions and the standard of care which they provided. We will then go on to look at what is known about the girls' history from reports produced by Romanian and UK-based professionals as well as from the eye witness accounts given by their adoptive parents. Finally, we examine the girls' progress immediately after adoption under the following headings: 1) physical development, 2) non-verbal cognitive development, 3) socio-emotional and communicative development and 4) language development.

2.2 The Romanian state orphanage system

The organization and infrastructure of Romanian child-care institutions have been documented in a number of studies (e.g., Johnson, et al., 1992; Ralph, 1994; Groza and Ileana 1996; Serbin, 1997). Although these institutions are commonly referred to as "orphanages", as we will here, many "orphans"[1] had been given up by living parents and caregivers for a variety of personal, social and economic reasons.

---

[1] For the purposes of the book, the legal definition of an orphan in the United States will be used: "A child may be considered an orphan because of the death or disappearance of, abandonment or desertion by, or separation or loss from, both parents." (Retrieved 28 October 2013 from http://www.uscis.gov/tools/glossary/orphan).

Until the early 1990s, orphaned or abandoned children underwent medical and psychological assessment at the age of 3 years and then at 7 years to determine their placement at one of three types of orphanage: the Prescolare ("preschool"), for those who passed the assessment at 3 years and were judged developmentally healthy, the Scoala Ajutatoare ("helping school"), to which Prescolare children who passed the assessments at 7 years were sent, and the Camin Spital ("home hospital") where children labeled *nerecuperabili* ("irrecuperables", Ralph, 1994, p.37) who failed the assessments either at 3 or 7 years were sent (Johnson, et al., 1992; Ralph, 1994). The "irrecuperable" label was applied to children with a broad range of medical and behavioural problems who were thought to have no developmental potential and, therefore, little or no chance of recovery. According to Vigilante (1993, p.138):

> "Children with mild deformities such as learning disabilities, visual or hearing impairments, cleft palates or even those who merely resided in the lower percentiles for height and weight were condemned to these inhuman facilities."

Although home to around 100,000 children, the existence of Camin Spitals had been kept a well guarded secret in the Romanian society controlled by Ceausescu (Serbin, 1997) until they attracted worldwide media attention in 1989.

All three of the children were adopted in the early 1990s before 1993. Two of them, Gabrielle and Ingrid, had been placed in Camin Spitals, while Serena had been placed in a Prescolare. Although the conditions of the "irrecuperables" were undoubtedly far worse than those of children in other orphanages, the living conditions generally for all children adopted between 1990 to 1993 were "abysmal" (Groza and Ileana, 1996, p.546). Romanian orphanages provided no educational provision and psychological stimulation of children was considered pointless (Ames and Carter, 1992). Institutional care was seen "as custodial care rather than meeting health, social, emotional and developmental needs" and such treatment had "detrimental health and psychological effects" (The Children's Health Care Collaborative Study Group, 1994, p.294). Only minimum levels of food, clothing and shelter were provided and many children were extremely malnourished. Such conditions were due to a number of factors.

Firstly, child to caregiver ratios, particularly in Camin Spitals, were unusually high, ranging from 8:1 to 35:1 (McMullan and Fisher, 1992) with reports of 60:1 in some orphanages (Ames and Carter, 1992; Johnson, et al., 1992). Many children had "propped bottles supplying their only feeding experience and nutrition" (Serbin, 1997, p.83).

Secondly, the lack of training and motivation amongst caring staff meant that there was neither expertise nor incentive to make the extra effort to communicate or interact with children. Childcare staff "receive low pay and little in the way of in-service education or training" (Children's Health Care Collaborative Study Group, 1992, p. 557). As a consequence, staff had no professional knowledge of children's developmental or emotional needs:

> "Owing to lack of equipment, appropriate staffing, and staff training children have limited opportunities to develop gross motor coordination, fine motor skills, social skills and language" (1992, p. 557).

Groza and Ileana (1996) note that child-care staff in institutions typically possessed no formal qualifications and were often unaware of and even disinterested in interacting with infants and young children, particularly those with special needs. In addition, there was virtually no structured programming in state-run child-care institutions and thus "children were left to their own devices for stimulation" (Groza and Ileana, 1996, p. 545). There were no nurses, occupational therapists, psychologists, social workers or teachers. Consequently, children had no remedial or educational input and did not attend schools. Medication was a common form of controlling children's behaviour. After visiting state run child-care institutions in Gradinari, Ralph (1994) observed:

> "Staff in charge had little or no concept of needs beyond clothing the children and providing them with basic medical care. In many instances this meant wanting sedatives to maintain docile behaviour in the most disturbed" (p.37).

Ralph (1994) also noted that,

> "In the Home Hospital situation, children too weak to feed themselves simply starve to death. Most terrible of all is the way that lonely and neglected children, unused to contact are unable to play with, or even look at each other. They have never learned how to" (p.37).

These practices created a downward spiral: overburdened child-care staff had no time or inclination to interact with children, children who were too lively were sedated, children who were ignored or sedated were less likely to seek attention, and so on.

Thirdly, caregivers were simply not encouraged to nurture "irrecuperable" children because of the lack of status these children had in the wider Romanian society (Johnson and Groza, 1993). In fact, "irrecuperable" children like Gabrielle and Ingrid were considered to be of similar status to non-human animals, as noted by Johnson and Groza (1993, p.50):

> "Quickly the primary caregivers attached labels to children, classifying them as either human beings or 'animals'. If a child could not communicate, feed itself, or walk, then it was an 'animal'. Animals do not need the same care as human beings, so care was rationed out."

Indeed, the very existence of children deemed "irrecuperable" was viewed as detrimental to the ideologically framed self-image of Romania and needed to be hidden:

> "the explicit or implicit pressure was to 'hide them away'; usually the facilities housing 'handicapped' children were located in rural areas to support the official policy of 'no handicapped children' in Romania" (Johnson and Groza, 1993, p.49).

A further obstacle to the children's receiving basic health care was a lack of official documentation as to their family backgrounds:

> "Hospitals also were reluctant to treat children who had no official family identity, a situation that contributed to the view that these children were non-persons" (Johnson and Groza, 1993, p. 51).

These, then, were the institutions to which Serena, Gabrielle and Ingrid were consigned more or less from birth. How did they fare?

2.3 Life in the orphanages

2.3.1 Serena

Serena was born in a Bucharest orphanage in March 1987. Although Serena's birth name and date and place of birth are known, there are no details about her birth history. At some point, she was transferred to a "laegun" ("home") for 0 to 3 year olds. Around 3 years, Serena was moved to a mainstream childcare institution ("Prescolare") until 7;5. Although her adoptive parents were never allowed access to the children's wards, a rough picture of her living conditions can be gained from contemporaneous accounts.

Serena was confined to a room with six or seven other children of the same age with no access to toys. The children were very rarely allowed outside. Serena never received any schooling. Her adoptive mother, J., commented:

> "We asked the lawyer what he thought and he said that they were probably kept in a bedroom or a room, all day, because there didn't seem to be a lot of time difference at all. I suppose time just didn't mean anything to them."

J. described her first impressions of the orphanage where Serena lived in June, 1994:

> "They were very careful not to let us go anywhere other than the office. Serena was brought to us actually in the office where the Director was and as usual in Romania, there were loads of toys - in the cupboards! *(laughs)*. The children weren't using them. It was very artificial. I assume some toys were brought in by Western aid volunteers. There was one great, big doll, which we'd actually seen before. It was obviously their pride and joy *(laughs)*, but the kids weren't allowed to play with it."

J. also described her first impression of Serena:

> "Her skin was very grey and wrinkled and she was like a little old woman, I thought, or a wizened monkey *(laughs)*. They wouldn't let them drink very much and it was really hot. So, she actually came out into the garden with us and we sat on this very rusty old swing and she was quite excited, so I don't think she'd been out very much really."

Nevertheless, J. spotted some hidden potential and later wrote:

> "When we first met her in the orphanage … we were impressed with the eye contact and general behaviour and felt that she would respond very well to stimulation, love and the attention of a family."

Of Serena's social relationships, J. commented:

> "I don't know whether she actually had relationships with other children. I do know that she didn't form any attachments to the care workers, no, none at all. She probably wouldn't have had much opportunity to hear people talk either. There always seemed to be so many more children than there were helpers and the helpers just didn't seem to talk very much, not when the children were there. And she didn't get out and go anywhere. She would hear the other children, but a lot of them didn't talk either."

In March 1994, 6 months before she came to the United Kingdom, Serena received a medical and psychological evaluation from a Romanian paediatrician. According to the report written in English, Serena, aged 7, was in a "satisfactory state of health" with a "good general appearance" but her "psycho intellectual" development had been inhibited. Language comprehension and production were reportedly performed "with difficulty." Serena was recommended to have specific follow-up treatment to "remedy the educational deficiencies" as well as "to stimulate speech development."

Serena was adopted at the age of 7;5. At the time of leaving the orphanage, she weighed 16.3 kilos and was 161.29 cms tall, the 3rd centile[2] (-3 SD) for height. She appeared to have no awareness of the outside world. Serena was extremely dehydrated, as indicated by her skin which was dry, wrinkled and putty in colour. She could barely walk. J. described Serena's appearance at this stage:

> "She was a mess. She was very grey, wizened, looking very, very anxious. When we first picked her up, her jaw was really prominent, really sticking out and her eyes were sort of always screwed up and there were these dark rings under her eyes, as if she was really worried and anxious the whole time. Sore. Her hands were absolutely covered in sores. Every time she touched anything, almost the skin came off. It was horrible."

J. described Serena's early language ability:

> "We think she probably knew about fifteen, twenty Romanian words when she came out of the orphanage. Quite a few people think that she was bright enough to have realized that there was no point in learning to talk, because nobody was going to take any notice of her anyway. But she just didn't talk. She made weird noises and sounds and pointed at things. Certainly when we came home, she would point at things and grunt (*makes grunting noise*), just sounds and that's what she would do all the time".

> "I think the first English word she used was 'look'. When we picked her up to bring her back to Bucharest, she stood up the whole time and we kept saying, 'Ooh, look Serena, there's a stork', or 'Look, Serena, there's a...' and she was so excited because the Romanian for 'look' is 'uite' but she

---

[2] Centile charts can show how a point on a scale compares with the same measurement in other individuals. For example, if height is on the 3rd centile, this indicates that for every 100 children of the same age, 3% would be likely to be shorter and 97% taller.

used the English word 'look'. She picked that up in a few minutes and so she learned that quite quickly. Actually, she didn't need encouraging because she wanted to talk. She was motivated."

In her new family setting, the profound impact of orphanage life became all too apparent. As J. says, "She hadn't a clue about anything." Her lack of spatial coordination meant that she was very unsteady on her feet and fell over furniture or knocked into things. Serena had to be held up for the majority of the time. She did not know how to play or pretend and was uncomprehending of tactile affection:

"If we tried to get her to sit on our knee, it was almost like a sort of stick or piece of wood. You almost had to bend her in the middle to get her to sit on your knee. It was really quite strange. You'd bend her and sit her on your knee and she'd sort of sit there, but she didn't really know how to behave or what to do."

Serena was eager for social contact but did not discriminate between strangers and family members:

"She just wanted to touch them and hold their hand. Well, sort of friendly, but sidling up to people and then holding their hand, but not wanting to get too close."

Serena ate ravenously, devouring meals as quickly as possible as if expecting them to be snatched away. In the institution, Serena had been deprived of water for long periods and had drunk by "cupping her hands under a tap or running water" which she continued to do. For almost three weeks, she clutched a cup for hours at a time and asked for water whenever she saw a tap.

She demonstrated limited real world knowledge. Serena had never seen a television before and many everyday household objects were completely unfamiliar to her, although she displayed no interest in these. She could not recognize objects that were represented by drawings and did not know how to navigate books; she held books upside down and started looking at the pages from the back.

2.3.2 Gabrielle

Gabrielle was born in Romania in June 1985 and, according to a later psychologist's report, there is no evidence to suggest that she was born with any physical or cognitive disabilities. Gabrielle's biological mother gave a false name and address and abandoned her at the hospital one day after birth. Gabrielle remained at the hospital for 2 years and 6 months. She was fed only a liquid diet and was swaddled from early infancy until the age of 2 years. Exploratory behaviour and gross motor development were restricted. She was then moved to an orphanage for 1-3 year olds where she was kept in her cot for 24 hours a day and, according to her Romanian paediatrician, "made no development". After 18 months, because of her lack of progress, Gabrielle was moved to an institution for "irrecuperables" (Camin Spital). During April 1991, Gabrielle's adoptive mother, K., went to Romania as a Western aid volunteer and saw Gabrielle for the first time when she was 5;9. K. describes her initial impressions:

> "I think I was well prepared for the state of the orphanage from all the media stuff that had come through, but the smell was the one thing I wasn't prepared for. You think you can imagine it, but you can't. The little children like Gabrielle were all sort of sat in pots, kept in their cots in their rooms. There were no other rooms to go to apart from the rooms where they slept. Their whole lives were spent in their rooms. The whole thing's difficult, seeing one hundred and forty kids in one building, and just the lack of attention. Even the women that were looking after them were so obviously worn out with their own lives, they didn't have any energy to give to the job. All these toys came in from the West, but the Romanian women had to be taught how to play with them as well as the kids. They hadn't much idea. But the most disturbing thing was where the big children were kept down stairs and they really were ordered about like animals, and I found that very difficult. They were sleeping three or four in a bed and lacked clothing because they'd never been used to clothing. They were given clothing by western volunteers but they didn't keep them on."

K. reported that Gabrielle was rarely spoken to by the carers and so the only opportunity for spoken language stimulation would have been with the other children who occupied the room. Spoken interaction would have been unlikely, however, since the other children, like Gabrielle were only just beginning to talk.

Describing Gabrielle's appearance at that time, K. said:

> "She was underweight and minute. I still couldn't believe her age, because at that time she was 5. She just had a 5-year-old size trunk with really spindly arms and legs. I supposed just like little sticks and not really able to bear her weight. She was beginning to pull herself up in the cot, but she was very easily tired, but she could sit up."

In August 1990, at 5;2, Gabrielle was visited by her adoptive father, M., who reported that she did not have any productive speech but exhibited "very good eye contact". Around 6 months before her adoption, Gabrielle's developmental level, at 5;9 was estimated by her adoptive mother, K. to be below that of a child aged 18 months. Gabrielle could not walk and used her arms to pull herself around on the floor. She could not eat solid foods and was not toilet trained. K. described Gabrielle's early language learning efforts during their visits to the orphanage:

> "I think she had about five words when we first went to see her, but she very quickly was learning words all the time and copying sounds. She looked as though she was going to be able to learn fairly quickly just given the stimulation. At the time I gave her 18 months to 2 but looking back I don't think she was as far on as that really. She was beginning to speak words. Like when there was a big, soft dog there, she'd go, 'woof, woof, woof', and she sussed it very quickly that the dog said, 'woof, woof', and she'd copy the 'woof, woof', so like a baby learning to talk really. She'd copy sounds you made to her. She tried to say the whole word like you were saying it. She was trying to learn to talk all the time."

Gabrielle appeared to prefer one-to-one interaction and took little notice of the other children. Although Gabrielle did not demand attention, she was responsive when this was given. This was evident in her non-verbal reactions, since she would establish and maintain eye contact with anyone who was attentive to her and smile at them. She was also reported to use gestures, such as pointing, to some degree. It was this aspect of Gabrielle's behaviour that was first noticed by K.:

> "It was the very strong eye-contact that attracted us to her right from the very first time we saw her. She would just sit in the corner of the cot and watch the world go by - just watch everything."

In October 1991, Gabrielle came to England to live with K. and M. and was adopted by them under British law in July 1992. Then aged 6;3, she still could not walk unaided or eat solid foods and was still in nappies. She was extremely malnourished and physically similar in size to a healthy 18 month to 2-year-old child. Productive language was virtually absent and she had a limited capacity for play.

2.3.3 Ingrid

Ingrid was born in October 1987 and spent her first months in hospital. Unconfirmed reports suggest that a Romanian paediatrician had inititally diagnosed numerous disabilities and had given a negative prognosis for recovery. In March 1988, at 5 months, Ingrid was discharged from hospital and moved to an orphanage where she lived for the first 3 years of her life. This institution functioned as a clearing house for children of varying abilities. At the age of 3, Ingrid was assessed and sent to a Camin Spital as an "irrecuperable". Her adoptive mother, M., describes Ingrid's living conditions:

> "Contrary to popular belief, where Ingrid lived was warm, dry and clean. In fact, it was very hot and stifling. It was quite bright, lots of windows, so physically the conditions weren't too bad. Some children were in a group of favourites. The orphanage was broken up into small units of fifty children of different ages. In each group of fifty, there was a smaller sub-group of perhaps eight children who were considered favourites. The care that they received was very good. They were always taken out of the cots. They were played with regularly. They were given extra tit-bits to eat. So they were quite chubby and well fed and developed reasonably normally on a physical level".

Ingrid, however, was not regarded as a favourite due to her perceived disabilities:

> "The rest of the children were treated really in isolation. In the unit where Ingrid lived, they were young children under 3 so most of them were still bottle-fed, still in nappies. They were given a bottle in the cot. The nappy was changed at the same time. In between the feeds, they were generally not played with or stimulated in any way."

Ingrid experienced physical ailments, including two bouts of bronchopneumonia. She resembled an average 1-year-old child, weighed around 11 kilos, was still in nappies. She became very frightened if she was lifted out of the cot and had no productive language. Ingrid had never been weaned and could not chew, since she had always been fed "mush" from a bottle (as per standard practice, Fisher et al., 1997). Ingrid also exhibited stereotyped behaviours which included rocking backwards and forwards and bouncing up and down while holding onto the cot rails. She started walking in August 1990 aged 2;10. In 1990, aged nearly 3 years, Ingrid's developmental level was estimated by her adoptive mother to be equivalent to an infant aged 9-10 months. In November 1990, aged 3;1, Ingrid was examined by a British paediatrician living in Romania who found that, while Ingrid was "a healthy but pale and small child", her motor skills as well as her social and cognitive skills were inhibited. On Ingrid's speech and language, the report states:

> "Both expressive and comprehension language were severely delayed. With the language difficulties it was not possible to test her formally but she had no expressive language in either Romanian or English though she did make some meaningful grunts."

Ingrid could not dress or undress herself and was not toilet trained. Her fine motor control was poor due to mild muscle hypotonia and her weight was 9.4 kilos. While Ingrid's development was "grossly delayed", she demonstrated an interest in play activities and a potential for learning. The report concluded that Ingrid's language ability was the most significantly inhibited area of development.

M. soon began adoption proceedings and in September 1991, at the age of 3;10, Ingrid went to live with her new adoptive family, then living in Romania. That same month, Ingrid was re-examined by the British paediatrician whose new report states that Ingrid still manifested stereotyped, repetitive behaviours, but that her motor skills (which were one of Ingrid's "best areas") had improved significantly. Her social and cognitive skills had also progressed to the point that she could now dress and undress herself and she demonstrated increasing interest in explorative and imaginative play. She also appeared to recognize some people with whom she interacted regularly, but Ingrid's expressive and comprehensive language continued to be inhibited. The medical record noted that, "She had no words, but is more attentive to others talking and was beginning to develop some listening skills."

Ingrid's weight had increased to 10.4 kilos, while her head circumference had increased to 44.5 cms. She had gained almost 7 cms in height (to 89 cms), but was still considerably below the 3rd centile for her age for European children. The paediatrician's conclusion was that while Ingrid had "shown excellent improvement of her developmental skills and has good capacity for learning", her acquisition of speech was still very inhibited. The further point was made that as Ingrid had not had the opportunity to form an attachment to a primary care giver during the first two years of her life, "she will have some emotional stress which may affect her development." The following, rather bleak, evaluation is added:

> "Some of the damaging effect of the lack of stimulation and support in the vital and formative first few years will be permanent."

By 4;0, Ingrid still had not spoken her first words. As M. noted:

"She had no speech at all at 4. She cried occasionally, but it wasn't something she did for attention. She cried if she was scared or something frightened her that she didn't understand. She cried when you tried to make her eat or drink from a cup or showed her a spoon, things that were associated with behaviour from the orphanage. We understood that an edict had gone out that children over 3 must be spoon fed and if they didn't respond they were held down and force fed, and so you only had to give her a spoon and she would really scream. She did giggle as well to games like 'peek-a-boo' or teddies, and tickling her because she was quite ticklish. That was nice because that was the more normal sort of reaction *(laughs)*."

2.4 Life after adoption

The three accounts above paint a broadly similar picture of children whose developmental states - physical, social, intellectual and linguistic – were the result of years of adaptation to the extremely impoverished conditions of their respective institutions. To what extent, however, had their potential for learning in general and for language learning in particular been compromised by their early experiences?

In this section we look closely at the progress the girls made in the days, months and years after adoption.

2.4.1 Serena

1.   Physical development

Within 2 and a half months of her arrival in the United Kingdom, Serena had grown 3.81 cm and gained 6.4 kilos in weight but she was of still of small stature, under the 3rd centile (-3 SD). Aged 7;8, medical evaluations found Serena's vision and hearing were "clinically satisfactory", but her co-ordination was immature. Serena was described as a healthy child, but with "some signs of developmental delay probably due to lack of stimulation." Serena was a natural left-hander, "but in Romania this was not allowed." By 8;8, a parental report suggested Serena's physical growth (height and weight) was slowing down after a rapid acceleration. She was smaller and lighter than the average 7 to 8 year old child. An annual school review for Serena aged 9;8 noted she tended to switch from using her left hand to her right. Serena entered puberty at around 10 years. By 10;2, Serena's gross and fine motor coordination had developed to the point where she was adept at ball games.

2. Non-verbal cognitive development

When adopted, Serena's spatial awareness and representational skills were limited, but she was very inquisitive. 3 months later, Serena's mother wrote:

> "We feel that she is an intelligent little girl who has lots of potential. She has achieved so much in such a short time that we are confident that with the right help, attention and stimulation she could well catch up with those of her biological peers who have not had her bad start to life."

An educational psychologist reported that, at 7;8, Serena's test age equivalent scores on the Wechsler Pre-School and Primary Scale of Intelligence - Revised UK Edition were between 3;6 and 3;9 years:

> "Although her abilities are still very delayed in terms of her age, the progress she is making daily strongly suggests that this delay is probably largely environmentally created, due to lack of opportunity and stimulation. It seems probable that Serena's intellectual functioning will, in time, be within the normal range".[3]

An annual school review noted that Serena, at 8;8, had progressed in all areas of the school curriculum and that her academic skills were at the 5-6 year level. A parental review in the same month recorded worries concerning her grasp of general knowledge and "reasoning skills", adding that Serena needed to learn to think independently and to generalize from experience. A speech and language therapist (SALT) reported that Serena, at 8;9, had weak spatial observation skills, found it difficult to do jigsaw puzzles and could not discriminate shapes. Serena's trial and error approach to problem-solving was considered characteristic of a younger child. Her nonverbal cognitive ability was assessed using the Goodenough Draw-A-Man test (see Chapter 7) which indicated a 5+ developmental level. Serena's annual school report at 9;9 states that her attention frequently had to be redirected when working alone and she found some subject areas in geography, history and science difficult to understand. For example, while she enjoyed and related to the topic of "Humans" - "as they were tangible" - it was "much more difficult for her to grasp the basic concepts" for the topic of "Sound and Light".

---

[3] However, there was no official follow-up assessment and so, between 1994 and 1999, there remains a gap in the information concerning Serena's intellectual progress.

Serena found using money difficult. She could not count very well and confused concepts of quantity such as "more" and "less". By 10;2, Serena attended the same classes as children who were 3 years younger. She received additional tuition during daily small group sessions, but there was still unease over her ability to concentrate for long periods, work independently, and understand basic mathematical concepts. At 11;5 Serena had made significant academic progress and was now in a class with children who were 2 years younger. She was a conscientious pupil, her school report for summer 1998 noting that she consistently scored As or Bs for "attitude and application to work". According to J.:

> "They say she's a miracle child at school. They can't believe where she's come from, what she was like when she came to their school. They say it's incredible. They say she's so determined. She wants to get things right. She's desperate to learn. I mean, she's like blotting paper - she just absorbs everything and she really sticks at things."

3.   Socio-emotional and communicative development

When adopted at 7;5, Serena's social awareness was limited. She seemed to have no idea of how to participate in play and pretend activities or to respond when affection was given. At 7;6, Serena was placed in the reception class of her local primary school alongside her brother, N., aged 3;10 and also adopted from Romania aged 1 year. The head teacher commented:

> "Serena is unable to communicate with her peer group. At break time she does not play with the other children and frequently goes back into school. Serena displays aggressive behaviour towards objects and sometimes towards other children. She bursts into tears frequently. She addresses the class teacher only as 'mummy'."

Serena appeared to have "extreme developmental delay" according to the school report and continually sought adults' individual attention. At times, she found group activity distressing and would hide under furniture. However, the educational psychologist reported a dramatic improvement in Serena's social behavior at school aged 7;8:

> "She generally appears calmer, happier, more able to concentrate and much more socially conforming than she did when I first met her. She is now keen to join in activities with the other children. She has learnt to wait or put up a hand for attention in a class group situation. She no longer seeks prolonged physical contact with her teacher."

At 7;11, Serena's parents described her as a determined child who responded well to explanations and routines. Serena liked to play "dolls going to bed" games. Serena now related well to the family pets, whereas before she had been afraid of them. Serena's relationship with her brother, N., was thought to be an important factor in her overall progress:

> "She relates well with her brother (3 and 3 quarters her junior) and in many ways they are like twins! He has played an important part in her adjustment to her new lifestyle."

At 8;7, a school report noted that Serena integrated well with other children from her own age group or younger. Her social level was estimated to be equivalent to a child aged 5 to 6 years. At 9;8, Serena's popularity, confidence and verbal abilities had increased. In the annual school review for November 1996, her parents wrote that she had recently cried about memories of the Romanian orphanage. However, Serena was also described as a "happy" and "settled" child, who enjoyed new challenges and was "able to relate these experiences to other things." At 11;5, Serena was still attending a mainstream school in a class with children aged around 2 years younger. Serena was very motivated to do well at school. She was extremely talkative and was becoming more integrated with her peer group. She no longer called out, held onto teachers' clothing or made inappropriate comments. The onset of puberty was also evident and Serena was displaying "almost normal" emotional reactions: on one occasion, Serena became upset when J., her mother, spent a brief period in hospital:

> "The night I came home, she actually disappeared upstairs for quite a while and then she came into the bedroom and she'd written just loads and really poured her heart out. I sat there and looked at it and said, 'Ooh, Serena, this is lovely,' and she looked at me and just burst into tears and cried and cried, really sobbed and I was absolutely over the moon because, I thought, 'Great, that's the first time, she's actually shown *real* emotion, that's she's just part of us.' Oh, it was lovely *(laughs)*, it really was."

Serena was described as an engaging child who would "sort of smile at people". J. observed:

> "I think for the first time, we're getting somewhere *(laughs)*. In the last few months, she just suddenly seems to have blossomed and she can talk like any little girl. She'll come and sit beside me and just *chat away* like any little child would do, whereas at one time, she wouldn't have done

that, or she just comes up for a cuddle or says, 'Would you like a cup of tea?' *(laughs)*."

4. Language development

When Serena left the orphanage her productive vocabulary consisted of less than twenty words. However, it quickly became apparent that, Serena displayed a "natural cautious curiosity" about her environment and that she was very motivated to speak. According to J.:

> "It was just the odd words to start with but enough of the word to know what she was talking about. Serena could actually understand sentences, but she didn't actually use them for a long time. Well, she always did understand a lot more than she could actually say. I suppose we just signed."

Within 3 months, Serena's vocabulary had increased and she was beginning to formulate more complex utterances such as "I've done it", "No, you stay over there", although her pronunciation was not always clear. She also easily established eye contact with other people. At 7;8, her educational psychologist observed:

> "Serena's expressive language as used in class has improved from a few single words and two word utterances accompanied by noises with speech like intonation, to a greatly increased vocabulary of single nouns, many familiar phrases and creative use of word combination. Serena now verbalises to herself as she does tasks. She continues to enjoy naming pictures and repeating new words and phrases."

At 8;8, a parental report states that Serena's verbal communication had improved and, while she liked to acquire new words, she did not always speak in sentences. A speech and language therapist (SALT) reported that Serena, at 8;9, enjoyed conversation and produced basic grammatical forms with an emphasis on communicating rather than using "correct language". At 9;8, Serena's expressive language as measured by the Action Picture Test (APT; Renfrew, 1988) was at the 8;5 year level for information and the 6;0 to 6;5 year level for grammar. Serena produced "clear, connected speech" of five to six words in length. Serena's language development was clinically monitored for nearly 2 years (from 9;8 to 11;7) via the APT and her results on this test were used to inform Serena's special needs program at school. At 10;8, Serena's receptive language as measured by the Test for Reception of Grammar (TROG, Bishop, 1989b), was reported by a SALT to be at the 7 year level, while expressive language (as measured by the APT) was still at the 8;5 year level. She "articulated all English speech sounds correctly", but did not yet use auxiliaries "is", "has", "was" and produced "incorrect" past tense forms e.g., "catched". By 11;5, Serena's comprehension and expression of language were described in a school report as approximately equal, with reading and spelling at the 7 year level. J. describes Serena's language ability at this point:

> "We're only just beginning to get a full sentence now. When she's writing she doesn't sort of write or doesn't seem to think it in sentences, but now she's actually talking, she very often will talk in a sentence. She's really got quite a grasp of English now and understands a lot."

It was in the area of receptive vocabulary that Serena made the most obvious and rapid gains, as periodically documented by her increase in test age equivalents on the British Picture Vocabulary Scale (BPVS). Between the ages of 9;9 and 11;6, her test age equivalent increased from 4;0 to 8;10 years - an increase of 4;8 years in 1;8 years.

At 11;7, Serena received her last formal SALT assessment. Many of the structures noted as absent the year before were now identified: auxiliaries, passives, subordinating conjunctions and relative pronouns, but there was inconsistent use of irregular verb forms (e.g., "catched" instead of "caught"). Serena's language development was not assessed as being clinically impaired since her "speech and language are commensurate with her general abilities".

2.4.2 Gabrielle

1. Physical development

Within 6 months of her coming to the UK Gabrielle learned to walk and she was fully toilet trained after 1 year. About 8 months post-adoption, Gabrielle's weight and height were increasing rapidly. From having been considerably below the 3rd centile, she was now much nearer the 3rd centile in height and at slightly below the 50th centile for weight, despite an early X-ray indicating delayed bone age associated with severe malnutrition. Gabrielle's hearing was tested and found to be satisfactory. A psychological report stated that, aged 7;8, Gabrielle's gross motor skills were very immature and her fine motor coordination needed to be improved. Gabrielle still would not chew and preferred to eat liquidized food. Her overall developmental level at 7;8 was placed between 3;0 and 3;6.

2. Socio-emotional and communicative development

8 months post-adoption, Gabrielle obtained a part-time placement at a nursery. Here she was encouraged to integrate with children aged at least 4 years younger. The school reported Gabrielle's friendships took time to emerge because of her inhibited language capacity. Gabrielle was reported by her parents to exhibit behaviours thought to stem from her experience of deprivation, such as looking at her poised fingers with a fixated gaze. They also reported she found it difficult to express her emotions or to tell others when she was hurt. There were "irritating obsessions" involving her toys and clothes and she sometimes made repeated requests "beyond the normal length of time a child would do." A paediatrician described Gabrielle as: "[a] happy, alert and friendly child who is eager to explore her environment and to communicate with those around her."

The educational psychologist described her as having a lively and forceful personality. She was sociable and outgoing but not indiscriminately friendly and could tell close family members from friends or acquaintances, even displaying a certain wariness of strangers. At this stage, her family considered Gabrielle to be "remarkably" well-adjusted given her early circumstances. Although contacts with other children in the orphanage were meagre, they "may have been sufficient to provide some basic emotional protection" according to the educational psychologist. At 8;5, Gabrielle obtained a part-time placement at a school for children with moderate learning difficulties. She quickly established a close relationship with the class teacher who described her as a happy, friendly child. It took longer for Gabrielle to make satisfactory relationships with the children. Gabrielle also continued to attend the mainstream lower school, where she was placed with Year 1 children. A school report for Gabrielle, at 9;2, noted she still found it difficult to express her emotions and would make comments such as "Do I say sorry now?" Gabrielle's play skills appeared to be still developing. She did not actively initiate or join in play with other children but played alongside them. Gabrielle did not appear to have any close friends, although she was liked and accepted by other children.

Aged 10;8, Gabrielle was now attending school full-time in a class with children of average age 8 years. Gabrielle was described as "going through a very awkward phase," by K.:

> "She relates well to other people. She's always quite a friendly child and willing to talk to other people and very keen to admire their clothes and their shoes and their possessions *(laughs)*. But she's also very skilled at the moment in the use of the negative and opposite. That's the sort of stage of development she's at."

Gabrielle sometimes disrupted the conversations of others, particularly those involving her adoptive mother, interrupting with her own comments. As Gabrielle matured, her parents often found it difficult to gain her cooperation. She could be argumentative and it was not easy to reason with her. It was not clear to them whether these reactions were due to teenage awkwardness or a problem in understanding what was being asked of her. At 11;11, the clinical psychologist reported that Gabrielle found tasks requiring "social awareness or understanding of the implications of actions" very difficult. She had several friends outside school and enjoyed playing with her Barbie dolls, skipping and riding her bicycle. Gabrielle preferred routinized activities and displayed "some preference for sameness". She was described as a "strong-willed" child who found emotional expression difficult.

3.   Non-verbal cognitive development

Around 8 months after adoption, Gabrielle's parents noted in a school report that she was easily distracted and had a short attention span. However, by 7;8, Gabrielle appeared to be progressing well according to an educational psychologist's report:

> "The picture since Gabrielle came to her new family has been one of steady and most encouraging progress which has followed a very 'normal' pattern, and which has been much greater than might have been expected given her age, history, and level of development at the time she left Romania."

In the psychologist's opinion Gabrielle had "shown not just progress but some degree of 'catch-up' i.e. though still very delayed, the degree of delay is less than before." At 7;7, an educational review reported that Gabrielle was not always able to grasp the meaning or purpose of particular verbal tasks, and could not understand the meaning of some pictures and their relation to reality. For example, in a silly/sensible game which involved negating a statement or question judged to present untrue information, Gabrielle replied "Yes" when asked "Can cows fly?" The game was "particularly difficult for Gabrielle who tends to take every statement as the truth". Gabrielle's thinking was thought to be rooted in the "here and now", and activities were created in order to develop her imagination. At 8;0, Gabrielle was moved (with a full-time helper) into the reception class of a mainstream school and after several months, as noted above, she also began to attend a school for children with moderate learning difficulties on a part-time basis where she was in a small class of Year 3/4 children. It was noted that Gabrielle was highly observant but distractible. At 8;7, a school report expressed worry that, after rapid early progress, Gabrielle's rate of development might have stabilized or slowed down.

At 9;11, Gabrielle's test performance on the Wechsler Intelligence Scale for Children, administered by an educational psychologist, indicated that she was functioning at a level where "learning difficulties" might be expected. Gabrielle's scores put her at a 4;5 to 5;5 year level. However, the educational psychologist also commented that, "The notion of "age equivalence" should be regarded cautiously" (see Chapter 4). It was found that she appeared to lack "listening focus" in that she had reduced concentration and a short attention span. Gabrielle's lack of real world knowledge was noted once more by a speech and language therapist:

> "She can still display great gaps in her general knowledge, i.e., she was not sure why a picture was particularly funny, as she tends to accept anything as being possibly true."

In the same month, a school report noted that mathematical concepts were particularly hard for Gabrielle to understand. At 10;8, she was reported to find it easier to understand concrete factual information rather than abstract concepts. In contrast to her early rapid development, Gabrielle's rate of progress had now become steadier. At 11;11, Gabrielle's intellectual ability was assessed by a clinical psychologist using Raven's Coloured Progressive Matrices and the British Ability Scales and found to be similar to that of a child aged 6 to 7 years. Gabrielle apparently had most difficulty with understanding highly abstract or non-meaningful visual-spatial tasks. Gabrielle also obtained low scores on tests of working memory including a visual recall measure (Recall of Designs subscale BAS). The psychologist concluded that: "Gabrielle has a fairly consistent pattern of skills with no marked discrepancies between her verbal and non-verbal abilities."

4.   Language development

Gabrielle's language development immediately after adoption was described by her mother, K.:

> "She came knowing about twenty odd words. She knew the word for 'going out', and 'here' and some that were Romanian and English. As soon as she came to live with us, she very quickly started stringing two words together. She started saying words, before she ever made any sentences. She used to make a lot of strange, demanding noises to get what she wanted. For example, if she wanted something to eat, she'd point at what she wanted and make a noise *(points and grunts)*. Then if you told her what it was, she'd try and say the word. One of the first things we taught her to say was, 'Oh dear' *(laughs)*. She would put it into all sorts of different situations, but appropriately, just like a baby learning language."

At 7;0, Gabrielle started to attend a nursery for one day a week, mixing with children aged 4 years younger. The school reported that Gabrielle "internalised" her language and "conversed" with her dolls. At 7;7, Gabrielle's head teacher described her language as telegrammatic but functional. Despite limited linguistic ability, she attempted to relate past, present and future events. Gabrielle's syntactic innovations, e.g. "off coat", were thought to be reminiscent of speakers learning English as a second language. Her basic vocabulary was growing almost daily, according to a speech and language therapist's report. At 7;7, she understood a variety of prepositions, could name all the colours and count to 5. She was able to select objects by their function and was beginning to understand and use temporal terms such as "yesterday", "later", "tomorrow". She produced mainly three-word utterances, was eager to talk and recount past events, ask questions and communicate some needs. She also loved singing, stories and joining in with nursery rhymes. Gabrielle appeared to have no articulatory difficulties. The report concluded: "Gabrielle continues to make good progress in her speech and language skills, following the normal developmental pattern." Gabrielle's early receptive lexicon was not tested formally, but developmental reports for February 1993 for Gabrielle aged 7;7 years state that her vocabulary for verbs and nouns was growing almost daily.

A SALT reported that Gabrielle, at 8;11, could now respond to WH-type questions and comprehend some complex sentences. She could understand and use tenses in speech and appropriately include morphological forms and function words like possessive 's, auxiliary verbs "has" and "is" and the determiners "the" and "a". However, she continued to show a lack of confidence in producing utterances to fulfill task demands. A SALT reported that Gabrielle, at 9;11, had become more accurate in guessing true/untrue statements during a game, understanding before/after concepts, and storytelling activities using pictures. However, the Reynell Developmental Language Scales scores suggested difficulties in processing lengthier instructions possibly due to auditory short-term memory limitations. Reportedly, Gabrielle's ability to use past tense inflections and plural endings was underdeveloped, but generally her expressive language had improved significantly so that "word order in sentences tends to conform more to the norm." No specific "speech sounds" needed attention and intonation patterns were unexceptional. Gabrielle had apparently made reasonable progress over the year and her overall speech and language skills were equivalent to those of a child aged 4;5 to 5;0 years.

At 10;2, Gabrielle's speech and language were re-assessed as being equivalent to children within the age range 4;0 to 5;8 years. Gabrielle had difficulty understanding some words (e.g. "between", "few", "whole", "second ", "after", "behind"), singular/plural contrasts ("dog" vs. "dogs"), and comparative adjectival structures ("older than", "bigger than"). She tended to speak mostly in the present tense and to omit auxiliaries. At nearly 12;0, Gabrielle was assessed by a clinical psychologist obtaining a test age equivalent of 7;0 on the Verbal Comprehension Scale of the Reynell Developmental Language Scales. Her score on a digit span test (Recall of Digits sub-scale of the British Ability Scales) suggested inhibited auditory short-term memory. Gabrielle's speech was described as "monotonic" and she tended to inappropriately use phrases she heard others use. She understood routine commands, but there were concerns she did not fully comprehend complex instructions. Gabrielle had "a good working vocabulary".

2.4.3 Ingrid

1. Physical development

When Ingrid entered her adoptive home at 3;10., her physical development was globally inhibited, but several months post adoption, she had made rapid progress with walking and self-help skills and had learnt to eat and chew. At 6;11,, Ingrid's hearing was reported to be satisfactory. At 7;1, an educational psychologist commented that "in gross skills like swimming, gymnastics she is well up to age-level." However, by 10;5 years, aspects of Ingrid's fine motor development worried her parents. An occupational therapist reported that Ingrid's low muscle tone (hypotonia) meant she found it difficult to control a pen or pencil for long periods. She continued to have difficulty in establishing a definite hand preference for fine motor tasks, particularly hand-writing. However, Ingrid's numerous sporting activities improved her coordination and gross motor skills. She particularly enjoyed swimming and football and was playing rounders, cricket and bowling. A medical report for Ingrid at 11;0 stated that, "She is growing well and her height is now average for her age". She was also approaching puberty. At 11;1, a paediatric occupational therapist reported that Ingrid's fine motor skills would no longer require occupational therapy because of the progress she had made.

2. Non-verbal cognitive development

At 6;6, Ingrid was found to have a "delay" in number skills and visual discrimination. In addition, Ingrid had difficulties with concentration and the ability to work unsupervised. At 7;1, Ingrid was in a class of children 1 year younger than herself. An educational psychologist reported that she was highly distractible but curious to experiment with test toys and books. Her nonverbal abilities were assessed using the McCarthy Scale of Children's Abilities and the psychologist's report concluded:

> "All these assessments broadly concur with the picture of a child making rapid progress from a very delayed starting point, progress that is normal in sequence and form. She is at present functioning much like a very ordinary child of between 5 and 6."

At 9;4, a school assessment reported Ingrid's noticeable progress in mathematical ability over a year, although not yet to an age-appropriate level. An educational psychologist reported Ingrid's general developmental (including non-verbal cognitive) level to be at least 3 years younger than her age. By 10;8, Ingrid's parents were becoming increasingly concerned about Ingrid's under-developed numeracy skills, which, according to a later report, were between 2;2 and 3;6 years behind her chronological age. At 11;0, an educational psychologist confirmed that Ingrid still showed a general developmental delay. Despite this, she had made further progress in acquiring mathematical concepts. Ingrid was still distractible and found it difficult to concentrate within a classroom setting. The psychologist commented: "The combination of her distractibility and her underdeveloped educational attainment limit her ability to function as an independent learner." The report attributed Ingrid's learning difficulties to her early deprivation.

3.   Socio-emotional and communicative development

At 3;10, a paediatrician predicted that Ingrid's socio-emotional development would be negatively affected by the lack of bonding with a primary caretaker early in life, implying that there might be an issue with forming social relationships with others, particularly children. The first opportunity that Ingrid had to mix with her peers was when she was placed in a Romanian day nursery ("gradanitza") at 5;0, 14 months after she was adopted. Here, Ingrid interacted with children between the ages of 3 and 7 years. She learned important play skills and everyday rituals such as washing hands and hanging up towels. She enjoyed play activities with other children and joining in with their games. By 6;0, it appeared that Ingrid related better to children younger than herself, and attended a class for children 2 years below her chronological age. At 6;6, Ingrid started to attend a mainstream primary school in the United Kingdom, mixing with children 1 year younger than herself. A teacher reported that Ingrid was "prone to mimic her peers' more undesirable actions." Ingrid's progress was monitored at regular intervals by the learning support teacher. At 7;1, an educational psychologist reported that she interacted well with her peers and "is accepted as a full and ordinary member of the class." She was described as a "delightful child, eager to relate to others and to learn", which was "a very good foundation for future progress." During her interview with the psychologist, Ingrid constantly asked questions, made comments or laughed and shared jokes. The psychologist noted that Ingrid's social behaviour resembled that of a child of 5 or 6 years.

Over three years later at 10;6, Ingrid was described by her child minder:

> "Watching Ingrid play with the other children, it is very noticeable that she feels more comfortable playing with children younger than herself,

mainly between the ages of 6 and 8. I've also noticed that Ingrid is easily led into situations that she knows are wrong. Socially she is below average for her 10-and-a-half years."

At 10;8 years, Ingrid's parents were becoming increasingly worried about her social skills and, at 11;0, a parental report noted:

"Social skills development remains a major concern for us, particularly as she approaches her transfer to secondary education. The concern centres around problems such as indiscriminate friendliness and delay in the development of age appropriate behaviour. Appropriate social skill building has been a problem for the past 4 years or so. She is very impressionable and gullible and goes with anyone who may request her to do so and as she approaches puberty is a major concern."

At 11;0, an educational psychologist reported that Ingrid tended to depend on other children for help with organizing herself and her belongings, but appeared to be aware of her strengths and weaknesses. Her main interest was still sport, particularly football, and she was a member of a youth club and school choir. Ingrid was most confident when interacting with a younger peer group amongst whom she had several long-standing friends. Although she was now able to differentiate between appropriate and inappropriate social behaviour with adults at school, there were worries that Ingrid was "most likely to behave in an over-familiar manner with acquaintances."

4. Language development

After 8 months in her new foster environment, Ingrid spoke her first words around 4;6. She produced single words first, followed by two-word and three-word utterances. Her first words referred to names of familiar people. She also imitated words. M. describes her early linguistic progress:

"She would say 'Mummy' and 'Daddy'. She noticed all the names of people that were in her immediate circle. Well, she understood a lot. Before she started her speech she knew what we wanted with language rather than gestures. We treated her like we would have done any other toddler of a year or 18 months. There was always somebody talking to her or playing with her. I mean she didn't start off with sentences. She first used words."

According to a language diary kept by M., Ingrid's acquisition of vocabulary between 4;6 and 4;9 was rapid and she was able to remember people's names "really well". Shortly after Ingrid's first words. M. wrote:

"Your language development is really coming on now. You have quite a big vocabulary but are not very good on pronouncing things - but we usually know what you mean. You are quite vocal and it is lovely to hear you when you got to bed at night and lie and chatter away, going through all our names. Sometimes you go through a phase of pointing to everything."

At 4;8, Ingrid communicated using a combination of manual gestures, such as pointing, and words that referred to everyday objects "usually with the end syllable pronounced" (e.g. "ba-th" for "bath", "sha-her" for "shower" and "wa-sh" for "wash"). Occasionally, she would pronounce the words without final consonants: "ba" for bath, "ta" for "tap" and "so" for "soap".

At 6;6, Ingrid started to attend a mainstream primary school in the United Kingdom and at 6;8 was assessed using the Bury Infant Check, which indicated a "delay" in language. Ingrid's communicative patterns could include repetitive questioning (according to a head teacher's report) and precise mimicking of regional dialect and accent forms with "the same little phrases and lisps." Once, Ingrid returned home talking in a broad Yorkshire accent after playing with one of her school friends. At 7;1, an educational psychologist predicted that Ingrid would continue to have residual difficulties with reading and spelling. A speech and language therapist first saw Ingrid at 7;3 and made annual assessments until age 9;3. According to M., the clinical opinion was that, at 9;3, Ingrid's understanding and use of language was equivalent to a 7;6 year old:

"It was certainly encouraging for me to say, 'Oh that's really good,' because Ingrid didn't start to talk until she was 4 and a half. If she was already up to the average 7 and a half year old, that meant within 4 and a half years, she gained 7 and a half years of speech which was pretty good."

At 9;4, her school informally tested Ingrid's receptive language using the BPVS and her results were equivalent to a child aged 6;11: "Progress in understanding of spoken language is roughly in line with chronological age, but is still an area which needs development." In fact, Ingrid's receptive vocabulary level (as measured by the BPVS) increased by 2;7 years between the ages of 9;4 and 10;9 - a period of 1;5 years.

Her accuracy range on a reading measure was at the 4;8 to 6;2 year level, while her performance on a spelling measure approximated that of a child aged 6;7. There were reportedly limitations on auditory short-term memory. Concerning Ingrid's phonological skills, it was reported that she could articulate words with C-V-C syllabic structure, could pronounce initial consonants such as "sh" (/ʃ/), "ch" (/tʃ/) and "th" (/Ө/) and could read some simple written words with the corresponding letters.

Between 9;4 and 10;3 some aspects of Ingrid's language development demonstrably improved each year according to standardized test scores. Her verbal receptive language increased by 15 months, reading accuracy by 26 months and reading comprehension by 20 months. However, auditory sequential memory remained an area of weakness and her ability to define the meaning of words (Aston Index Vocabulary Scale) was 2;9 years below her chronological age of 10;3. The school report states: "However, there is still a mis-match between attainment and chronological age so she continues to need close monitoring of progress." M. reported that Ingrid had subtle word finding difficulties, e.g., "tooth club" for "youth club", and that she occasionally made word order errors, e.g., "cloth-table" for "table-cloth."

At 11;0, an educational psychologist reported Ingrid still showed a general language "delay" relative to her chronological age. Her reading skills were at the 7;6 year level (on the Wechsler Objective Reading Dimensions Assessment) with spelling and writing skills at a similar level. On a verbal reasoning task (pointing out why two items are similar), her scores were at a low average level for her age. Ingrid could find it difficult to process verbal instructions unless information was presented in small chunks.

2.4.4   Children's overall progress following adoption

1.   Physical development

The children entered their adoptive homes suffering from the negative impact of undernutrition combined with poorly developed gross and fine motor control. Serena and Ingrid were unable to walk unaided and Gabrielle could not walk at all. Neither Gabrielle nor Ingrid could chew solid foods. All three girls were extremely underweight and of short stature (at or under the 3rd centile). However, within several months of adoption, each child's weight and height were increasing rapidly. After 6 months, each child had learned to walk properly. Serena and Ingrid could now chew their food, although Gabrielle took longer to adjust to a non-liquidized diet. Physical catch-up continued rapidly for at least 2 years after adoption and then appeared to continue at a slower, steadier rate. Nevertheless, their prior deprivation appeared to have longer-term negative effects on the girls' physical development. At 7;8, Gabrielle was found to have delayed bone age, which was associated with severe malnutrition. Serena also continued to be of a short stature. By 10;5, Ingrid was found to have visual-perceptual and fine motor difficulties. Hand dominance was still not established and she could not hold a pen for long periods due to muscle laxity (hypotonia). However, Serena and Ingrid, according to records, appeared to have a typical onset of puberty between 10 and 12 years of age. Gabrielle's case was less clear.

2.   Non-verbal cognitive development

Early post-adoption assessments, together with parental observations, paint a picture of global "delay" in perceptual and cognitive functioning and a virtual absence of knowledge of everyday life as typically experienced by children of similar ages. However, all the girls made rapid strides in discovering and negotiating their new physical and social environments. Perhaps the most significant marker of the girls' overall cognitive development was their ability to attend school, albeit in classes with younger children. Within the first few years of life post-adoption, Serena, Gabrielle and Ingrid all made significant academic progress according to the evaluations of educational psychologists. Each child was considered to display considerable learning potential and to be making rapid progress from a very "delayed" start. Cognitive development was described as following a pattern consistent with that of younger children so that Serena at 8;9, for example, was described as having the trial and error problem solving strategies of a 5 year old. In each girl's case, the psychologists suggested that inhibited intellectual functioning appeared to be "largely environmentally created" rather than due to innate learning disabilities. Despite undoubtedly rapid progress, certain non-verbal cognitive skills at first appeared to be problematic or slow in coming. For example, Serena and Gabrielle had difficulty recognizing objects represented by drawings and with tasks that required some depth of imagination and hypothetical reasoning. However, there was no reference to these issues in later developmental reports. Early worries concerned the girls' ability to concentrate for long periods and their distractibility although they all made noticeable improvements in this area, with the possible exception of Ingrid whose progress was less obvious. In science subjects at school, Serena, Gabrielle and Ingrid were reported to be better at understanding words relating to concrete or tangible notions as opposed to abstract, theoretical concepts. The girls also struggled with any activities involving numbers or numerical values. Both Serena and Gabrielle were reported to have weak visuospatial skills, finding difficulty, for example, with jigsaw puzzles or "non-meaningful visuospatial tasks" (e.g., copying geometric patterns). These weaknesses persisted over several years. Serena and Gabrielle also continued to display gaps in their general knowledge. Assessments by health care professionals on the basis of standardized tests consistently reported several years post adoption that the non-language cognition of all three girls was commensurate with their language abilities.

3.   Socio-emotional and communicative development

Despite their lack of social and communicative skills upon adoption, Serena, Gabrielle and Ingrid were curious about their surroundings and responsive when given attention, sharing eye-gaze, smiling and pointing. These affective responses are similar to those displayed by infants and toddlers within the first two years (Locke, 1997). Longer term, each of the girls was able to develop positive social relationships with others, including adult family members and other children. Serena, in particular, formed a selective attachment to her younger brother, and Gabrielle and Ingrid enjoyed their younger friends' company. In general, the girls were able to develop appropriate and effective informal and formal relationships with others in a variety of contexts. However, the cases of Gabrielle and Ingrid also suggest that the early absence of opportunities for significant socio-emotional contact and bonding may continue to subtly influence interactional behaviours and attitudes for some time. For example, Ingrid continued to show indiscriminately friendly behaviour (up to age 11) as frequently observed in previously institutionalized children (Chisholm et al, 1995; Chisholm, 1998; Wilson, 2003) and, in Gabrielle's case in particular, there were reports of continuing difficulties in expressing emotion.

4.   Language Development

When Serena, Gabrielle and Ingrid entered their adoptive environments they had virtually no productive language, at best a repertoire of less than twenty words. However, their expressive vocabularies began to expand immediately and, within a few weeks or months, had rapidly increased.

Such accelerated word learning in older internationally adopted children has often been noted (e.g., Snedeker, Geren and Shafto, 2007). Each child's early word use involved names of objects or familiar people and was accompanied by non-verbal behaviours such as pointing and shared eye-gaze. This rapid acquisition of vocabulary between the age range 4;6 (Ingrid) to 7;8 (Serena) appears to parallel the early word explosion of children who do not have histories of extreme neglect up to the age of 24 months (Locke, 1997). In addition, Gabrielle and Ingrid appeared to display the "nominalizing" tendency reported for typically developing children (Curtiss, 1977, p.89). Serena, Gabrielle and Ingrid produced single words first, followed by two- and three-word utterances (e.g. "banana for school"), in common with most typically developing younger children according to many accounts (Crystal, 1997a).

Within 2 years, each child was speaking in full sentences of up to five or six words and making use of the English tense system to some degree. Characteristic of the early grammatical development of Serena and Gabrielle was the frequent omission of non-lexical words such as auxiliaries and determiners and morphological markers such as past tense inflections. Inconsistent usage of such elements is typical of the language production of younger children up to the age of 5 years (Brown, 1973; Peters, 1995), but particularly of children between the ages of 2 and 3 years (Locke, 1997). In the cases of Serena and Gabrielle, variability in the use of such elements continued for at least 4 years post adoption until 10;0 and beyond. Serena and Gabrielle also regularized irregular past tense forms ("catched"), as has also been noted in 2-3 year olds (Pinker, 1999; Locke, 1997). Difficulties with working memory for language persisted over time according to standardized tests. Nevertheless, as Chapter 3 will show, they had developed into highly skilled conversationalists by the time this study began.

2.5 Beginnings: conclusions

All the evidence about Serena, Gabrielle and Ingrid that it was possible to obtain enables us to draw two main conclusions. On the one hand, the state-organized deprivation factories of the Romanian orphanage system failed to provide any of them with adequate opportunities for physical, mental, social or linguistic development. Compared with typically developing children of the same age from the general community without histories of deprivation, the girls, prior to adoption, appeared to be severely disadvantaged and completely dependent on others for their most basic needs. On the other hand, these years spent in the most impoverished conditions had not apparently impaired, let alone destroyed, their ability to learn on any front. From their first days, sometimes their first minutes, with their new families, the children changed, became enlivened, hungrily sought out and seized opportunities to act and interact, and began to develop along lines which are quite familiar from studies of younger children in more typical life conditions. This suggests that the behaviours which Serena, Gabrielle and Ingrid exhibited while still in the orphanages, and for some time post-adoption, were not signs of irreparable damage done to their minds and bodies. On the contrary, their subsequent progress implied that these behaviours were acquired, and, therefore, contingent, adaptations to the restricted opportunities for action and interaction that could be had under such conditions and which they could begin to transcend, or unlearn, once those conditions improved, although to what extent remained ultimately unclear.

Serena, Gabrielle and Ingrid were able to make fundamental and significant strides in forming positive social relationships with others and successfully integrating into a variety of social contexts. The girls were able to make good academic progress at school relative to the time they had spent in their new homes, with no sign of marked disparities between different aspects of cognitive development (see Chapter 7).

The capacity for language learning proved to be particularly resilient once the girls found themselves in a more encouraging environment. Indeed, the rapid development of language skills in Serena, Gabrielle and Ingrid closely parallels that reported for younger children without histories of extreme neglect. Linguistic catch-up of this order has been noted in other cases of severe deprivation (Chapter 1). Language ability also reportedly developed in step with non-verbal cognition, according to conventional tests, offering no obvious evidence for alleged "dissociations" between linguistic and non-linguistic cognition (see Chapters 4, 5 and 6). The virtual absence of productive language in the children when adopted, coupled with clear signs of immediate and rapid learning of English, strongly suggest that the girls' linguistic development is best seen as *first language learning* rather than either second language learning, as is the case with many internationally adopted children, or as "second first-language acquisition" (Scott, Roberts and Glennen, 2011) as has been proposed for many globally deprived adoptees (see Chapter 1).

In sum, the picture which emerges from the accounts of the early and post-adoption lives of Serena, Gabrielle and Ingrid is one of substantial and rapid recovery of physical abilities and learning capacities, with language no exception, a picture which is consistent with many accounts of the development of internationally adopted post institutionalized children (Chapter 1). All the same, such a positive picture of resilient developmental potential should not lead us to misunderstand or underestimate the scale of the learning task that the girls faced when entering their new homes. The attitudes and expectations from others that a 6 year old child has to deal with, for example, are not the same as those that surround a 2 year old. Similarly, the behaviour of a 6 year old will not be interpreted and responded to by adults or other children like the behaviour of a 2 year old. The learning task for an older child, therefore, can simply never be the same as for a younger child. As Glennen (2007a) notes, this general circumstance also poses the most difficult challenges for those charged with assessing children's progress after years of deprivation, since the usual developmental yardsticks do not apply.

CHAPTER THREE

LIFE IN CONVERSATION:
TALK IN EVERYDAY SETTINGS

3.1 Introduction

In this chapter we look closely at the children's development as conversationalists. Conversation provides perhaps the best and most direct view of the children's progress in both linguistic communication and social interaction and also affords rich insights into their development as unique personalities.[1]

Existing psychological and linguistic literature generally appears to pay little attention to spontaneous conversation as a window on the social and communicative development of extremely deprived or previously institutionalised children. To our knowledge, there are no published studies of Romanian adoptees' spontaneous talk in naturalistic contexts and it is rare to see any transcribed utterance material at all in the literature on internationally adopted children.

However, conversational skills have been explicitly noted in some relevant studies. In the case of Genie, for example, Curtiss concludes the following:

"in total, Genie performs few normal or appropriate acts and, in large measure, appears to be *conversationally incompetent*. Verbal interaction with Genie consists mainly of someone's asking Genie a question repeatedly until Genie answers, or of Genie's making a comment and someone else's responding to it in some way" (1977, p.233).

Curtiss goes on to consider the reasons for Genie's "conversational incompetence":

---

[1] In this chapter, aside from the researcher's name, Lisa, pseudonyms are used for friends and acquaintances of the girls, while initials will be used for close family members.

"It is not surprising, I think, that Genie displays incompetence in this area. Her failure to perform many of the behaviours requisite for successful conversational interaction is most probably a result of her social and psychological deprivation. Genie grew up in an environment devoid of verbal interaction. Never or practically never having witnessed the performance of these sociolinguistic behaviours, she did not develop them" (Curtiss, 1977, p.233).

Curtiss goes on to speculate that "individuals with developmental social and psychological disturbance" might be expected to "display general and pervasive impairment in the social and communicative functions of language" (p.233). However, in line with the prevailing theoretical wisdom of the time (and of much later times), it never occurs to Curtiss to make a close link between conversational skills (which she refers to as "sociolinguistic behaviors") and linguistic competence. That is, she never considers that Genie's lack of conversational inclination and experience might be a key factor in explaining the *structural* "economy" of her utterances (cf Jones, 1995, p. 279, footnote 3).

Serena, Gabrielle and Ingrid, like Genie, missed out on the experience of the early patterns of socio-emotional interaction between child and primary carer which are considered by some to be a prerequisite for the successful development of social (and conversational) skills in late childhood and adulthood (Bowlby, 1951, 1969; Locke, 1995). Also like Genie, when Serena, Gabrielle and Ingrid were adopted (at the respective ages of 7;5, 6;3 and 3;10), they had not learned to talk. Nevertheless, as this chapter will show, within a few years the girls had developed a conversational competence arguably indistinguishable from that of many older children or teenagers, at least in those contexts that were accessible for research purposes.

Methodologically, the chapter is influenced by Conversation Analysis (CA) in its examination of key aspects of the organization of talk-in-interaction (Sacks, Schegloff and Jefferson, 1974; Whitworth, Perkins, and Lesser, 1997). We will be looking at some of the most basic and common techniques for engaging co-operatively and coherently in everyday conversational exchange, including turn-taking (3.2.1), fixing troubles in ongoing conversations (3.2.2), respecting etiquette and being polite (3.2.3) and adapting conversational style according to the context (3.2.4).

CA is a useful methodology to adopt, and suits our qualitative research goals, since it is non-reductionist in theory and flexible in practice. It does not attempt to shoe-horn observed behaviour into a finite set of preconceived categories but attempts to account for conversational participants' own strategies and understandings as these are displayed in their handling of live utterances. Furthermore, CA is broader in scope than traditional linguistic analysis since it takes into account not only the syntactic, lexical, morphological and phonological aspects of spoken language, but the "communicative acts in discourse that are not part of conventional languages – eye gaze, gestures, nods, smiles and manifest actions" (Clark, 1996, p.57). This allows for an open-minded and open-ended examination of the entire repertoire of creative communicative strategies used by children to interact with the people around them and can also shed light on the strategies unique to a particular child. Nevertheless, "analysis" along these lines remains an interpretative enterprise on the part of researchers rather than an "objective" description and, therefore, readers may disagree about the interpretations of utterances we have given below. While what follows, then, is not intended as a conventional "assessment" of the girls' communicative abilities, we hope that it will have interest in illustrating the levels of interactional attunement, communicative sensitivity and creativity, as well as the linguistic sophistication more narrowly, which are demonstrably at play in the talk of Serena, Gabrielle and Ingrid.

3.2 Conversations

Here we present selected extracts from conversations involving Serena, Gabrielle and Ingrid which were observed over a 2 year period. Where relevant, the girls' conversational behaviours are compared to those of Genie (Curtiss, 1977), since the latter case study is unusual for the detail that it gives about particular episodes of interaction.

3.2.1 Turn-taking

In order to participate in everyday talk, speakers must be able to initiate conversations, respond to the initiatives of others, and elect to take turns to talk during conversations. Speakers must also be able to propose, pick up on and sustain appropriate conversational topics. The following extracts give examples of these aspects of the girls' turn-taking skills.

Asking questions

One of the most frequent strategies used by Serena, Gabrielle and Ingrid for initiating and continuing a conversation was to ask questions. They employed a range of syntactically marked question types including aux-inverted, WH-type, tag and intonated forms. WH-type question structures were often utilized as a conversational device for selecting the next speaker or requesting clarification of the conversational partner's previous turn. Serena, Gabrielle and Ingrid used questions to maintain a topic relevant to the conversational partner's previous turn and to initiate their own topics. In contrast, Genie's attempts at conversation were noticeable for the absence of syntactically marked questions (WH-type or subject-auxiliary inversion):

> "Genie has never asked a syntactically marked question. Her attempts to construct questions (in attempts to teach her to do so) have led to the most ill-formed, least English-like structures she has produced (e.g. *Where is may I have a penny?; Where is tomorrow Mrs. L?; I where is graham cracker on top shelf?*). She can decode the linguistic structure of questions and appears to know the constituent structure of WH-question word she hears ... but is unable to produce spontaneous interrogatives" (Curtiss, 1977, p.191).

The following examples illustrate the three girls' ability to use questions to initiate and maintain topics in conversation or to join in with others' discussions.

Serena: (16.10.99, aged 12;7)[2]

Scene: Serena, Gabrielle and Lisa have been talking in the sitting room. There is a brief lapse in the conversation. Serena initiates a new topic.

T1	S:	Have you got a g-boyfriend?
	L:	*{nods}*
T2	S:	Who?
T3	L:	His name's John.
T4	S:	John? *{looks confused as if she has never come across this name before}*
T5	S:	D'you like him?
T6	L:	Ye:s he's nice=
T7	S:	=What does he look like?
T8	L:	Well, he's tall.

---

[2] Utterances will be dated as follows: 16.10.99 (i.e., 16th of October 1999).

Serena: (20.05.00, aged 13;2)

Scene: Lisa has just administered a standardized test to Serena. After a brief pause, Serena initiates a conversation.

T1	S:	D'you have to do this to somebody else now or?
T2	L:	Yeah=
T3	S:	=Do you? Who? Who d'ya have to do?
T4	L:	Well actually no I don't I don't have to do it to anybody else now.
T5	S:	Don't ya? I thought ya did.
T6	L:	No I already did it to somebody else earlier on in the week.
T7	S:	Why? Who was it?
T8	L:	e:rm another child who I'm (1) visiting like I'm visiting you.
T9	S:	Who is that child's name?
T10	L:	Her name is Ingrid.
T11	S:	Who?
T12	L:	Ingrid.
T13	S:	That's _ strange name.
T14	L:	Well she's Rom-She's from Romania as well.

Gabrielle: (17.09.98, aged 13;2)

Scene: Conversation between Gabrielle and friend, Dana. After a brief pause, Gabrielle starts a new topic.

T1	G:	So what did y do in school today?
{pause: Dana is licking her lolly}		
T2	D:	Lots of things.
T3	G:	Work?
T4	D:	mm: (3) loads of boring stuff.
T5	G:	Oh, movin' round, goin' to different teachers?
T6	D:	mm:
T7	G:	Yep, that's what we did (1) tsk! Well, that was a bit boring (2) Work is borin' init? and school (2) Definitely is.

Gabrielle: (16.10.99, aged 14;4)

Scene: Gabrielle is styling Lisa's hair.

T1	G:	D'ya want to know what I want for Christmas then?
T2	L:	e:rm [[You tell me then
T3	G:	[[Reebok Classic Trainers.

Ingrid: (02.12.98, aged 11;1)

1. *Scene: Ingrid is playing with her yo-yo and asks Lisa about the other children in the study.*

T1	I:	Who else d'you see?
T2	L:	Who else do I see?
T3	I:	Yea:h=
T4	L:	=As in which of the children do I see?
T5	I:	Pardon?
T6	L:	As in what other children do I see?
T7	I:	Yea:h.

{Slight pause}

T8	L:	A few others.
T9	I:	What're their names?
T10	L:	Serena Gabrielle Carrie Eleanor Tommy Terrie and Nicholas.
T11	I:	And me.
T12	L:	Yeah.
T13	I:	What-What's the matter with them? Why d'ya need to see them?
T14	L:	Because they're like you They were all born in Romania and came to England (2) like you did.
T15	I:	Do they all come from Romania?
T16	L:	Yep (.) yeah.

2. *Scene: Ingrid is eating dinner with her family, including her mother, M. The conversation has just changed topic to the subject of vegetarianism. Lisa has just said that she likes to eat some types of vegetarian food. Ingrid tries to enter the conversation.*

T1	I:	Are you a vegetarian?
T2	L:	Yeah.
T3	I:	Why?
T4	L:	I just don't like eating meat very much.
T5	I:	D'ya like chickens?

T6	L:	I used to like chicken yeah.
T7	M:	mm:
T8	L:	I'm not strictly vegetarian though I eat fish but I never used to eat fish before.
T9	I:	I don't like fish very much.

Serena, Gabrielle and Ingrid also used interrogative forms to make requests, extend invitations and tell jokes (even if the punch-lines were not always clear), as illustrated by the following examples.

Serena: (08.09.98, aged 11;6)

Scene: Serena and her teacher, Mrs Taylor (T), are playing cards.

T1	S:	*{stands up and then goes into kitchen}* Am I allowed to have a biscuit?
	T:	*{does not directly answer Serena because is talking to her brother}*
T2	S:	*{comes back into dining room and stands in front of Mrs Taylor}* 'Scuse me am I allowed to have a biscuit?
T3	T:	Yes I think so=
T4	S:	=Thank you *{Serena then bounds into kitchen and opens biscuit tin and takes out a biscuit}*

Gabrielle: (17.09.98, aged 13;2)

Scene: Gabrielle and Dana are facing the camera, noisily slurping ice-lollies.

T1	G:	*{turns and looks at Dana}* Would you like to come to my school barbecue on Friday next week?
T2	D:	e:rm-
T3	G:	D'ya like barbecues?-burgers roll e:rm (2) D'ya like barbecue food? *{gazes up at Dana}*
T4	D:	er e:rm yeah.
T5	G:	Good! *{nods simultaneously}* Would ya like to come? Are ya doing anythink on Friday?
T6	D:	I don't know yet (2) What time d' it start? *{slight pause}*
T7	G:	Well I('ve) not had the letter. I've no idea (1) mm:

Ingrid: (13.04.99, aged 11;6)

Scene: Ingrid and Lisa are talking in the study.

T1	I:	What's an-What's an elephant up a tree? [[It's stuck
T2	L:	[[I don't know
		{slight pause}
T3	I:	Hm D'you get it? It's too fat to get in a tree [[D'you get it?
T4	L:	[[O:h yeah
		(2) yeah *{Lisa laughs}* That's good.

In some situations, Serena and Gabrielle asked their conversational partners lots of questions in quick succession. However, their motivations appeared to differ. Serena was always very curious about the lives and experiences of others and often used open-ended WH-type questions to enquire about a range of issues from cyber-pets to marriage. On one occasion, during an exchange with Gabrielle's adoptive mother, K., Serena asked fifteen questions in 30 seconds (28.10.98, see example below). Gabrielle, on the other hand, was noted to frequently use Yes/No (aux-inverted) questions when ascertaining the specific preferences of same age or younger peers. Note the following examples.

Serena: (28.10.98, aged 11;7)

Scene: Serena and K. (Gabrielle's mother) have been cooking together in the kitchen. Suddenly, Serena sees some school exam material belonging to K.'s son, J.

T1	S:	What-Who's gonna learn these?
T2	K:	Pardon?
T3	S:	Who's gonna learn this?
T4	K:	J.
T5	S:	Why?
T6	K:	'Cuz he's doing-'Cuz he's taking an exam. They have to know all about the body=
T7	S:	=Does he know it?
T8	K:	No, not ye:t *{switches on food mixer}*
T9	S:	Did he used to?
	K:	*{doesn't hear Serena's previous question, so switches off food mixer}*
T10	S:	Did he used to though?

T11	K:	No he doesn't know it. That's the trouble why he needs to learn it.
T12	S:	And what 'appens if he still can't learn it?
T13	K:	mm:?=Well he won't pass the exam. If he can't learn it he won't pass the exam.
T14	S:	And what would he do then?
T15	K:	He'll fail it. That will be that.
T16	S:	And then what [[stay at home?
T17	K:	[[mm: No: oh no he wouldn't stay at home
T18	S:	[[What would he do then?
T19	K:	[[He's got to go out to work and get a job (3) [[an' earn some money.
T20	S:	[[What 'appens if he can't get it?
T21	K:	Huh?
T22	S:	What 'appens if he can't get a job?
T23	K:	He will get a job doin' something.

Gabrielle: (17.09.98, aged 13;2)

Scene: Gabrielle and Dana talking in the bedroom.

T1	G:	D'ya wanna keep that Lypsol?
T2	D:	mm:
T3	G:	Would ya like to keep that doggy-here?
T4	D:	No it's all right I've got thousands of them.
		{pause: Gabrielle shows Dana some animal stickers in a book}
T5	D:	[[A:h!
T6	G:	[[D'ya want that one or that one?
T7	D:	*{Dana looks at Gabrielle and then points to a picture}*
T8	G:	What that one?
T9	D:	[[Yeah
T10	G:	[[Would ya like to keep that one? *{turns to look at Dana}* Well if I cut it out for you [[yeah?
T11	D:	[[No s'all right don't wanna keep (2) that.
T12	G:	e:rm What d'ya wanna keep then? *{clears throat}* I'm not-not- I'm not forcin' you I'm not shouting at you. *{simultaneously raises hands in supplication and then smiles and then lets out a breath}*
T13	D:	*{does not look at Gabrielle but giggles}*

T14   G: *{leans forward}* So what would you like to keep then?
               D'ya wanna keep anything-anything of here: or?
               *{slight pause: Dana ignores Gabrielle's previous
               question and examines posters on the wall}*

It was during group discussions that the differences between the
questioning styles of Serena and Gabrielle with adults were particularly
evident. For example, on one occasion (16.10.99), Serena, aged 12;7 and
Gabrielle aged 14;4, interrogated the researcher, Lisa, about her friend,
John. Gabrielle persisted in asking questions that seemed to relate to her
own experiences and preferences, while Serena made polite inquiries
about the circumstances of her conversational partner:

Serena and Gabrielle: (16.10.99, aged 12;7 and 14;4)

*Scene: Gabrielle, Serena and Lisa have been conversing together in the
sitting room. Gabrielle and Serena then begin to question Lisa about her
friend.*

T1   S: =Does he look sexy or not (.)[[or handsome?
T2   L: [[Yea:h *{starts to laugh.}*
               He does yeah.
T3   G: What does he wear sports clothes like me then?
T4   L: [[yeah.
T5   S   [[Does he live with you *{points to Lisa}* or d'ya live
               separate?
T6   L: No sometimes we live together and sometimes we don't
               I-I live in my own place an' he's got his own house an'
               I sometimes go and see him.
T7   G: *{slurps noisily on her lolly}* Has he got Kickers then
               Puma?
T8   L: Has he got?
T9   G: Has he got Reebok Classic trainers then?
T10   L: e:rm *{L. considers}*
T11   G: Nike Ellesse?
T12   L: I'm not sure if he has got Reebok Classic Trainers to be
               honest=
T13   G: =Tsk Oh you must know he's y- (1) you've got-You
               must know it's y-You must know he's your boyfriend
               {sighs}
T14   L: Well he's probably got just some (1) normal trainers but
               he hasn't got Reebok ones.

T15	G:	He hasn't got any make?
T16	L:	No: [[he's not into that.
T17	G:	[[Oh well that's a bit-[[Guess he must be stupid then in't he?
T18	S:	[[No *{comments on Lisa's previous statement.}*
T19	L:	He doesn't like that kind of thing=
T20	G:	=He's horrible then I hate 'im.

Replying to questions

The following extracts illustrate the ability of Serena, Gabrielle and Ingrid to comprehend and respond appropriately to WH-type, aux-inverted and intonated questions.

Serena: (08.09.98, aged 11;6)

Scene: Serena and Lisa talking in the conservatory.

T1	L:	You get detention if you do something wrong?
T2	S:	Well if you don't- *{proceeds to speak more slowly}* If you don't do your homework in time cuz like Sally James sez "I'm goin' ou:t" and then Miss Jones('ll) say "You've got to do homework by tomorrow" (an' I <u>say</u>) "I can't Mi:ss" (.) that an'-then she'll say "You'll-You'll have detention" *{Intonation rises at end of word}* Yeah cuz Sally James got detention an' she got gold certificate.

Gabrielle: (07.10.98, aged 13;3)

Scene: Gabrielle has just finished a bowl of Weetabix. Lisa initiates conversation by asking about one of Gabrielle's acquaintances.

T1	L:	So who's Taryn?
T2	G:	Tsk O:hh Serena's friend who goes to Winchester.

Ingrid: (10.09.98, aged 10;11)

Scene: Ingrid and Lisa talk about Ingrid's father, J., and his interest in walking.

T1	L:	Does he do lots of walking then?
T2	I:	No: I like walking though.

Serena, Gabrielle and Ingrid understood the point of *why* and *how* questions and always responded aptly to these. This is significant since, according to Crystal, full comprehension of *because* (in answer to *why* questions) is not acquired until the age of 8 years and beyond in children without histories of extreme neglect:

> "Children have often been observed to use structures without fully comprehending them - a point which is felt not to be surprising in the learning of vocabulary, but which is often neglected in relation to grammar. A well-studied example is children's use of *because*, encountered as a connective from around age three, but not fully comprehended until age eight and after, as shown by examples such as *My father never got sick because he catches cold* and *Why do wolves bite? Because they are from Little Red Riding Hood*" (Crystal, 1987, p. 106).

The following examples demonstrate the girls' apposite use of *because* to answer *why* and *how* questions:

Serena: (08.09.98, aged 11;6)
T1   L: Why's she better than you?
T2   S: 'Cuz she 'ad more practice than me (1) sometime.

Gabrielle: (27.07.98, aged 13;2)
T1   L: Why is Ruth with Phil?
T2   G: 'Cuz she loves him She wants to kiss him.

Ingrid: (22.07.98, aged 10;9)
T1   L: How do you know Shelby?
T2   I: Because coz er (2) my mum met her.

There was the odd occasion when the girls' responses to questions appeared to indicate misinterpretation or possible difficulty with comprehension, although this may have been due to a perceived ambiguity in the conversational context or, indeed, to the listener misinterpreting or mishearing the child's response. Note the following example for Serena:

Serena: (18.03.00, aged 13;0)

Scene: Serena and Lisa are talking in the dining room. Gabrielle is also present.
T1   L: D'you ever walk the dog?
T2   S: Yea:h hh. {*Nods*}

T3   L: Where d'you go?

{3 second pause: Serena looks at Lisa in a perplexed way, then looks out of the window. She seems to be having difficulty in answering Lisa's question}

T4   S: Only sometimes.

In Gabrielle's case, very occasionally, her responses to questions (including WH-type ones) appeared to be unrelated to the conversational partner's previous turn. For example, Gabrielle would not answer a specific question directed to her, but instead would ask the interlocutor another non-related question. However, this could have been due to interpersonal issues such as shyness rather than any problem with comprehension. Note the following:

Gabrielle: (24.04.99, aged 13;9)

Scene: Gabrielle is standing alone in the dining room when Serena's father, R., enters the room.

T1   R: Where's N. gone? D'you want to go upstairs and find him?

{2 second pause}

T2   G: D'you like my hair?

As mentioned earlier, in many conversational settings, Serena asked lots of questions. In answer to questions, however, Serena occasionally gave highly elliptical, often one word, answers. This is reminiscent of the one-word responses sometimes given by Genie to WH-questions during her early years of rehabilitation. Note the following example (Curtiss et al., 1975, p.147):

"Marilyn and Genie: 2-19-75
M: What does Marsha do in class?
G: Draw.
M: What does Marsha draw?
G: Sun."

Similar interactions were noted during the first few years after Serena's adoption:

Serena: (17.05.97, aged 10;2)[3]

1.		*Scene: Serena and her brother, N., are engaged in a colouring activity in the lounge. Their mother, J., who is filming them, asks Serena about an art lesson at school.*
T1	J:	mm: What other flowers did you do?
T2	S:	Daisy

2.   *Scene: J. talks to Serena in the garden with N. also present.*
T1   J: Now (2) What do you like about the Isle of Man?
T2   S: Beach (2) [[Collectin' shells
T3   J: [[And the beach (2) collecting shells yeah an'
                    You fell over Yep.

In one conversational exchange between the adoptive parents of Serena and Gabrielle, all twelve of Serena's turns consisted of questions (WH-type, aux-inverted and tag). In exasperation, Gabrielle's father, M., decided to ask Serena an open-ended question back. Note her response in turn 2:

Serena: (28.10.98, aged 11;7)
T1   M: What happens when you run out of questions?
T2   S: Quiet.
T3   M: You go quiet do you?
T4   S: Yeah No.

Statements: recounting events

Serena, Gabrielle and Ingrid often offered or maintained conversational topics by volunteering information about their views, opinions, likes and dislikes and by giving descriptions or explanations of events or situations. For example, Serena sometimes liked to talk about her school activities or friends, while Ingrid was quite effective at explaining unfamiliar activities or objects to her conversational partners, if they requested her to do so. Gabrielle enjoyed expressing her likes and dislikes and giving her opinions, particularly concerning clothes. In the following examples, Serena describes events that took place at her school, Gabrielle gives her

---

[3] The following two extracts of talk are taken from a videotape made by the family prior to the beginning of the study and made available by them for research purposes.

views on fashion and Ingrid describes a leisure centre, and gives a step-by-step explanation of an unfamiliar school activity.

Serena: (11.03.99, aged 12;0)

Scene: Serena, Gabrielle and her mother, K., are in the kitchen, talking. Gabrielle has just told K. that she has some maths homework to do. Serena, addressing K., continues the topic by describing a maths exam at school.

T1	S:	On Tuesday we had a difficult questions up to twenty-eight and we had a tape Mr Johnson who's our Maths teacher gave us all a sheet and then he told us about it (2) then lady on the tape say "If you get stuck put a cross on it."

{2 second pause: Serena looks at K. expectantly}

T2	S:	an' then-an' I got one out of twenty-eight (3)[[and that's not good.
T3	K:	[[And what's- You got one out of twenty [[eight?=Is it called SATS?
T4	S:	[[{giggly breath}

{3 second pause}

T5	S:	[[Well it's only a practice [[It was a practice one-
T6	K:	[[It sounds like- [[Practicing-practicing for the SATS?
T7	S:	-before before May

Serena: (20.05.00, aged 13;2)

Scene: Lisa has been talking about her school days to Serena.

T1	S:	Did you get in trouble in middle school (2)[[or in high school?
T2	L:	[[Sometimes yeah
		I got detention.
T3	S:	I've got a detention this Monday (.) [[for not signing my diary.
T4	L:	[[Did you? (4) Did you? *{sounds surprised}* We:ll

T5   S: Well I-I'm-I'm getting that one this Monday (1) but
                uhuhh *{voice trails off}* Well it's a mistake I had one tic-
                ticket for English (1) for interrupting class and I had erm
                (3) yeah and got some late tickets.

Describing ambitions and expressing likes and dislikes

Gabrielle: (24.04.99, aged 13;9)

*Scene: During test administration. Gabrielle and Lisa sit and talk in the
conservatory at Serena's parents' house.*

T1   L: Would you like to be a weather lady?
T2   G: No! *{said abruptly}* [[Don't be silly
T3   L: [[Why not?
T4   G: I want to be a (1) a gym-a gym-a gym-a gym teacher an'
                a sports- an work in a sports shop.
T5   L: Do ya?
T6   G: Ye-e-es! Plus- (3) That is my favourite thing doin'
                spo:rt. (2) mm:
T7   L: Is that your favourite subject at school?
T8   G: Spo:rt?
T9   L: Yeah.
T10   G: S'all right=I don't like P.E. but I like doin' sport.

Making comments and giving opinions

Gabrielle: (24.04.99, aged 13;9)

1.   *Scene: Lisa checks the video camera while Gabrielle observes.
        Gabrielle then initiates a new topic.*
T1   G: I bet ya haven't got a bright orange nail varnish (1) I bet
                ya haven't got a bright pink or a bri- or a bright orange
                nail varnish I('ve) got a bright orange.
{slight pause}
T3   L: You know Gabrielle I haven't actually got any nail
                varnish at all because really I don't use it [[I don't wear-
T4   G: [[That's   cuz
                your fingers are- Your nails are too short (2) an' mine
                are as well.

2.   *Scene: Lisa and Gabrielle talk about clothes.*
T1   L: You don't like my jacket?
T2   G: No it's no-your trousers are not fashion your top's not
                    an' your (1) jacket's not.
T3   L: So (2) what are (1) the latest fashions then Gabrielle?
T4   G: e:r Well I thi:nk (2) we:ll I think (1) hipsters are fashion
                    hipsters with skirts and (2) combat jeans.

Describing

Ingrid: (22.07.98, aged 10;9)

Scene: Lisa and Ingrid talk in the study.
T1   L: I didn't know there was an ice skating place in London
T2   I: "The Ice Centre"! You can get all sorts there You can
                    get bowlin' and you c- Yeah you can get bowlin' at
                    another place but I didn't go You can get swimmin' with
                    "The Ice Centre" ice skating and all sorts of games and
                    you can get tea there as well.

Explaining

Ingrid: (10.09.98, aged 10;11)

Scene: Lisa and Ingrid are sitting in the study, talking about Ingrid's choice of subjects at school. Lisa asks for clarification of a subject activity called "maps".
T1   L: What do you have to do in maps?
T2   I: Yeah okay We at school- I'm quite good because I've
                    done it in class It's like (2) you have to look in a map
                    okay?
T3   L: A map of anywhere?
T4   I: Yeah like in a country somewhere and if you wanted to
                    go you're there *{points}* aren't ya?
T5   L: mm:
T6   I: If you wanted to go on the other side you go in the car
                    that way *{points}* don't ya or something?
T7   L: Yeah
T8   I: Well you turn or something=
T9   L: =Yeah=

T10	I:	=and you keep going on and there's a corner what says "Shrewsbury" You turn that way.
T11	L:	Right Shrewsbury.
T12	I:	And then (2) I wanna get to the other side to Wales right I turn to Shrewsbury Right you keep goin' on (.) Oh I need to turn back cuz I've gone in the wrong place (2) Then you keep goin' on (1) and then there's this place what's called (3) Ya keep goin' on and there's this corner you have to turn at That's what maps are.
T13	L:	O:h! *[Lisa finally understands]* So you have to sort of find your directions to [[it-to a place?
T14	I:	[[Yea:h.

3.2.2 Fixing troubles in ongoing conversation (repair)

As Perkins (2003) notes:

> "An immense variety of trouble sources can arise ... in interaction, which obstruct the production of a sequentially implicated next turn. The organization of repair provides a mechanism to deal with such trouble sources. The organization of repair is the self-righting mechanism for the organization of language use in social interaction" (p. 148).

Throughout the 2 year duration of the study, Serena, Gabrielle or Ingrid were consistently able to use a range of repair devices when faced with possible communicative breakdowns in conversation in a wide variety of contexts, as the extracts below illustrate.

Repair on next turn

Serena, Gabrielle and Ingrid were able to repair conversational breakdowns due to simultaneous self-selection by both parties and include the use of "next turn repair initiators" (Levinson, 1983, pp. 335, 339) to prompt the conversational partner to repeat a turn:

Serena: (08.09.98, aged 11;6)

1.	*Scene:*	*Serena and Lisa are at the table.*
T1	L:	When are ya seeing Gabrielle again?
T2	S:	I'm not sure (2) I don' know
T3	L:	[[When was the la-
T4	S:	[[In-

{slight pause: 2 seconds}

T5	S:	What?=
T6	L:	=When-when was the last time you saw Gabrielle?=
T7	S:	=I don' know (2) Look at that (.) Keep it Keep it.

2.   *Scene: Serena and Lisa resume talking after a brief pause in the conversation.*

T1	L:	[[I sometime-
T2	S:	[[Sometimes I colour (2) pictures
T3	L:	Do you?
T4	S:	mm: What was yous gunna-yous gunna say?
T5	L:	I sometimes sit down and I draw pictures occasionally (1) but then I kind of erm (1) lose patience and it gets a (2) bit boring but I-I used to like it at school.

Serena: (16.10.99, aged 12;7)

Scene: Serena has just awakened from her sleep and walks into the lounge where Lisa is sitting.

T1	L:	What's your favourite erm *{voice trails off as Lisa picks up something from the floor}*
T2	S:	And what?
T3	L:	What's your favourite swimming (2)[[position?
T4	S:	[[I like all of them really.

Gabrielle: (16.10.99, aged 14;4)

1.   *Scene: Gabrielle and Lisa talk during a game of "hairdressers".*

T1	L:	When was the last time you did a picture?
T2	G:	Wha:t?
T3	L:	When was the last time you did a picture?

2.   *Scene: Gabrielle asks Lisa for clarification of Serena's previous turn.*

T1	G:	What?=What did she say?
		{brief exchange between Serena and Lisa}
T2	G:	What's she said?
T3	L:	She asked if I worked with old people.
T4	G:	O:h right.

Gabrielle: (20.05.00, aged 14;10)

Scene: Gabrielle has just said that she doesn't like a sweet because Lisa gave it to her.

T1	L:	Well that's not very nice is it?
T2	G:	Sorry?
T3	L:	Would you say you didn't like it if Serena'd given you the sweet?
T4	G:	Hm:?
T5	L:	Would you say you didn't like it if Serena'd given you the sweet?
T6	G:	What? What d'you say? What d'you mean?

Ingrid: (29.06.98, aged 10;8)

Scene: Family meal. Ingrid's mother, M., makes a comment about the date.

T1	M:	It's July tomorrow (2) eight or nine Yeah, I'm not sure.
T2	I:	*{looks sharply at M.}* What did you say?
T3	M:	It's July tomorrow.

Ingrid: (14.10.98, aged 11;0)

Scene: Ingrid and her friend, Carina, are out of camera range, playing with the computerized spelling game. Carina then moves into camera range.

T1	C:	Right come on We'll do them a dance there.
T2	I:	What did you say?
T3	C:	*{Carina talks to the camera}* We are going to do you a dance.

Serena, Gabrielle and Ingrid were also able to issue direct requests for clarification if they had not understood or misheard some aspect of their conversational partner's previous turn, as in the following examples:

Serena: (08.09.98, aged 11;6)

Scene: Mrs Taylor (T.), the teacher, and Serena are at the table playing cards. Serena asks for clarification of a word meaning.

T1	S:	*{sighs}*
T2	T:	Well you've won some more.

T3	S:	Mostly ca:rds
T4	T:	Oh dear [[you're never satisfie:d!
T5	S:	[[blah blah blah

{slight pause: Serena and Mrs Taylor continue to play cards for 4-5 seconds}

T6	S:	What's that sa-sa-What's-what's that mean "sa-sa-fied"? hh
T7	T:	"Satisfied"?
T8	S:	[[Yeah, what's that mean?
T9	T:	[[You always want mo:re (.) of something else.
T10	S:	(I think)
T11	L:	Don't you know what "satisfied" means Serena?
T12	S:	No *{puts thumb in mouth}* I want more *{blows a raspberry}* thank you.

Repair through completion of conversational partner's previous turn

Serena and Gabrielle were able to complete their conversational partners' previously unfinished turns, demonstrating their ability to predict what the other speaker was likely to say based on the preceding utterance:

Serena: (08.09.98, aged 11;6)

Scene: Serena and Lisa are in the conservatory and have been reading Serena's school report together.

T1	S:	*{maintains eye contact with Lisa}* D'you still like art?
T2	L:	*(ponders for a couple of seconds)* No: I don't like art any more I think it's a bit erm (3)
T3	S:	boring?
T4	L:	Yea:h Do you find it boring?
T5	S:	*{shrugs}* I don't mind it.

Serena: (16.10.99, aged 12;7)

Scene: Serena is talking with Lisa about diet.

T1	L:	I don't eat much chocolate though anyway because (2)[[erm
T2	S:	[[It makes ya fat?
T3	L:	Yeah.

Gabrielle: (16.10.99, aged 14;4)

1.   *Scene: Gabrielle styles Lisa's hair while they talk.*
T1   L: Let's play a game
T2   G: What game?
T3   L: We're goin' to play (3) *{Lisa's voice trails off as she
            thinks}*
T4   G: "Truth or Dare" okay.

2.   *Scene: Lisa is just about to administer a test.*
T1   G: Well this is a bit of a boring game.
T2   L: No it's not.
T3   G: It is.
T4   L: Well if you concentrate then it'll be (3) *{voice trails off}*
T5   G: even more boringish.

3.   *Scene: Lisa and Gabrielle talk before the administration of a test.*
T1   L: Oh before you go Gabrielle there's one (3) *{voice trails
            off)*
T2   G: one what?
T3   L: test=
T4   G: =*{yawns heavily and slumps against the sofa, sighs then
            giggles}*

Repair of misunderstandings through questioning and cross-checking

According to Crystal (1997a):

> "In everyday conversation, misunderstandings often take place as speakers
> make assumptions about what their listeners know, or need to know, that
> turn out to be wrong. At such points, the conversation can break down and
> may need to be 'repaired', with the participants questioning, clarifying, and
> cross-checking ... But it is quite common for participants not to realize that
> there has been a breakdown, and to continue conversing at cross purposes"
> (p. 117).

Like all conversationalists, Serena and Ingrid did not always make their
communicative intention clear to their interlocutors, which occasionally
resulted in conversational misunderstandings. They would, however,
attempt to clarify these mix-ups when they occurred, as the following
dialogue extracts show:

Serena: (08.09.98, aged 11;6)

Scene: Serena and Lisa are talking in the conservatory.

T1	S:	Has Gabrielle changed a lot (2) 'cuz I haven't seen her for long time
T2	L:	Has she changed a lot?
		{pause}
T3	L:	When was the last time you saw her?
T4	S:	*{looks at L.}* Mm? What?
T5	L:	When was the last time you saw Gabrielle?
T6	S:	Yeah erm I'm asking you has Gabrielle changed a lot (1) or not?
T7	L:	*{looks confused}* Well from when? 'cuz I don't=
T8	S:	=Before
T9	L:	Before when? When was the last time you saw her? ('cuz I-)
T10	S:	No you-you saw her. You went to see her, didn't you? *{Points to Lisa}*
T11	L:	I went to see her (2) about three months ago [[and then-
T12	S:	[[Yeah but-
T13	L:	I went to see her a couple of weeks ago and she hadn't *{shakes head}* she didn't change in the few weeks that I saw her.
T14	S:	I haven't changed have I?
T15	L:	No you haven't changed no.

Ingrid: (10.09.98, aged 10;11)

Scene: Ingrid and Lisa talk about Ingrid's father and his interest in walking

T1	L:	Does he do lots of walking then?
T2	I:	No: I like walking though
T3	L:	Where do you [[normally go?
T4	I:	[[I packed in it now.[5]
		{slight pause}
T5	L:	Who?
T6	I:	He doesn't like doing it anymore.

---

[5] Here Ingrid says "packed in it" rather than "packed it in". As a result, Lisa mishears, thinking that Ingrid had said someone's name ("Pat Dinnit").

T7	L:	What's that?
T8	I:	He sort o' packed in it He just did it in the winter [[I think.
T9	L:	[[Pat Dinnit?
T10	I:	D'you know pack You packed your bag?
T12	L:	Oh yeah
T13	I:	Pack in He packed in it.
T14	L:	O:h *{Lisa finally understands what Ingrid is talking about}*

Other-initiated self-repair

Sometimes the girls were misheard or misunderstood by their conversational partner and prompted to clarify. When this occurred, attempts might be made to "self-repair" by reformulating previous utterances:

Serena: (08.09.98, aged 11;6)

Scene: Serena and Lisa conversing about what Gabrielle did during a previous visit.

T1	L:	e:rm She played with my shoes She likes shoes a lot.
T2	S:	Yeah Does she come in shoe erm shop or not?
T3	L:	*{looks confused}* Does she go in a shoe shop?
T4	*S:*	*{laughs self-consciously}* She hhh *{breathy giggle}* Does she-Does she want to work at the shoe shop or? *{slight pause}*
T5	L:	I think she likes a shoe shop called "Shoe World" actually.

Ingrid: (11.11.98, aged 11;1)

Scene: *Ingrid is drawing a picture and Lisa has to guess what it is.*

T1	L:	e:rm (2) Is it an animal?
T2	I:	e:rm *{mumbles}* Sort of (2) Somebody dressed up That's a clue.
T3	L:	Somebody dressed up that's a clown?
T4	I:	No I said it's a clue:!
T5	L:	Right I'd better get my hearing sorted out.

Ingrid: (21.09.98, aged 10;11)

*Scene: Lisa and Ingrid are waiting for Ingrid's friend. Ingrid is facing
the camera.*

T1	I:	She maybe gone to somebody's friends
T2	L:	She made you what?
T3	I:	She maybe gone to somebody else's friend
T4	L:	She made you go to somebody else's friend?
T5	I:	No She's maybe gone to her friend's. Friend? Y'know children (1) as your friends?
T6	L:	Oh yeah.

Gabrielle: (17.09.98, aged 13;2)

1.		*Scene: Gabrielle and her friend, Dana, talk in the playroom.*
T1	G:	Are ya glad it's the weekend?
T2	D:	Hm?
T3	G:	Are ya glad it's the day off on Saturday?

2.		*Scene: Gabrielle is talking with Dana.*
T1	G:	I bought a clock.
T2	D:	Huh?
T3	G:	I bought a new clock.

3.		*Scene: Lisa and Gabrielle talk during administration of a test.*
T1	G:	I don't think it's the right shape?
T2	L:	Sorry?
T3	G:	That's the right shape innit?

3.2.3 Social etiquette and politeness

Politeness

Throughout the 2 year period of data collection, Serena, Gabrielle and Ingrid demonstrated their awareness of the social factors that warrant use of conventional markers of politeness like "please" and "thank you." These skills are said to usually develop between the ages of 3 and 5 years (Crystal, 1997a). In Serena's case, markers of politeness were a regular and routine element of her talk. During conversation, she was vigilant over the manners of others, even adults, and might instruct someone to say "please" or "pardon" if she felt that these expressions had not been used where needed:

Serena: (08.09.98, aged 11;6)

Scene: Serena is in the lounge with her teacher, Mrs Taylor (T.), and asks if she can have some biscuits.

T1	S:	Am I allowed to 'ave two pi-two biscuits?
T2	T:	Well I don't know about that!
T3	S:	Plea:se! *{puts hands together pleadingly}*

Serena: (07.10.98, aged 11;7)

Scene: Serena, Gabrielle, Gabrielle's mother and Lisa watch television in the lounge. Gabrielle then comments on her mother's new hairstyle.

| T1 | G: | It looks ugly on you |
| T2 | S: | Just watch (a) video please *{points to T.V.}* |

Serena: (16.10.99, aged 12;7)

1.   *Scene: Serena, Gabrielle and Lisa talk in the lounge.*

T1	L:	*{speaks to Gabrielle, then offers Serena some chocolates}*
T2	S:	No: I don't want your sweets thanks Thank you for your permission though.
T3	L:	That's okay Don't worry about it.
T4	S:	I'm not worrying about it Just don't want any sweets.

2.   *Scene: Lisa is about to leave Gabrielle's house, but first offers Serena and Gabrielle some chocolate.*

T1	L:	Maltesers chocolate
T2	G:	Ugh!
T3	L:	They're all right for you Serena because erm they haven't got any calories.
T4	S:	No I won't have any thank you.

Ingrid, like Serena, was characteristically polite when interacting with both children and adults:

Ingrid: (29.06.98, aged 10;8)

Scene: Family dinner where Ingrid, Lisa and Ingrid's mother, M., and sister, B., are present. The conversation revolves around football.

T1	L:	Is there anybody tipped to win tonight?
T2	I:	*{speaks in sing-song voice}* E:ngla:nd!
T3	M:	*(looks at Ingrid and makes a surprised sound)* Oh!
T4	B:	Probably Argentina I'm afraid
T5	M:	[[Well Argentina-
T6	I:	[[Na:::
T7	M:	They're 5/4 favourites aren't they Argentina?
T8	I:	*{Ingrid suddenly reaches out with her left hand and wriggles her fingers towards a bowl containing cheese}* B. can you pass that cheese, please?
	B:	*{passes the cheese to Ingrid}*

Unlike Serena and Ingrid, Gabrielle sometimes had to be encouraged to say "please" and "thank you" when with adults. However, with same-age or slightly younger peers, Gabrielle used these unreservedly:

Gabrielle: (17.09.98, aged 13;2)

1.   *Scene: Gabrielle and Dana talk with Lisa in the playroom.*
{Gabrielle takes a drink from a bottle of pop and passes it over to Dana}

T1	G:	You can have the [[rest
T2	D:	[[mm:
		Thank you.

{slight pause: Dana and Lisa talk briefly and then Dana passes the drink over to Gabrielle}

T3	G:	Thank you.

2.   *Scene: Gabrielle and Dana talk in Gabrielle's bedroom.*

T1	D:	*{turns to Gabrielle and proffers her lolly wrapper}* Have you got a bin?
T2	G:	A bin? *{gets up and takes Dana's lolly wrapper}* Thank you *{throws wrapper in the bin, then sits back down on the bed}* Right. Wha' shall we talk about?

Greeting and leave-taking

Serena, Gabrielle and Ingrid responded civilly to greetings directed to
them and issued salutations to others. Convivial exchanges such as the
following were observed on many occasions:

Serena: (07.10.98, aged 11;7)

Scene: Serena, Gabrielle and Lisa watch television in the lounge.
Gabrielle's father, M., enters the house and comes into the lounge.

T1	S:	Hello
T2	M:	*{walks further into room}* How ya doin'? [[All right? Hi *{speaks to Lisa}*
T3	L:	[[Hi Hi
T4	S:	Hello (2) Have you had a good day at work?
T5	M:	Yeah busy.

Serena: (16.10.99, aged 12;7)

1. *Scene: Serena has just awoken from her afternoon sleep and*
    walks into the lounge where Lisa is waiting.

T1	S:	Hello
T2	L:	Hi Have you been asleep?
T3	S:	mm: *{simultaneously sips her drink and goes to sit on the sofa}*
T4	L:	Are you ready to play a game then?
T5	S:	Yeah.

2. *Scene: Lisa has just finished administering some tests to Serena.*

T1	S:	I'm gonna go *{gets up from sofa and walks out of camera range}* What ya doin'? *{3 second pause}*
T2	L:	I'm goin' to leave now.
T3	S:	Bye bye then (2) Nice seein' you again.
T4	L:	Okay Serena it was nice seein' you too See you again soon.
T5	S:	Yeah *{walks into the kitchen}*

Ingrid: (02.12.98, aged 11;1)

Scene: Ingrid's mother, M., has just arrived home from work and Ingrid greets her.

T1	I:	Hi Mum
T2	M:	*{Has just walked through door}* Hi:!
T3	I:	How are you?
T4	M:	I'm fine How are you?
T5	I:	Oh we're upstairs
T6	M:	Are you? Right I'll make you a cup o' tea.

In contrast to Serena and Ingrid, Gabrielle did not habitually use greetings or partings with adults or respond to these spontaneously. Often Gabrielle had to be encouraged to reply to "hello" or "goodbye" and sometimes she did not reciprocate at all, but looked at the interlocutor silently. Conversely, Gabrielle's greeting and leave-taking behaviour was, it appears, always very polite and courteous when in the company of her peers, as in the following examples:

Gabrielle: (17.09.98, aged 13;2)

Scene: Gabrielle and Dana have been playing a game where they pretend to be at school and describe imaginary holidays.
{Lisa knocks on door and enters room}

T1	G:	Oh hello *{speaks in a pleasant, conciliatory manner}*
T2	L:	Hi how's everythin' going?
T3	G:	[[fine
T4	D:	[[okay
T5	L:	Sorry I didn't mean to interrupt
T6	G:	That's all right. *{speaks in the same pleasant manner as before}*
T7	L:	Sorry *{turns to leave room}*
T8	G:	That's [[okay
T9	D:	[[okay
T10	G:	*{continues with her imaginary holiday story}*

Gabrielle: (19.11.98, aged 13;5)

Scene: Serena has just arrived outside Gabrielle's house. Gabrielle's mother, K., opens the door to let Serena in and Gabrielle sees another friend, Tamara, outside.

T1   G: Hello Tamara
{pause and several voices overlap}
T2   S: *{enters the house and addresses K. and Gabrielle}* Hello
                    Hello
{pause: Tamara then walks down the drive to her mother who is parked outside}
T3   S: See you tomorrow Tamara
{slight pause: voices overlap}
T4   S: Good bye Tamara
T5   G: Bye Tamara

In the first example, below, Gabrielle and Dana have been asked by the researcher to simulate a conversation. In the second, Gabrielle and Dana are engaged in a game of pretence (with the researcher out of the room). Although these discussions are contrived, Gabrielle's turns show that, in structured situations and pretend play with peers, she had knowledge of appropriate social routines even if she did not always use these spontaneously with adults.

Gabrielle: (17.09.98, aged 13;2)

1.   *Scene: Gabrielle and Dana are talking with Lisa present.*
T1   G: Hello.
T2   D: Hello.
T3   G: How are you?
T4   D: Fine thank you how are you?
T5   G: Fine thank you *{smiles and lets breath in and out
                    sharply, while rubbing her hands together}*

2.   *Scene: Gabrielle and Dana play a pretend game called "shops."*
T1   D: Right (1) Right and you come-you come in and buy
                    something Just pretend you bought something=
T2   G: =Hello: Mi:ss *{puts on a "plummy" accent}*
T3   D: Hello:
T4   G: Can I buy a actually a doll-a Shellie one please?
                    {Gabrielle holds up a doll}
T5   D: *{Dana takes the doll from Gabrielle}* Let me see now.

3.2.4 Differences in conversational style according to context

As the above examples indicate, Serena, Gabrielle and Ingrid were able to adapt their communicative behaviour to different conversational partners and/or contexts. In this section the girls' conversational abilities in varying contexts are compared.

Serena

Serena's conversational style changed according to the situation or person to whom she was talking. She could be voluble and domineering with quieter children such as Gabrielle, but tended to be more reserved with family members such as her boisterous younger brother, N. During the early stages of the study, Serena's social interaction with N. was observed in detail. N. was both very talkative and competitive and would frequently try and overshadow Serena with his chatter. Thus, when N. was with Serena and their mother, J., he often vied for J.'s attention by interrupting Serena's turns or dominating the conversational floor with lively speeches. Serena usually deferred to N. by pausing patiently in order for him to finish speaking. Rather than show irritation or impatience, Serena politely tolerated N.'s disruptions. Serena also emulated aspects of N.'s behaviour, including his vocal characteristics and non-verbal gestures, and appeared to closely monitor his actions in order to predict what he was likely to do next. The following extracts illustrate Serena's interactions with N.

Conversations with N. (aged 6;6)

1   Serena: (12.05.97, aged 10;2)

Scene: N. and Serena are engaged in a game of football in the garden.
Their parents, J. and R., are filming them. J. calls Serena over.

T1	J:	What are we goin' to do next week-half term?
T2	S:	erm We_ not at school.
T3	J:	mhm:
T4	S:	We:=
T5	N:	=So we're goin' to a park=Oh one with a safari park or a zoo.
T6	J:	Let me ask Serena.
T7	N:	Yeah and what else are we gonna do Serena?
T8	S:	And (2) on Wednesday we're gonna see Gabrielle.

2   Serena: (07.08.98, aged 10;2)
Scene: Lisa is filming Serena and N. playing a storytelling game in the
playroom. Serena is describing to Lisa how she first met her friend
Gabrielle.

T1   S: mm: First of all I met Gabrielle at her house or she
                 comes round my house (3) and=
T2   N: =Serena you tell a story not repeating (things) *{suddenly*
                 gets up and stands directly in front of Serena, who
                 draws back in surprise. N. puts hands up in
                 frustration to emphasise point}
T3   L: No I wanted to hear about this actually N. Serena tell me
T4   S: and (3) and then (2) we met friends and then we played
                 together=
T5   N: =We met friends?
T6   S: Yea:h *{smiles shyly}*

In the third example below, N. attempts to dominate the conversational
floor by talking almost continually in order to overlap with what Serena
and J. are saying. He even explicitly requests that Serena "be quiet". In
contrast to N.'s forceful and direct behaviour, Serena is quieter and takes
her turns almost hesitantly.

3   Serena: (17.05.97, 10;2)

Scene: J. attempts to talk to Serena about colouring activities. N. competes
for J.'s attention by presenting his own patterns to the camera.

T1   J: D'you prefer doin' your colouring?
T2   S: Yes
T3   N: And I did this one How do you think I make that one?
                 [[I-I put a (fan) [[and er cut shapes in it y'see Serena be
                 quiet when I'm talking-
T4   S: [[erm o:h Mum I-
T5   J: [[(Y-You can come to the pool with us)
T6   S: I can do th-I can do those two the same.
T7   J: That's right.
T8   S: So
T9   J: [[(N. N. (1) That'll do
T10   N: [[And and I did that one and I did that one and I did that
                 one and I did that one and (2) I did that one and I did er
                 {whispers} which one? And I did the mask one *{growls}*
T11   J: [[Yes it looks like a mask that one

T12	S:	[[Yes
T13	N:	[[Does it?
T14	J:	mhm
T15	N:	And I did this one Lots
T16	S:	Can I tell= *{puts hand up}*
T17	N:	=<u>And</u> I did this one.

Conversation with Gabrielle

In contrast to her compliant, almost passive conversational behaviour with N., Serena was more assertive, even domineering, with quieter children such as Gabrielle. Serena often occupied centre-stage with her animated turns, whereas Gabrielle, sometimes argumentative with adults, was deferential in Serena's presence. Particularly during role playing games, it was observed that Serena often interrupted Gabrielle's turns or instructed Gabrielle on what to say next. The majority of Gabrielle's turns consisted of one word replies or comments controlled by Serena and incomplete sentences (due to Serena's disruptions). The following example, typical of the exchanges between Serena and Gabrielle, occurred when they were respectively aged 11;7 and 13;3 and occupied in a pretend play activity involving the acting out of imaginary scenes from school.

Serena: (07.10.98, aged 11;7)

Scene: Serena and Gabrielle have been playing "schools" in the sitting room. After a brief interruption by Gabrielle's brother, J., Serena resumes the game.

| T1 | S: | *{starts to sing to herself}* Then we got ho-at school an' then I said "Sorry I 'aven't done my homework 'cuz I've got my colouring"=Pretend you was a teacher an'-l-l-look *{holds up her coloured picture in front of Gabrielle}* an' then you said "O:h   look at- Mi:ss I've done my colouring" then ya saying- Then don't shout just whisper like I'm talking *{looks at Gabrielle to emphasize her point and gestures simultaneously}* Pretend "Miss I've done my colouring" (2) You say "Detention" *{looks expectantly at Gabrielle}* |
| T2 | G: | *{Gabrielle has been looking at Serena rather blankly throughout her monologue}* Detention. |

T3   S: O::h Mi::ss *{then raises voice}* But I love detention a::h
            de-dah-dah-dah Then I'm um-m-m-m *{gestures to
            herself}* an' then-an' then (1) an' then you-an' then I
            went in your room an'-an' then you: had to say (1) say
            "Why did you get detention?"
T4   G: Why did ya get detention?
T5   S: 'Cuz I didn't-I didn't know the colour of my picture so
            pip squea:k! You do the colouring [[Boring I wish I
            could (hold)
T6   G: [[I know but you('ve)
            got to do it.
T7   S: *{pretends to cry}* scribbly scribbly nah nah nah-nah nah
            [[Oh Then w-then we went home but er sister "I got
            detention I love homework" an' then you told it to my
            Mum.
T8   G: [[Well scribble on the-
            Mum
T9   S: N-no you *{points at Gabrielle}* (2) I say it to you 'cuz
            you pretend you're my mum yeah [[You're everything
            like you'll pretend you're teacher an' mum an' friends
            yeah?
T10   G: [[Mm:*{nods
            simultaneously}*
            mm: *{nods quietly then turns back to her colouring}*
T11   S: Sister (2) erm Mu:m I got detention.
T12   G: Why:?
T13   S: 'Cuz I('m) want to get detentio:n.

Gabrielle

Gabrielle was more likely to talk at length or describe her experiences
when interacting with peers. Her behaviour with familiar adults was often
monosyllabic or argumentative, whereas with same-age or slightly
younger peers she was more conciliatory, even deferential, and voluble if
not garrulous. According to her mother, K., Gabrielle was eager for and
enjoyed the company of other children, preferring to be with them rather
than with adult family members. The next two examples illustrate these
contrasting conversational styles.

Conversation with familiar adult

Gabrielle: (24.04.99, aged 13;9)

Scene: Gabrielle has been playing a board game with Serena's brother,
N. Serena's father, R., comes into the lounge to observe the game.

T1	R:	Have you played this before Gabrielle?
T2	G:	No. *{speaks rather abruptly and does not look at R.}*
T3	R:	No?
	G:	*{wipes hand across forehead self-consciously}* *{brief exchange between N. and R.}*
T4	R:	What games d'you play at home Gabrielle?
T5	G:	*{looks at R}* Nothink
T6	R:	You don't play any games?
T7	G:	No!
T8	R:	No board games?
T9	G:	No!
T10	R:	What d'you do all the time then?
T11	G:	*{sits back, looks away from R. and mumbles}* Play outside with my friends That's all. *{looks down at table, still not maintaining eye-contact with R.}*
T12	R:	At nights when it's dark?
T13	G:	Yeah! *{turns to looks at R.}* No! *{smiles self-consciously}*
T14	R:	What d'you do when it's dark? *{humorous undertones in voice}*
T15	G:	e:rm (2) *{turns head to look out of the window}*
T16	N:	Go to sleep. *{supplies Gabrielle's answer for her}*
T17	G:	No. *{looks up at ceiling}* Mess about. *{Smiles self-consciously}*
T18	R:	What in the house?
T19	G:	*{looks at R. and smiles shyly}* Yep!
T20	R:	D'you watch television a lot?
T21	G:	Nope!

{slight pause: R. is visibly trying to think of something else to say}

Gabrielle's demeanour during this conversation will probably be familiar to anyone who is used to teenage communicative behaviour in a family setting.

Conversation with peer

In contrast, with Dana, a friend, Gabrielle is talkative and animated, her turns quite lengthy and descriptive. She appears to enjoy the activity of narrating imaginary holiday scenes and skilfully maintains the conversational topic. Her non-verbal behaviour is confident and demonstrative and she often uses hand gestures while simultaneously vocalizing in order to emphasize a point that she is making. She establishes and maintains eye contact with Dana when taking her turns or gazes fondly at Dana when she is talking.

Gabrielle: (17.09.98, aged 13;2)

Scene: Gabrielle and Dana play a game of pretence where they describe imaginary holiday experiences.

T1	G:	I went to-I went to Devon and look what I bought today (1) in Devon *{reaches behind her and picks up a small doll to show Dana}* a Shellie doll just to show.
T2	D:	A:w that's ni:ce *{lowers voice conspiratorially}* Pretend the erm teacher's pulling a face because he wore that on top *{refers to a hat}*

{pause: Gabrielle gazes at Dana for a few seconds}

T3	G:	Shall I take it back home?
T4	D:	O:h no: You do whatever you want with it It's yours Gabrielle.
T5	G:	And when after that when we went doin' we sun bathe on the beach and erm after-Just pretend I bought you photographs and leaflet okay? Just pretend Shall we pretend?
T6	D:	*{whispers}* Oh thank you Gabrielle.
T7	G:	I bought a clock.
T9	D:	Huh?
T10	G:	I bought a new clock.

{pause: Dana whispers inaudibly and touches the clock that Gabrielle is holding. Gabrielle then puts the clock on the shelf}

T11	G:	And after that when I was in Devon I had restaurant I had lasagne erm and I had apple-apple pie and custard [[and black currant-
T12	D:	
		[[*{coughs}*

{pause: Gabrielle looks up at Dana's face}

T13	D:	Yea:h?
T14	G:	mm: *{nods simultaneously}* And then we went to be:d then I shared bedrooms with (2) just a friend-just me and erm when I went-and I did <u>all</u> *{simultaneously waves arms around to emphasise "all"}* those holidays everythink That's it now.
T15	D:	Well done Gabrielle.
T16	G:	It's you that('s) got to tell me about your holiday.

Ingrid

Ingrid's social and communicative behaviour also subtly differed according to situation or conversational partner. This was most evident when Ingrid's conversational interactions with her mother and with peers were compared. In the context, below, her mother, M., influenced their conversational exchange by suggesting to Ingrid what to say or introducing conversational topics. Ingrid rarely asked questions or initiated topics herself and appeared to be quite shy and self-conscious, speaking quietly, almost inaudibly. This impression was reinforced by her non-verbal behaviour: she often did not establish direct eye contact with M., choosing instead to look down at her hands.

Conversation with mother

Ingrid: (09.06.98, aged 10;8)

Scene: Ingrid is sitting on M's lap. M. asks Ingrid about a previous football experience.

T1	M:	How many matches did you play?
T2	I:	Three.
T3	M:	And who (2) who scored the goals?
T4	I:	Simeon W.
T5	M:	mm: Is he a good player?
T6	I:	Nearly (1) scored it.
T7	M:	Nearly scored it?
T8	I:	Yeah=
T9	M:	=Well, who actually scored it?
T10	I:	*{speaks very quietly}* Don't know who actually scored it Joachim-Joachim H- Oh don't know I forgot.
T11	M:	<u>Who</u> scored the first goal? *{pause}*

T12   I: They got ten We got one.
T13   M: Mm:?
{pause and Ingrid does not answer}
T14   M: What about (1) the class play that you did?
T15   I: Oh I was in the da-dragon
T16   M: And what was the play called?
T17   I: "George"? "St. George and the Dragon."
T18   M: Well tell me the story about St. George and the dragon
                 {pause}
T19   I: St. George came up and fighted dragon.

Ingrid was much more outgoing with her friends than with her mother. The following extracts are taken from an exchange between Ingrid, at 11;0, and her friend, Carina, aged 10;9, who was observed to be noticeably quieter than Ingrid and quite reserved in the researcher's presence. Ingrid was clearly sensitive to Carina's relative quietness and employed a range of communicative strategies designed to draw her friend into the conversation:

Conversations with slightly younger peer

Ingrid: (14.10.98, aged 11;0)

1.   *Scene: Ingrid and Carina have been talking about Carina's sister over dinner. There is silence for a while as they eat, then Ingrid picks up the topic again.*
T1   I: Y'know your sister?
T2   C: Yeah
T3   I: She wan't there She weren't in year six very long O:h then when we helped (.) Mr Soames put all the stuff in the van and he gave us a lolly=
T4   C: =Yea:h
T5   I: Yeah y'know Class 3 they jus-Y'know Class 3 they just went in just ignorin' the stuff just takin' their own bag and go straight home didn't they?
                 {Carina nods}
T6   I: An' then-An' then we should have gone to rounders with Leanne A bit late for rounders weren't we?
T7   C: Yeah.

2.   *Scene: Ingrid begins to talk about the joint serving of drinks during the dinner hour at school.*

T1   I: D'ya know know the partner you do drinks on?

{2 second pause: Ingrid leans towards Carina slightly, looking at her face. Carina nods without looking at Ingrid, and glances around kitchen}

T2   I: You're not allowed to swap it.

{2 second pause: Ingrid gazes at Carina, who looks down at her plate, while eating}

T3   I: I wanna be with you.

{2 second pause: Ingrid looks at Carina, waiting for her response. Carina still does not return Ingrid's eye-gaze, but smiles and carries on eating}

T4   I: You're not allowed to swap it.

{2 second pause}

T5   C: Yvette nearly always asks to do it wi' me an' I don't like it.

T6   I: Yeah I know You're not even allowed to swap You have to keep to that partner *{Ingrid is looking at Carina who nods slightly but does not establish eye contact with Ingrid}* She nearly does it with everyone.

3.   *Scene: End of meal. Long pause then Ingrid introduces completely different topic.*

T1   I: D'ya like it when if you do hard work Mr. Ross goes [["Yeah!" {*stretches out hand towards Carina in a thumbs up sign}* It's funny int it? He always does it to me when (he says) "Are you going to football match?" and I goes "Yeah" *{again waves hand up and down in thumbs up sign}*

T2   C: [[*{Nods}* Yeah.

3.3 Life in conversation: conclusion

Overall, Serena, Gabrielle and Ingrid gave the impression of being effective conversationalists in a variety of different interpersonal contexts. They demonstrated skills at talk that would appear typical of many older children and adolescents, including the use of a range of appropriate politeness forms and non-verbal behaviours. Some individual differences were evident in the choice of strategy used to relate to particular conversational partners. The children's sophisticated linguistic skills in everyday talk are clear testimony to their success in overcoming their early social isolation. More particularly, these conversational behaviours are quite unlike those of children with disorders from the autism spectrum and do not show signs of the "quasi-autistic patterns" noted for other previously institutionalised children by Rutter et al. (1999) and Rutter, Kreppner and O'Connor (2001).

Conversational proficiency of this order requires exquisitely timed intersubjective communicative coordination with conversational partners in open-ended encounters, practical and discursive, on myriad topics. Such communicative abilities, we would argue, are the clearest and most convincing evidence for the intact linguistic and cognitive potential of the three girls. The cases of Serena, Gabrielle and Ingrid, therefore, suggest strongly that extreme and prolonged global deprivation in early childhood does not preclude the full development of socio-communicative, linguistic and cognitive skills in later life as manifest in the most fundamental and important context for the development of language, namely everyday conversation.

CHAPTER FOUR

PUTTING LANGUAGE TO THE TEST

4.1 Introduction

This chapter reports on the performance of Serena, Gabrielle and Ingrid on standardized language tests. The tests were administered when Serena and Gabrielle were already in their early teens and Ingrid was approaching her teenage years. A range of tests designed to assess different aspects of language ability, including syntactic, lexical and semantic areas, was selected and administered. Our first objective was to obtain an overall developmental profile for language for each of the girls. Our second objective was to consider whether their test results offered any sign of critical period effects on the girls' linguistic progress. Our third objective was to see if there was any evidence for within-language dissociations of the kind reported in other studies (see Chapter 1).

4.2 Use of standardized tests

Standardized tests are frequently used measures in psychological, educational, and speech and language therapy contexts. They have been used as the main tools for linguistic analysis and assessment in studies of internationally adopted children, including Romanian orphans, and sometimes the only tools used. The advantage of such tests is that they allow a view on the linguistic abilities of an individual child in relation to a wider population of same-age children. At the same time, however, test results should always be treated with caution for a number of reasons.

First of all, standardized tests, particularly those involving test age equivalents, have inherent methodological limitations which compromise their reliability (Howlin and Cross, 1995; Bishop, 1989a).

Secondly, the use of standardized tests to assess language outcome in post-institutionalized internationally adopted children is particularly problematic because such tests have not been developed on the population of children in question (Meacham, 2006; Glennen, 2007a). Gindis (2005, p. 295) also notes that results on standard psychometric tests may obscure the extent to which children have been culturally deprived and, therefore, give a quite misleading view of their learning potential. Particularly significant in relation to our study is the fact that such tests involve norms based on *chronological age* (CA) and therefore presuppose a common cultural background and a "typical" developmental trajectory which Serena, Gabrielle and Ingrid did not experience. Accordingly, we have included in the reporting of results an additional temporal measure, namely *time since adoption* (TSA) ("time home", Glennen, 2007a, p. 544), which, we will suggest, is a more relevant factor in understanding the rate and quality of linguistic development for each of the girls, at whatever age their language learning began.

Thirdly, test scores reflect performances of particular children at particular times in the artificial, and possibly stressful, interactional setting that test protocol requires. Consequently, test results should be viewed carefully, if not sceptically, in the light of other evidence about children's communicative abilities and with due regard for personal and contextual factors.

Finally, these tests build in problematic assumptions about the nature of the linguistic skills they purport to measure, something we take up in chapter 6 in relation to the analysis of syntactic structures in the girls' spontaneous speech.

4.3 Behaviour during tests

During the testing, Serena was always cooperative and would view the test session as an interesting challenge. She was usually eager to perform well and would be disappointed or concerned if she thought that her responses were incorrect. She often appeared to be very unsure of her abilities, saying that she had not done very well despite lavish praise for a particularly successful test performance or for continued effort. Serena was always alert and showed sustained concentration during formal tasks, although her behaviour could be controlling or abrupt at times. She could be relied upon to give responses without constant prompting and needed little encouragement to stay motivated. Serena's test performances remained consistent throughout the duration of the study.

Gabrielle was rather reserved at times and displayed little enthusiasm for these tasks. She was, however, cooperative, appearing to want to do well, and would remain quiet and introspective although occasionally she became challenging. She would be eager for her parents to know that she had done well and would ask about her progress ("Was I tryin' hard then?", 16.10.99). Gabrielle could concentrate for long periods although occasionally her attention would wander and she would have to be redirected back to the task in hand. Gabrielle could be very patient when test games became monotonous, choosing to stay quiet rather than complain. She also appeared to lack confidence in her abilities and would often deny that she had done well even if she had.

Ingrid was often extremely "chatty" during testing, making it difficult sometimes to explain the rules of a game. She would get excited, laugh, giggle or tell school jokes. Ingrid's behaviour was animated, cooperative and charming, but, occasionally, came across as over-friendly. For example, she would touch the jewellery, clothes or hair of the researcher and would talk incessantly. This sociability meant that she did not always concentrate on the tasks and her attention had to be redirected to the test games. Occasionally, Ingrid's actions were so exuberant that her mother had to reprimand her, but she was generally able to sustain her concentration during test administrations.

4.4 Testing procedure

4.4.1 The tests

The tests applied here include two which offer a "global" view of language development, that is, a view of various aspects of language development taken together, along with eight individual measures which focus on particular aspects of linguistic production and comprehension.

Global measures

The two global measures are:
1 Clinical Evaluation of Language Fundamentals Preschool (CELF-Preschool, Wiig, Secord and Semel, 1992), used with younger children up to 6;11 years to assess various aspects of receptive and expressive language. It contains the following subtests: Concepts and Following Directions, Word Structure, Expressive Vocabulary, Recalling

Sentences, Sentence Structure, Basic Concepts, Recalling Sentences in Context, Word Classes and Phonological Awareness.

2 Clinical Evaluation of Language Fundamentals Third Edition (CELF-3, Semel, Wiig and Secord, 1995), used with children and young people aged between 6;0 and 21;11 years to assess aspects of syntax, morphology, semantics, and working memory for language. It has six core subtests: three Receptive Language subtests (Concepts and Directions, Word Classes, and Semantic Relationships) and three Expressive Language subtests (Formulated Sentences, Recalling Sentences and Sentence Assembly). Two supplementary measures, Word Structure and Sentence Structure, are standardized for younger children up to 8;11 years.

Individual measures

The eight individual measures were selected to allow a more detailed focus on the following areas of linguistic ability: vocabulary and concepts, grammar and syntax, narrative ability, reading, and working memory for language.

Vocabulary and concepts

1 British Picture Vocabulary Scale (BPVS, Dunn et al., 1982), standardized for children and young people up to 19;0 years.

2 The Word Finding Vocabulary Scale (WFVS, Renfrew, 1992), standardized for children up to 8;6 years.

3 Boehm Test of Basic Concepts (BTBC, Boehm, 1986), standardized for children up to 8 years, but gives percentile ranks rather than test age equivalents.

Grammar and Syntax

1 Test for Reception of Grammar (TROG, Bishop, 1989b), standardized for children between 4 and 12 years.

2 Action Picture Test (APT, Renfrew, 1988), standardized for ages up to 8 years.

Narrative ability

Bus Story Test of Continuous Speech (Renfrew, 1991), standardized for children aged 3 to 8 years.

Reading

Salford Sentence Reading Test (form B) (Bookbinder, 2000), standardized for children aged 5 to 10+ years.

Working memory for language

1 Recall of Digits Forward sub-test of British Ability Scales, Third Edition (BAS-III, Elliott, 1996), standardized for children and young people aged 5;0 to 17;11 years.

2 Recalling Sentences subtest of CELF-3, standardized for children and young people aged between 6;0 and 21;11 years.

3 Children's Test of Nonword Repetition (CNRep, Gathercole and Baddeley, 1996), standardized for children between 4;0 and 8;11 years.

4.4.2 Global measures: results and discussion

The overall scores for the girls on CELF-Preschool and CELF-3 are given in Table 4.1. Table 4.1a presents details of CELF-3 subtest scores and Table 4.1b reports CELF-3 Receptive, Expressive and Total Language Scores.

Table 4.1 Results on global language tests: chronological age (CA), time since adoption (TSA), test age equivalent (TAE), percentile rank (PR) and standard deviation from the mean (SD).[1]

	Serena		Gabrielle		Ingrid	
CELF-Preschool						
CA	12;0		13;8			
TSA	4;7		7;5		N/A	
TAE	4;7		4;5			
PR	10		6			
SD	-1.26		-1.53			
CELF-3						
CA	12;1	13;2	13;9	14;10	11;5	12;7
TSA	4;8	5;9	7;6	8;7	7;7	8;9
TAE	5;0	5;0	5;0	5;0	5;0	5;0
PR	1	1	1	1	1	1
SD	-3	-3	-3	-3	-3	-3

Table 4.1a CELF-3 subtest scores: chronological age (CA), time since adoption (TSA), subtest raw scores (RS), subtest standard scores (SS), percentile ranks (PR) and standard deviation from the mean (SD).[2]

	Serena		Gabrielle		Ingrid	
CA	12;1	13;2	13;9	14;10	11;5	1;7
TSA	4;8	5;9	7;6	8;7	7;7	8;9
Concepts & Directions						
RS	7	21	7	8	19	18
SS	3	4	3	3	5	4
PR	1	2	1	1	5	2
SD	-2.3	-2	-2.3	-2.3	-1.6	-2
Word Classes						
RS	9	14	12	15	15	22
SS	3	3	3	3	3	6
PR	1	1	1	1	1	9
SD	-2.3	-2.3	-2.3	-2.3	-2.3	-1.3

---

[1] For CELF-Preschool, percentile ranks (and deviations from the mean) were derived by comparison with the scores obtained by children aged 6;6 – 6;11.
[2] For Word Structure and Sentence Structure subtests, percentile ranks and distances from the mean were derived by comparison with scores obtained by children aged 8;0 - 8;1.

Semantic Relationships						
RS	2	2	5	1	4	4
SS	3	3	3	3	3	3
PR	1	1	1	1	1	1
SD	-2.3	-2.3	-2.3	-2.3	-2.3	-2.3
Formulated Sentences						
RS	20	28	14	13	16	28
SS	3	5	3	3	3	6
PR	1	5	1	1	1	9
SD	-2.3	-1.6	-2.3	-2.3	-2.3	-1.3
Recalling Sentences						
RS	15	17	20	26	20	24
SS	3	3	3	3	2	3
PR	1	1	1	1	1	1
SD	-2.3	-2.3	-2.3	-2.3	-2.3	-2.3
Sentence Assembly						
RS	1	4	2	0	1	3
SS	3	3	3	3	3	3
PR	1	1	1	1	1	1
SD	-2.3	-2.3	-2.3	-2.3	-2.3	-2.3
Word Structure						
RS	19	18	17	18	22	27
SS	6	5	5	6	7	10
PR	9	5	5	5	16	50
SD	-1.33	-1.66	-1.66	-1.33	-1	0
Sentence Structure						
RS	17	20	15	19	15	18
SS	8	15	6	11	6	10
PR	25	95	9	63	9	50
SD	-0.66	+1.66	-1.33	+1.66	-1.33	0

Table 4.1b CELF-3 Receptive, Expressive and Total Language Scores: chronological age (CA), time since adoption (TSA), test age equivalent (TAE), standard scores (SS), percentile ranks (PR), standard deviation from the mean (SD).

	Serena		Gabrielle		Ingrid	
CA	12;1	13;2	13;9	14;10	11;5	12;7
TSA	4.8	5.9	7.6	8.7	7.7	8.9
TAE	5;0	5;0	5;0	5;0	5;0	5;7
Receptive Language						
SS	50	50	50	50	53	57
PR	1	1	1	1	1	1
SD	-3.3	-3.3	-3.3	-3.3	-3.1	-2.8
Expressive Language						
SS	50	50	50	50	50	53
PR	1	1	1	1	1	1
SD	-3.3	-3.3	-3.3	-3.3	-3.3	-3.1
Total Language						
SS	50	50	50	50	50	52
PR	1	1	1	1	1	1
SD	-3.3	-3.3	-3.3	-3.3	-3.3	-3.3
Sum of Six Sub-test Raw Scores	54	86	59	62	75	99

CELF-Preschool

CELF-Preschool was administered once to Serena and Gabrielle[3] in March 1999, purely as a trial run for subsequent administration of CELF-3, and is not standardized for the girls' chronological ages. Test age equivalent scores for Serena (12;0) and Gabrielle (13;8) were 4;7 and 4;5 respectively when compared to the test norms for children aged up to 6;11 years with percentile ranks of 10 and 6. Their times since adoption (4;7 and 7;5 respectively) were a much closer match to test age equivalents when compared to the test norms. The trial run appeared successful and so it was decided to go ahead with the administration of CELF-3.

---

[3] Ingrid was not available for testing on the scheduled visit.

CELF-3

CELF-3 was administered to Serena, Gabrielle and Ingrid on two occasions: the first (March/April, 1999) when they were aged 12;1, 13;9 and 11;5 respectively and over one year later (May 2000) when aged 13;2, 14;10 and 12;7. On the first occasion, Serena, Gabrielle and Ingrid all obtained a test age equivalent of 5;0 years, a score more typical of children significantly below their actual ages by approximately 7;1, 8;9, and 6;5 years respectively. A similar picture was obtained when they were retested after a year: their scores corresponded to the same test age equivalent of 5;0 and were respectively 8;2; 9;1, and 7;0 years below their actual ages. As their test performances deviated by as much as –2.3 SDs below the mean, this would be interpreted as indicating clinical "delays" of language ability (Semel, Wiig, and Secord, 1995) for their chronological ages with no marked difference between their receptive and expressive ability. However, if time since adoption is considered, a different picture emerges. Serena's time since adoption values (4;8, 5;9) are close to her test age equivalent, Gabrielle's (7;6, 8;7) and Ingrid's (7;7, 8;9) are somewhat further apart, but still a closer match than chronological age.

From Table 4.1a, which presents data on the girls' scores across all core language subtests of CELF-3, there is no appreciable difference between performances on different linguistic tasks that might hint at possible disparities between aspects of language competence (e.g., syntax in Formulated Sentences and Sentence Assembly subtests versus vocabulary and semantics in Concepts and Directions and Semantic Relationships subtests). This is because percentile ranks were all between 1 and 5 and standard deviations were mostly -2.3 from the mean of children's performances in the same chronological age groups. Exceptions were Ingrid's CELF-3 scores on Concepts and Directions for both years tested which were respectively -1.6 and -2 SDs from the mean, her second scores on Word Classes and Formulated Sentences which were both -1.3 SDs from the mean, and Serena's performances on the Concepts and Directions and Formulated Sentences of -2 and -1.6 SDs respectively

Furthermore, there appears to be no correlation between age of adoption and test results with each girl obtaining the same test age equivalent, although this could simply mean that CELF-3 is not a sensitive enough tool for analysing language performance in children from "non-standard" linguistic backgrounds (see also Glennen, 2007 on "local norms").

CELF-3 subtests

As Table 4.1a indicates, CELF-3 does not provide test age equivalents for subtest performances, but does provide (in addition to percentile ranks) standard scores, converted from raw scores, which provide a means of comparing the participant's performance to the normative data. The standard score scale that CELF-3 uses has a mean of 10 and a standard deviation of 3 with a standard deviation of +1 or −1 from the mean considered to be within the typical range of any given age group. About two thirds of all typically developing participants will obtain standard scores between 7 and 13, considered to be the typical range (Semel, Wiig and Secord, 1995). The standard scores of Serena, Gabrielle and Ingrid on the six core subtests were between 3 and 6 on both test occasions. These scores corresponded in general to percentile ranks of 1, about −2.3 SD from the mean of children in the girls' age groups. On one of the supplementary subtests (Sentence Structure), the girls' most recent scores were like those of younger children aged 8;0 - 8;11 for whom this measure is standardized. When compared with the test norms, their scores either exceeded or were equivalent to the average child's in this age range.

The subtest (standard) scores for Serena, Gabrielle and Ingrid for both test sessions are given in Figures 4.1 and 4.2. These indicate how their subtest scores relate to the average performance (represented as 0). As shown, their scores on the CELF-3 core subtests were in general −2.3 SDs from the mean of children in their chronological age groups. There was a slight increase to raw scores when the girls were retested 13 to 14 months later but not enough to raise the standard scores and the overall percentile rankings or test age equivalents. In contrast, Figure 4.2 shows that the girls' scores on Sentence Structure increased appreciably over a year: the scores of Serena and Gabrielle increased to within +1.66 SD *above* the mean whilst Ingrid's score raised to the mean range. This appeared to suggest an area of relative strength in the girls' subtest performances, albeit on the supplementary measures.

Figure 4.1 Standard deviations from the mean for CELF-3 subtest scores (March-April 1999).

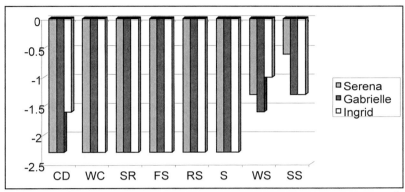

Subtests: CD = Concepts and Directions, WC = Word Classes, SR = Semantic Relationships, FS = Formulated Sentences, RS = Recalling Sentences, SA = Sentence Assembly, WS = Word Structure, SS = Sentence Structure.

Figure 4.2 Standard deviations from the mean for CELF-3 subtest scores (May 2000).

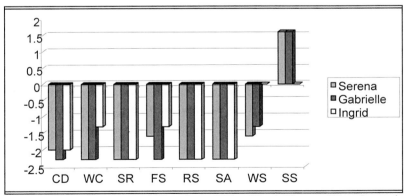

Subtests: CD = Concepts and Directions, WC = Word Classes, SR = Semantic Relationships, FS = Formulated Sentences, RS = Recalling Sentences, SA = Sentence Assembly, WS = Word Structure, SS = Sentence Structure.

Receptive, Expressive and Total Language Scores

CELF-3 subtest standard scores can be used to compute a Receptive Language Score (RLS) and Expressive Language Score (ELS). These scores can be compared with each other to ascertain whether a child has primarily a receptive or expressive language difficulty or both. When these two scores are combined the total converts to a standard score which comprises the Total Language Score (TLS) indicating the participant's overall performance on CELF-3. The Receptive, Expressive and Total Language Scores have a mean of 100 (which represents an average performance) and a standard deviation of 15. About two thirds of all participants with typical linguistic ability obtain standard scores of 85 to 115 – considered to be within typical limits (Semel, Wiig, and Secord, 1995).

As Table 4.1b shows Receptive, Expressive and Total Language standard Scores for Serena and Gabrielle for April 1999 and May 2000 were all 50 and Ingrid's increased from 50 to 57. Thus, their (composite) scores were below the average range of children from their chronological age groups and corresponded to percentile ranks of 1, about –3 SD below the mean. This means that around 99% of children from the same chronological age groups as the girls would be expected to obtain higher scores. Total Language Scores on CELF-3 for both years corresponded to test age equivalents of 5;0 for Serena and Gabrielle and 5;7 for Ingrid's most recent performance.

There appeared to be no difference between the Receptive and Expressive Language Scores of Serena and Gabrielle for both years tested or any difference between their scores on expressive and receptive tasks. For Ingrid, on the other hand, her Receptive Language Score was slightly ahead of her Expressive Language Score for both years tested. No obvious disparity between the girls' expressive and receptive language was indicated by CELF-3.

Let us now turn to the results of the individual standardized tests.

4.4.3 Individual measures: results and discussion

Vocabulary and concepts

Test results concerning vocabulary and concepts are summarized in Table 4.2.

Table 4.2 Results on tests of vocabulary and concepts: chronological age (CA), time since adoption (TSA), test age equivalent, (TAE), test raw scores (RS), test standard scores (SS), percentile ranks (PR), standard deviation from the mean (SD).[4]

	Serena	Gabrielle	Ingrid
British Picture Vocabulary Scale			
CA	11;5 12;7	13;2 14;4	10;8 12;0
TSA	4;0 5;2	6;11 8;1	6;10 8;2
TAE	9;6 8;3	8;3 10;2	9;6 8;11
RS	20 18	18 21	20 19
SS	86 71	69 79	92 78
PR	18 3	2 8	30 7
SD	-0.93 -1.93	-2.06 -1.4	-0.53 -1.46
Word Finding Vocabulary Scale			
CA	13;0	14;9	11;6
TSA	5;7	8;6	7;8
TAE	5;4-5.	5;9	5;9
RS	34	37	37
Boehm Test of Basic Concepts			
CA	11;9	13;5	11;2
TSA	4;4	7;2	7;4
RS	41	33	48
PR	3	1	50

---

[4] Boehm Test of Basic Concepts: percentile ranks of 3, 1 and 50 in comparison with the scores of children aged up to 8 years; Word Finding Vocabulary Scale: test age equivalents derived in comparison with scores obtained by children aged 8;6.

1 Receptive Vocabulary - British Picture Vocabulary Scale (BPVS)

The girls' verbal receptive language abilities ranked lower than the average range of children in their chronological age groups (percentile ranks between 2 and 30; distances from the mean −0.93 to −2.06 SDs). Scores for Serena and Ingrid declined over a year, whereas Gabrielle's did not. While test age equivalents (ranging from 8;3 to 10;3) were low compared to chronological age, time since adoption values – all "ahead" of their test age equivalents – indicate stronger performance than test norms indicate.

2 Expressive Vocabulary - Word Finding Vocabulary Scale (WFVS)

At the respective ages of 13;0, 14;9 and 11;6, the raw scores for Serena, Gabrielle and Ingrid on the WFVS corresponded to test age equivalents of 5;4-5, 5;9, and 5;9, a wide divergence. Over 25% of their naming responses were inaccurate (according to test guidelines), while a typically developing child of 8;6 (the oldest age range the WFVS is standardized for) would be expected to score close to 100%. Time since adoption values (5;7, 8;6, 7;8) are, again, much closer to test age equivalent than chronological age.

3 Conceptual Awareness - The Boehm Test of Basic Concepts (BTBC)

Compared with the norms for second graders, the girls' percentile ranks were 3 (Serena), 1 (Gabrielle) and 50 (Ingrid), indicating that 97%, 99%, and 50% of children aged 7-8 years might be expected to respond more accurately than the girls at the respective ages of 11;9, 13;5, 11;2. However, respective time since adoption values of 4;4, 7;2, and 7;4 may provide useful context for these scores.

Grammar and Syntax

Test results concerning receptive and expressive grammar and syntax are summarized in Table 4.3.

Table 4.3 Results on tests of grammar: chronological age (CA), time since adoption (TSA), test age equivalent (TAE), test standard score (SS), percentile rank (PR), standard deviation from the mean (SD).[5]

	Serena		Gabrielle		Ingrid	
Test for Reception of Grammar						
CA	11;7	12;7	13;2	14;4	11;1	12;0
TSA	4;2	5;2	6;11	8;1	7;3	8;2
TAE	6;0	6;0	5;9	6;0	8;0	7;0
SS	73	67	63	67	81	71
PR	1-5	1-5	1	1-5	10	1-5
SD	-1.8	-2.2	-2.46	-2.2	-1.26	-1.93
Action Picture Test						
CA	11;9	13;0	13;5	14;9	11;1	12;0
TSA	4;4	5;7	7;2	8;6	7.3	8;2
TAE: Grammar	5;0	6;6	4-4;5	6-6;6	6-6;5	7-7;5
Information	8;5	8;5	7-7;5	6-6;11	5-5;5	7-7;5
RS Grammar	22	27	19	27	26	29
Information	37	37	35.5	34.5	30	35

1 Receptive Grammar - Test for Reception of Grammar (TROG)

The girl's performances on the TROG appeared to be several years behind their chronological ages according to the test norms. As Table 4.3 shows, percentile ranks were between 1 and 10 meaning 90% to 99% of children of similar chronological ages would be expected to obtain higher scores. The distances from the mean of their chronological age groups ranged from −1.26 to -2.46 SDs. Over the year, Serena's test age equivalent remained at 6;0, Gabrielle's 5;9 increased slightly to 6;0 and Ingrid's 8;0 decreased to 7;0. However, Serena's time since adoption values (4;2, 5;2) were "ahead" of her test age equivalents, Gabrielle's (6;11, 8;1) were much closer to her test age equivalents, and Ingrid's (7;3, 8;2) were respectively slightly "ahead" and slightly "behind" in relation to test age equivalents.

---

[5] Standard deviation from the mean derived for Gabrielle by comparing her scores with those obtained by children aged 12;0 - 12;11. Action Picture Test test age equivalents derived by comparing the girls' scores with those of children aged 8;5.

2 Expressive Grammar – Action Picture Test (APT)

The APT was administered twice when the Serena, Gabrielle and Ingrid were approaching or within their early teens. The girls' scores were either equivalent to or below what would be expected of an average ability child aged 8 years (according to the APT norms). Serena (aged 11;9 and 13;0) had test age equivalent scores for information content of 8;0- 8;5, Gabrielle's scores (aged 13;5, 14;9) decreased from 7;0-7;5 to 6;6-6;11, and Ingrid's (aged 11;1 and 12;0) rose from 5;0-5;5 to 7;0-7;5. Time since adoption values were closer to test age equivalent as usual: Serena's scores of 4;4 and 5;7 put her "ahead", Gabrielle's scores of 7;2 and 8;6 put her very close to test age equivalent and Ingrid's scores of 7;3 and 8;2 put her a little "behind". On the grammar component, time since adoption values were generally hovering around test age equivalents. Serena's time since adoption values (4;4, 5;7) were "ahead" of test age equivalent (5;0, 6;6), Gabrielle's (7;2, 8;6) were "behind" (4;0-4;5, 6;0-6;6), and Ingrid's (7;3, 8;2) were slightly "behind" (6;0-6;5, 7;0-7;5). Furthermore, the girls' scores for grammar all increased over the testing period: Serena's by 1;6 years in 15 months, Gabrielle's by 2;1 years in 15 months and Ingrid's by 1 year in 10 months.

Narrative Ability, Reading and Working Memory for Language Measures

Test results for the above areas are presented in Table 4.4 below.

Table 4.4 Results on tests of narrative ability, reading and working memory for language: chronological age (CA), time since adoption (TSA), test age equivalent (TAE), test standard score (SS), ability score (AS), percentile rank (PR), standard deviation from the mean (SD).

	Serena		Gabrielle		Ingrid	
Bus Story Test of Continuous Speech						
CA	11;9	13;0	13;5	14;9	11;2	12;2
TSA	4;4	5;7	7;2	8;6	7;4	8;4
TAE: Information	4;0-4;5	6;0-6;5	3;9-3;11	4;6-4;11	5;0-5;5	8;5+
TAE: Subordinate Clauses (No.)	4;0-4;5	4;0-4;5	4;0-4;5	5;1-5;11	8;5+	7;6-7;11
TAE: Sentence Length	4;1-4;11	5;1-5;11	3;9-3;11	5;1-5;11	6;0-6;5	6;0-6;5
SD from the mean	-0.47	0	-0.30	-0.37	-0.25	+0.30
Salford Sentence Reading Test						
CA	13;2		14;10		12;7	
TSA	5;9		8;7		8;9	
TAE	8;1		7;5		7;5	
Recalling Digits Forward (BAS)						
CA	11;8	12;7	13;4	14;4	12;0	
TSA	4;3	5;2	7;1	8;3	8;2	
TAE	4;4	5;7	4;4	4;1	6;10	
Ability Score	105	111	94	88	131	
PR	1	2	1	1	14	
Recalling Sentences (CELF-3)						
CA	12;1	13;2	13;9	14;10	11;5	12;7
TSA	4;8	5;9	7;6	8;7	7;7	8;9
SS	3	3	3	3	2	3
PR	1	1	1	1	1	1
SD from the mean	-2.3	-2.3	-2.3	-2.3	-2.3	-2.3

Children's Test of Nonword Repetition (CNRep)			
CA	13;0	14;8	12;2
TSA	5;7	8;6	8;4
TAE	5-5;11	5-5;11	4-4;11
PR	<10	<10	<10

Narrative Ability – Bus Story Test of Continuous Speech (BSTCS)

The BSTCS was administered twice to Serena, Gabrielle and Ingrid when they were approaching or just in their early teens.

The girls' scores for Information, Number of Subordinate Clauses, and Sentence Length were generally below what would be expected of an average ability child aged 8 years according to the test norms. However, time since adoption values are, once more, a closer match with test age equivalent on all test components, although there are some quite striking divergences on individual measures. In Gabrielle's case, for example, her time since adoption of 7;2 contrasts with the test age equivalents of 3;9-3;11 (Information), 4;0-4;5 (Subordinate Clauses), and 3;9-3;11 (Sentence Length). However, the marked increases in Gabrielle's test age equivalents on the later test session (4;6-4;11, 5;1-5;11, 5;1-5;11 respectively) may suggest that Gabrielle was still acquiring these aspects of linguistic competence. In fact, all the girls increased their test age equivalent scores on the Information measure over the testing period.

Reading - Salford Sentence Reading Test (SSRT)

When aged 13;2, 14;10, and 12;7 respectively, Serena, Gabrielle and Ingrid obtained test age equivalents on the SSRT comparable to that of younger children (aged 8;1, 7;5, 7;5 respectively). Time since adoption values, again, are a closer match to test age equivalent with Serena "ahead" (5;9) and Gabrielle (8;7) and Ingrid (8;9) marginally "behind".

Working Memory for Language

1 Recall of Digits Forward (BAS-II)

RDF (BAS-II) was administered twice to Serena (aged 11;8 and 12;7) and Gabrielle (aged 13;4 and 14;4) and once to Ingrid (aged 12;0).[6] The respective test age equivalents for Serena and Gabrielle were 4;4 and 5;7 and 1 year later were 4;4 and 4;1, whereas Ingrid's test age equivalent was 6;10. Percentile ranks ranged from 1 to 14 suggesting around 86% to 99% of children from the same chronological age groups would have been expected to obtain higher scores. Time since adoption values of 4;3 and 5;7 (Serena), 7;1 and 8;3 (Gabrielle) and 8;2 (Ingrid) were much closer overall to test age equivalent.

2 Recalling Sentences (CELF-3)

This test was administered to Serena, Gabrielle and Ingrid twice, between the ages of 12 and 14 years. Their performances on both occasions were scored as percentile rank 1, meaning that 99% of children of similar chronological ages would be expected to obtain a higher score, although their time since adoption values may help to contextualize this result.

3 The Children's Test of Nonword Repetition (CNRep)

The CNRep was administered once to Serena, Gabrielle and Ingrid between the respective ages of 13;0, 14;8 and 12;2 years. Their scores when compared to the norms for children aged 8;0 to 8;11 (the oldest age the measure is standardized for) yielded percentile ranks of 10 or below and corresponded to test age equivalents of 5;0-5;11 (Serena), 5;0-5;11 (Gabrielle), and 4;0-4;11 (Ingrid). Time since adoption values (5;7, 8;6, and 8;4 respectively) are a closer match to test age equivalent, although Ingrid's result is still markedly "behind" her time since adoption value.

4.5 Within-language "dissociations"

Though the girls' scores on core CELF-3 subtests were consistent (with no marked differences) across both syntactic and lexical/conceptual areas of receptive and expressive language, results on individual tests indicated areas of inconsistency. For example, test age equivalents on the British

---

[6] The RDF (BAS-II) was unavailable on the day that Ingrid was visited.

Picture Vocabulary (BPVS) of 9;6/8;3 (Serena), 8;3/10;2 (Gabrielle) and 9;6/8;11 (Ingrid) (Table 4.2) noticeably exceeded respective test age equivalents of 6;0/6;0, 5;9/6;0 and 8;0/7;0 on the Test for Reception of Grammar (TROG) (Table 4.3). Might this disparity be evidence of "dissociation" between lexical and grammatical skills, as hypothesised by nativist scholars?

A closer look at the test evidence suggests not. First of all, as noted earlier, we must exercise caution in interpreting standardized test results based on test age equivalents, particularly for children with early experience of deprivation. In principle, these quite striking differences in test age equivalents for the two tests may not say anything at all about the actual abilities of Serena, Gabrielle and Ingrid or their progress in these linguistic areas. However, in order to pursue the issue rather more stringently, it was considered useful to make statistical comparisons between the girls' performances on the TROG and the BPVS using z-scores (or standard scores) which express how many standard deviations a performance is from the mean (Gleitman, 1995). In other words, the use of z-scores made it possible to compare how far the girls' TROG and BPVS performances were from the average range. The z-scores - together with the percentile ranks - corresponding to the girls' performances for the years 1998 and 1999 are presented in Table 4.5.

According to the data, the most noticeable difference between TROG and BPVS scores was for the first test performances of Serena and Ingrid and Gabrielle's second performance. In these cases the difference between the TROG and BPVS scores was almost 1 standard deviation. However, the between-score differences of -0.87, -0.8 and –0.73 are not statistically significant; a difference of at least 1.64 on the z-score scale would be needed to reach significance.[7] On the basis of the statistical comparison using z-scores, then, there is no evidence of a within-language "dissociation" between grammar and vocabulary of the type proposed by supporters of modularity (e.g., Locke, 1994)

---

[7] Calculation of statistical significance was carried out with expert assistance from the Department of Human Communication Sciences, University of Sheffield.

Table 4.5 Results of z-score comparison between TROG and BPVS: chronological age (CA), percentile rank (PR), z-scores, difference between z-scores for both tests

	Serena		Gabrielle		Ingrid	
TROG CA	11;7	12;7	13;2	14;4	11;1	12;0
BPVS CA	11;5	12;7	13;2	14;4	10;8	12;0
TROG PR	1-5	1-5	1	1-5	10	1-5
BPVS PR	18	3	2	8	30	7
TROG z-scores	-1.8	-2.2	-2.46	-2.2	-1.26	-1.93
BPVS z-scores	-0.93	-1.93	-2.06	-1.4	-0.53	-0.47
Difference	-0.87	-0.27	-0.4	-0.8	-0.73	-0.47

TROG and BPVS z-scores are depicted graphically in Figures 4.3 and 4.4.

Figure 4.3 BPVS scores for test times 1 and 2: standard deviations from the mean.

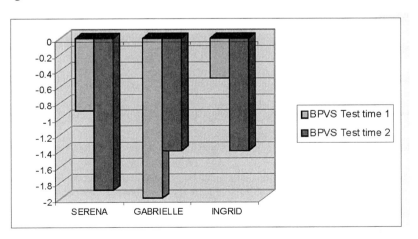

Figure 4.4 TROG scores for test times 1 and 2: standard deviations from the mean.

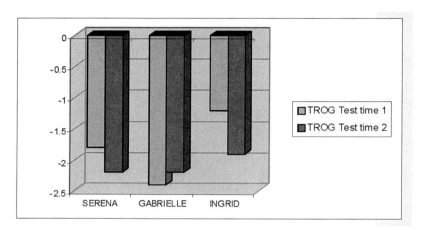

Moreover, a comparison between TROG results and results for other non-syntactic measures on the basis of percentile ranks suggested a close association rather than dissociation between these language skills. For example, the scores on TROG were similar to the scores of all tests of working memory for language: Recall of Digits Forward (BAS), Recalling Sentences (CELF-3), Children's Test of Nonword Repetition (CNRep). For results see Table 4.6.

The results indicate that percentile tasks were quite similar between TROG and tasks of working memory for language. For example, the TROG percentile ranks for all test occasions were, in general, 1 to 5 (except for 10 for Ingrid's first score) which are comparable to the percentile ranks of 1-2 for RDF(BAS) and RS(CELF-3) (again except for Ingrid's score of 14 for the former test). All the non-syntactic tests including the CNRep were similar to the TROG in having percentile ranks of 10 or below. General caution about test results notwithstanding, neither the z-score nor percentile rank comparisons appear to provide any grounds for suspecting a marked divergence between aspects of linguistic or psycholinguistic ability.

In summary, the girls' performances overall on a range of individual standardized assessments offer no clear evidence to contradict the view that their abilities with respect to different areas of linguistic ability had developed, and were possibly still developing, in step.

Table 4.6 Comparison of results of syntactic and non-syntactic tests: chronological age (CA), time since adoption (TSA), percentile ranks (PR).

	Serena	Gabrielle	Ingrid
TROG			
CA	11;7 12;7	13;2 14;4	11;1 12;0
TSA	4;2 5;2	6;11 8;1	7;3 8;2
PR	1-5 1-5	1 1-5	10 1-5
RDF(BAS)			
CA	11;8 12;7	13;4 14;4	12;0
TSA	4;3 5;2	7;1 8;3	8;2
PR	1 2	1 1	14
RS (CELF-3)			
CA	12;1 13;2	13;9 14;10	11;5 12;7
TSA	4;8 5;9	7;6 8;7	7;7 8;9
PR	1 1	1 1	1 1
CNRep			
CA	13;0	14;8	12;2
TSA	5;7	8;6	8;4
PR	<10	<10	<10

4.6 Putting language to the test: conclusion

During a 2 year period, Serena, Gabrielle and Ingrid were tested on a variety of receptive and expressive language measures, obtaining scores that would have been expected for much younger children. Going on their chronological ages, the results may have indicated global "delays" in language ability. However, introduction of the time since adoption measure allows a different picture to emerge, namely that Serena, Gabrielle and Ingrid had made progress in first language acquisition after adoption which was similar to that of many younger, typically developing children in terms of both its rate and its general course. This suggests that the girls' early years of global deprivation had not irreversibly affected their language learning abilities. Furthermore, there was no evidence to suggest any obvious relationship between their progress in language and the age at which they were adopted, a finding mirrored in other studies of older internationally adopted children with early experience of social and linguistic deprivation (Scott, Roberts and Glennen, 2011) (Chapter 1).

Though there were certain differences between the results for Serena, Gabrielle and Ingrid on different aspects of linguistic ability (e.g., vocabulary versus grammar), a closer examination of their scores did not reveal anything of statistical significance. Nor did a broader comparison of results on grammar on the one hand and tasks of verbal working memory on the other point up any obvious differences between types of linguistic ability.

Overall, then, the girls' performances on standardized tests of language ability appear to offer no evidence either for critical period effects on their language learning or for the kind of within-language dissociations that nativist theory might predict.

CHAPTER FIVE

WORDS AND WORD FORMATION: THE ACQUISITION OF MORPHOLOGY

5. 1 Introduction

While Chapter 4 presented the results obtained by Serena, Gabrielle and Ingrid on a range of standardized language tests, here we begin our examination of structural linguistic features in their spontaneous speech. This chapter will concentrate on morphological and morphosyntactic features of the girls' utterances, looking out in particular for evidence of their ability to infer and apply morphological rules. In this way we hope, firstly, to obtain a more fine-grained picture of the girls' linguistic progress in relation to well established descriptions of morphological development and, secondly, to address issues of particular theoretical significance in relation to possible critical period effects on linguistic development.

We will begin by examining transcriptions of the girls' spontaneous speech for evidence of the acquisition of morphosyntactic forms following Brown's (1973) treatment of morphological development. We will then present a more detailed exploration of morphological patterns and inconsistencies in their spoken language. Finally, we will turn to the phenomenon of so-called "over-regularizations" of regular morphosyntactic patterns (e.g., "catched", "mouses") which has acquired immense significance in theoretical debates over language acquisition. We will attempt to describe and quantify the over-regularizing tendencies on display in the girl's utterances and will then ask whether the data provide any support for the idea that there is an innate modular-like system for grammar subject to its own critical period.

5.2 Acquisition of morphology

One of the first systematic studies of the acquisition of grammatical morphemes was carried out by Roger Brown and his associates (Cazden, 1968; Brown, 1973). Using naturalistic data from three very young children, Brown investigated the production of 14 non-lexical (grammatical) morphemes, some bound and some free. It was found that some morphological forms, such as the present progressive *-ing*, prepositions *on* and *in* and regular plural and possessive inflections, were produced early on in the acquisition process (between 27 and 30 months), but that consistent usage of these morphemes did not occur for many months (until around 41 to 46 months). Other grammatical morphemes, such as the third person singular ("she walk*s*"), emerged later (between 39 and 42 months) and were acquired more slowly, usually by the age of 5 (Cazden, 1968; Wolf-Nelson, 1993; Peters, 1995). The reported order of emergence of the 14 morphemes is given in (5.i).

(5.i)   Brown's (1973) order of emergence of 14 grammatical morphemes.

present progressive *-ing*	1
preposition *in, on*	2-3
plural *-s*	4
past irregular e.g., *went*	5
possessive *–'s*	6
uncontractible copula *be* e.g., *am, was*	7
articles *the, a*	8
past regular *-ed*	9
third person regular *-s*	10
third person irregular e.g., *does, has*	11
uncontractible auxiliary *be* e.g., *were, is*	12
contractible copula *be* e.g., *– 's, - 're*	13
contractible auxiliary *be* e.g., *– 's, - 're*	14

Brown argued that the children's progress in language learning was marked by "distinct developmental achievements" which he somewhat arbitrarily termed "stages" (Miller, 1981, p. 25). Brown assessed utterance complexity by using a quantitative measure - the "mean length of utterance in morphemes" (henceforth MLU) - which he associated with his "stages", thereby allowing a child's developmental "stage" to be defined by an MLU value. Brown's stages of structural development are summarised in Table 5.1.

Table 5.1 Brown's (1973) stages of structural development

Brown's stage	Expected MLU	Age (Predicted)
Early Stage I	1.01.- 1.49	19 – 23 months
Late Stage I	1.50 – 1.99	23 – 26 months
Stage II	2.00 – 2.49	27 – 30 months
Stage III	2.50 – 2.99	31 – 34 months
Early Stage IV	3.00 – 3.49	35 – 38 months
Late Stage IV – Early Stage V	3.50 – 3.99	39 – 42 months
Late Stage V	4.00 – 4.49	43 – 46 months
Post Stage V	4.50+	47 – 58 months

MLU provides a gross quantitative measure of syntactic complexity for children up to the age of 5 years (Stage V; MLU = 4;0) and is a common method used by researchers and clinicians alike for assessing language development in children with or without communicative disabilities (Miller, 1981). MLU is calculated by dividing the total number of morphemes by the total number of "communication units" (C-units) in which those morphemes are contained.

MLU was calculated for Serena, Gabrielle and Ingrid using extracts of spontaneous speech from the beginning, middle and closing stages of the data collection period of around 23 months. In order to evaluate the reliability of the researcher's transcriptions, a second transcriber examined a small subset of conversational data, half an hour for each child. Five-minute speech samples were selected from the beginning, middle and end of the data collection period. For each transcript, the number of words agreed upon by both coders was divided by the total number of words (Balason and Dollaghan, 2002). The inter-rater agreement rate for each child is shown in Table 5.2. The overall inter-rater agreement for all transcripts was 80%. Inter-rater agreement on past tense over-regularizations (see 5.4.1, 5.4.2) was 100%.

Table 5.2 Inter-rater agreement on transcription by child

Serena	Gabrielle	Ingrid	Overall Agreement Rate
84%	73%	83%	80%

The calculating procedure for MLU was adapted from Brown (1973) and followed Chapman (1981) in using 50 rather than 100 utterances as a sample. Results are presented in Table 5.3.

Table 5.3 MLU between June 1998 and May 2000

	Date of Visit	Age	Mean Length of Utterance (MLU)
Serena	04.06.98	11;3	5.18
	11.03.99	12;0	6.24
	20.05.00	13;2	5.68
Gabrielle	17.09.98	13;2	7.08
	16.10.99	14;4	5.60
	18.03.00	14;9	6.01
Ingrid	09.06.98	10;8	5.74
	13.04.99	11;6	6.28
	16.05.00	12;7	5.14

As can be seen, all MLU values for all of the girls over the period of data collection were 4.50+ which corresponds to Post Stage V of language development and a predicted chronological age of 47+ months (range 47 to 58 months). The level of complexity of the girls' productive language, then, was either equivalent to or beyond that of children aged 4 to 5 years on this measure. At this most advanced of Brown's stages, children are considered to be able to use the full range of morphemes.

However, use of the MLU measure obscures some interesting quirks of grammatical construction in the girls' speech which we will now illustrate.

5.3 Morphosyntactic idiosyncracies

A range of morphosyntactic idiosyncrasies or "errors", occasional rather than frequent, were evident in the spoken language of Serena, Gabrielle and Ingrid throughout the study. The girls would alternate between "correct" and "incorrect" forms over several months, within the same visit, or even within the same turn at talk.[1] Here we give examples from different grammatical processes at clause and phrase level:

5.3.1 Verbal system

1)   Subject-verb agreement

Serena:	(12.05.97)	No, he *do* a different one.
	(04.06.98)	This *have* to be by Monday, phew!
Gabrielle:	(18.09.98)	*Do* I be nice to you?
	(24.04.99)	*{Gabrielle's response to test item}* While the boy *are* cooking.
	(18.03.00)	What *is* his names?

2)   Use of auxiliary verb

Serena:	(27.05.97)	My yellow *didn't* be my favourite colour.
	(24.04.99)	That were meant to be that, *should*n't it?
Gabrielle:	(16.10.99)	*Will* you think Serena('d) be havin' her sleep by now?
Ingrid:	(11.03.99)	O:h, I know what you were gonna do. You were gonna do that *don't* ya?

3)   Tense marking in auxiliary - main verb structures

a)   Tensed auxiliary + tensed main verb (same tense)

Serena:	(08.09.98)	Just as well you *didn't brought* me a proper one.
	(20.05.00)	*Did* I *got* half of that?
	(11.03.99)	*Is* that battery *works*?

---

[1] Our use of scare quotes around "error", "correct", "incorrect" etc., is intended to signal distance from an overly prescriptive attitude to creative departures from conventional or standard usage.

Gabrielle:	(24.04.99)	Why *did* ya *came* to Serena_ house to play games with me and Serena?
	(24.04.99)	When *did* Lisa *came*? (1) So when *did* Lisa *came*?
Ingrid:	(11.11.98)	And I di:d some shopping. I *did got* some red 11 nail varnish.

b)   Tensed auxiliary + tensed main verb (different tense).

Serena:	(04.06.98)	Oh wish I *can watched* it.
Gabrielle:	(18.09.98)	*Can* you *sent* her out, please?
	(11.03.99)	*{Gabrielle picks up her doll}* She'*ll came* and throw honey at you.
Ingrid:	(21.09.98)	*Shall* we *stood* up?
	(02.12.98)	You *could* have *came* with us.

c)   Finite verb + tensed verb complement structures

| Serena: | (19.11.98) | Ah yeah but you *saw* me *went* on the floor, didn't you as well? |
| Ingrid: | (11.03.99) | I'm tryin' to press that one. The one what ya *told* me to *pressed*. |

d)   Other uses of tense marking

Serena:	(07.10.98)	I *be* a baby if I'm a teen-teenager huhh hahh.
	(20.05.00)	He *known* him when he was at lower school.
Gabrielle:	(18.09.98)	*{Gabrielle tells Dana about a holiday}* I went to-I went to Devon and look what I bought today (1) in Devon (1) a Shellie doll, just to show *(pause)* -and when after that when we went doin'- we *sun bathe* on the beach.
	(28.10.98)	I hope you *be* dead tomorrow.
Ingrid:	(14.12.98)	I liked the ending, but I *hate* the beginning.
	(11.03.99)	I *be* Ingrid. My name's called Ingrid.

e)   Use of non-finite forms (i.e., use of infinitive instead of participle forms)

Serena: (09.12.98)   Well then, have you *write* it down?
Ingrid: (13.04.99)   I an't *hold* one for ages.

5.3.2 Nominal system

a)   Singular determiner with plural marked nouns

Serena: (18.03.00)   D'you wanna have *a play times*?
Gabrielle: (16.03.96)   L: What else are ya gonna get?
                                       G: (2) *A clothes and shoes.*

b)   Singular determiner with non-count noun

Serena: (08.09.98)   Oh yeah, well had *a fruit* y'know. I've already had *a fruit* this morning.
                 (20.05.00)   Why ya got *a sand* in there?
Ingrid: (16.05.00)   Is it-Need *a* paper.

c)   No overt plural inflection in plural nouns (although determiners may be inflected)

Gabrielle: (19.11.98)   *Those metal ball*, look there. They come off.
Serena: (09.12.98)   I'm lookin' at *these box.*
Ingrid: (02.12.98)   *{Ingrid's response to item of expressive grammar task}*
                                      L: Tell me what the man is doing.
                                      I: He's climbing up *some ladder* and getting' a cat down.

d)   Singular determiner with plural marked noun

Gabrielle: (24.04.99)   Let's play these cards (1) Let's play *this cards* (2) here-there.

e)   Lack of noun-pronoun number agreement

Serena:	(18.03.00)	*{Serena and Lisa talking during test}* L: I haven't got any trainers but I do like Gabrielle's Reebok Classic Trainers. Do you? S: Yes *it's* very nice.[2]
Gabrielle:	(11.03.99)	G: D'ya like *our new beds* mummy what we brought from the D.F.S.? K: Mm very nice. G: We brought *it* with our money yesterday.

f)   "failure to observe co-occurrence restrictions between determiners and nouns", e.g., "much bricks" (Scott, 1988)

Serena:	(08.09.98)	I'm getting' mostly cards. Look you've got that *mu:ch*.
	(28.10.98)	Not very much now is there? Not very *much* eggs; you've taken them all.[3]
Ingrid:	(02.12.98)	How *much* things are you going to play?

g)   No agreement in number between subject and subject complement

Serena:	(20.05.00)	*That's* long sentences.
Ingrid:	(17.12.99)	You had some pictures and you asked me to (1) say things and *it was* so easy things.

h)   Case in pronouns: genitive unmarked

Serena:	(04.06.98)	*Who* turn was it?
Gabrielle:	(11.03.99)	*{Talks about her doll}* Just-Who could it be?=What name can ya tell me could this be? Mummy?=Can you tell me *who* name could this be?

---

[2] Alternatively, Serena could have meant, " it's very nice, that line in trainers".
[3] A few seconds previously, Serena said, "How *many* eggs have you had?"

5.4 Over-regularization

One aspect of the morphosyntactic constructions of Serena, Gabrielle and Ingrid is of particular significance, namely the extent of application of "regular" inflections to words showing "irregular" formations (in Standard English at least). "Over-regularization" has been observed in the speech of typically developing children from the age of 2;6 in forms like "goed", "mouses" and "gooder" (Marcus, 1995). Over-regularization "errors" are considered one of the most significant developments during the earliest language learning years (MacWhinney, 1995) and have been singled out for special attention by some theorists for the support which the phenomenon allegedly gives to a particular conception of language and its associated model of language acquisition (Pinker, 1999), as we shall see below.

5.4.1 Rates of over-regularization

Marcus et al. (1992), on the basis of spontaneous speech transcripts of 83 children (obtained from the CHILDES computer database, MacWhinney and Snow, 1985), found that the mean over-regularization rate was 4.2%. In other words, the children studied used the "correct" past tense version of an irregular verb (such as "broke") around 96% of the time.[4]

Speech transcripts for Serena, Gabrielle and Ingrid covering the entire 2-year period of data collection were examined for over-regularizations. A summary of findings on over-regularizations is presented in Table 5.4.

Serena produced the most over-regularizations (30 in total) and so four transcripts were examined, spanning a period of three years and corresponding to the dates 12.05.97, 09.12.98, 24.04.99 and 20.05.00 when Serena was aged 10;2 to 13;2. For these transcripts, the mean "error" rate was 4.5%. Gabrielle produced over-regularized forms less frequently and so two of her transcripts were studied from 28.10.98 and 20.05.00 when she was aged 13;4 and 14;10. Gabrielle's combined rate of over-regularization was 3.66%. Three of Ingrid's transcripts were examined from 09.06.98, 18.10.99 and 16.05.00 when Ingrid was aged 10;8 to 12;7. Ingrid's mean over-regularization rate was 3.33%. Table 5.4a gives a summary of over-regularization rates for each child. These results are

---

[4] Marcus mentions that the ages of the children in the CHILDES database range from the 2s into the school-age years.

comparable to those obtained by Marcus et al. (1992) for typically developing children.

Table 5.4 Total over-regularizations in spontaneous speech
(The number of times the form was heard, if more than once, is in brackets)

	Irregular past tense verbs	Irregular plural nouns	Irregular third person singular	Irregular comparative adverbs
Serena	drived, hurted, comed(2), heared, teared(3), drawed(4), throwed(2), shined, broked(3), blowed, knowed, choosed, falled, writed, catched(3) breaked, seed, stoled, steeled(2)	gentlemans(7) mouses(2), feets(2), childs(2), childrens	[du:z] (for 'does')	gooder(2), goodest(2)
	Total = 31	Total = 14	Total = 1	Total = 4
Gabrielle	broked(2), blowed, feeded, teached(8), lighted(2), drawned(2), drawed	foots(2), childs, childrens	[du:z](4)(for 'does')	badder, gooder
	Total = 17	Total = 4	Total = 4	Total = 2

Ingrid	fighted, thinked, bited, throwned, brokeden, chosed, token, brokened, drived(2), singed, goed, wroten, sticked, catched(2), hided, runned, wroted, catched	mices(4), chickens, dices, themselfs, childs, scarfes, tooths		boringest
	Total = 20	Total = 10	Total = 0	Total = 1

Table 5.4a Rates of over-regularization for each child

Child	Dates of Transcripts Examined	Age Range	Rate of Over-regularization	Age when adopted	Time since Adoption
Serena	12.05.97; 09.12.98; 24.04.99 20.05.00	9;10 to 13;2.	4.50 %	7;5	2;9 4;4 4.8 5.9
Gabrielle	28.10.98 20.05.00	13;4 to 14;10	3.66 %	6;3	6;11 8;7
Ingrid	09.06.98, 18.10.99 16.05.00	10;8 to 12;7.	3.33 %	3;10	6;9 8;2 8;9

5.4.2 Types of over-regularization

Here we look more closely at the *types* of over-regularization that Serena, Gabrielle and Ingrid produced.

Verbs

Irregular past tense verbs with the regular /-ed/ suffix[5]

Serena:	(17.05.97)	You **driv*ed*** in the car first.
	(07.10.98)	Why-Why is this **tear*ed*?** Hey why is this **tear*ed*?** Why was it **tear*ed*?**
	(24.04.99)	Catty: Catty:! Somebody **draw*ed*** look! Now somebody's **draw*ed*** a cat
	(20.05.00)	L: Tom saw Peter. David saw Frank. Who was seen; Tom, David, Peter or Frank? S: Tom **see*d*** Peter (1) and Dave saw Frank.
Gabrielle:	(28.10.98)	I just **brok*ed*** it mum (2) I **brok*ed*** it
	(09.12.98)	He **blow*ed*** a whistle.
	(20.05.00)	L: The student did not know the teacher who taught Year 5 last year. G: E:rm The student didn't know (1) know e:rm her who **teach*ed*** them last year.
Ingrid:	(09.06.98)	St George came up and **fight*ed*** dragon.
	(19.10.99)	I've **hid*ed*** those Smarties.
	(16.05.00)	L: Can you make a sentence out of this picture using the word "if"? I: If I get **runn*ed*** over I'll get told over-off I meant.

Like younger children, Serena, Gabrielle and Ingrid appeared to be fairly indiscriminate in the forms that they chose to over-regularize (Pinker, 1999, p. 191). They applied regular markers not only to irregular stems as in "fighted", "bited", "blowed", "throwed", "heared" and "teared" but also

---

[5] According to Curtiss (1977, p. 171), Genie only over-regularised once (in the Autumn of 1973) when she applied the regular past tense morpheme to the verb *break* to get *[brekt]*. In fact this was the only time that Genie used the /ed/ past tense morpheme throughout Curtiss's study and so it was concluded that the past regular had not been acquired. It was also claimed that Genie did not comprehend past tense.

took irregular past tense forms as stems as in "broked", "stoled" (Serena, 11;9 and 13;2), and "chosed", "wroted" (Ingrid, 10;11 and 12;7). Serena, Gabrielle and Ingrid applied regular tense marking to their own neologisms such as "magicked" and "rehearsalled" (Ingrid, 12;2). Gabrielle and Ingrid applied /ed/ to irregular past tense verbs that already had a suffix such as "drawned", (Gabrielle, 14;10), "throwned", (Ingrid 10;11) and "brokened" (Ingrid, 11;0). In addition, Ingrid was noted to over-apply the past participle /-n/ suffix to irregular past tense forms as in "tooken" and "wroten" and once applied the /-n/ ending to an already over-regularized form ("brokeden") (10.09.98).

Serena and Gabrielle over-regularized even when asked to repeat the correct past form of an irregular verb during a sentence repetition task (Recalling Sentences, CELF-3):

Serena:	(20.05.00)	L: The fielder caught the ball and the crowd cheered loudly. S: The fielder **catch*ed***-caught the ball and the erm e:r (2) and the people cheered.
Gabrielle:	(20.05.00)	L: The student did not know the teacher who taught Year 5 last year. G: E:rm The student didn't know know e:rm her who **teach*ed*** them last year.

Irregular verbs with singular /-s/ suffix

Three verbs, "have", "do" and "be", are irregular in the third person singular present tense and typically developing children overgeneralise the /–s/ suffix to all three (Pinker, 1999). Serena and Gabrielle (although not Ingrid) did the same for at least one of these verbs ("do"):

Serena:	(18.03.00)	mm: *{Shrugs}* Football netball (1) mm: dunno (1) tennis. Dunno what else. (1) Sometime_[**du:z**] cross country.
Gabrielle:	(24.04.99)	Well me an' Serena can play a game while N. [**du:z**] this.

Nouns

Typically developing children from the age of 2 will frequently extend the regular plural /-s/ suffix to irregular noun stems (Marcus, 1995), as did Serena, Gabrielle and Ingrid:

Serena:	(04.06.98)	Hello gentlemen-gentle**mans** and the ladies and welcome to the show.
	(24.04.99)	L: Here is one foot. Here are two:? S: **Feets**!
	(18.03.00)	I'm not good with **childs** toddlers huhh (1) or babies.
Gabrielle:	(24.04.99)	L: Here is one foot. Here are two:? G: **Foots**.
	(24.04.99)	L: Here is one child. Here are three? G: **Childs**.
	(20.05.00)	L: Here is one child. Here are [[three- G: [[Three **childrens**.
Ingrid:	(02.12.98)	L: What has the cat just done? I: Killed some **mices** (2) Getting some **mices**.
	(10.03.99)	L: Here is one child. Here are three...? I: **Childs** (2) children.
	(19.10.99)	L: The elephant is pushed by the boy. I: *{Points)* Number two. The **tooths** are pushing.

Adjectives

In Standard English, regular comparative and superlative forms of adjectives are derived using the /-er/ and /-est/ suffixes with the consequence that many children extend the suffixes to irregular forms (Pinker, 1995). For example, children will often say "gooder" and "goodest" (or "bestest") rather than "better" and "best". Similar things were observed for Serena and Gabrielle:

Serena:	(09.12.98)	I'm **worser** than Gabrielle. I'm **worser** than you.
	(20.05.00)	L: This picture is good, but his picture is eve:n? S: **Good*er*** L: and this picture is the? S: **Good*est***
Gabrielle:	(24.04.99)	L: This picture is good, but this picture is even? G: Bad-Badder-**Good*er*** (2) Good.

Typically developing children also have the tendency to over-generalize these regular suffixes to adverbs with two or more syllables such as "beautifullest". Something similar was noted for Ingrid who said "boringest" (11;2).

(Over-regularized forms were also noted in the speech of the girls' peers and siblings. Serena's younger brother, N., twice said "catched". Gabrielle's same age friend, Dana, over-regularised an irregular no change verb "resetted", while Ingrid's friend, Carina, aged 10;9, said "telled" and "singed". Over-regularizations are clearly still common in typically developing children at the age of 10 and beyond).

5.4.3 Variability in rule application

At times, Serena, Gabrielle, and Ingrid alternated between "correct" and over-regularized forms of a verb or noun within the space of a few sentences or even words, a pattern documented for younger children by Pinker (1995):

> "it looks as though over-regularization is fairly haphazard from one moment to another. In fact, children can use the correct and over-regularized version of the same verb in quick succession" (p.116).

These alternations were evident in the speech of all three girls. For example, on 13.04.99, Ingrid (11;6) swapped between "sticked"/"stuck", while on 07.10.98, Serena (11;5), alternated between "broked"/"broke", and "torn"/"teared" and between "mans" and "men". Note turns 2 and 6 in the following dialogue:

(07.10.98) *{Serena and Gabrielle talking just before a colouring game}*
T1	G:	You can sit here (1) right?
T2	S:	*(Talks to the camera)* Hello: Ladies and Gentle**men** (2) There's Gabrielle and me and Lisa here today (2) and we gonna-
T3	G:	[[do colouring
T4	S:	[[do colouring He::lp! Let me put this on *{Refers to her detachable microphone}*
T5	G:	Give (her a chance) Mada:m
T6	S:	Thank you Ladies and Gentle**mans**.

Similarly, on 29.06.98, at 10;8, Ingrid said "thinked" and "thought" while conversing with her mother.

Some "errors", such as the use of tensed auxiliary plus tensed main verb as in 3(a), appeared with some consistency, as the following instances in Serena's speech attest:

Serena:	(08.09.98)	Just as well you *didn't brought* me a proper one.
	(07.10.98)	I *did had* "Aliens" tamagotchi but that broke.
	(07.10.98)	*Did* ya *got* some toys?
	(28.10.98)	Why *did* you *went* like that?
	(28.10.98)	Yeah she's askin', "What *did* Serena *did*?"
	(19.11.98)	*Did* ya *saw* that?

(In fact, similar forms were also heard in the speech of the girls' friends. For example, Ingrid's friend, Rose, aged 9, said:

R:	(21.09.98)	1. Think she's just *came* up-Are you *Came* upstai:rs?
		2. Have you *came* upstairs?

It is also possible, therefore, that forms we have been referring to as "idiosyncratic" may in fact be more widespread in particular linguistic varieties in the local area).

Over the same time period, Serena also produced sentences with the "correct" pattern as in "*Did* you *get* that?" and "What *did* she *say*?"

During one visit (in May 2000, at 13;2) she said "*Did* you *get* in trouble in middle school?" but then a few minutes later "*Did* I *got* half of that?"[6]

On some occasions, over-regularization "errors" were self-corrected almost immediately:

Serena: (11.03.99)   L: This is a bubble. Yesterday he blew the
                            bubble. *{Points}* This is a ball. Yesterday he?
                            S: Threw (1) **Throw*ed*** He threw (.) He rolled
                            the ball.

Ingrid: (10.03.99)   L: Here is one child. Here are three:?
                            I: **Child*s*** (1) children.

Serena even "experimented" with past tense forms, as in the following example where she was asked to give a past tense for "write":

Serena: (24.04.99)   L: The boy is writing a letter. This is the
                            letter the bo:y *{points to picture of boy
                            writing}*?
                            S: Writ-wri:ten-writ or whatever.
                            L: Or we could say "This boy *is* writing a letter
                            This is the letter the [[bo:y?"
                            S: [[boy *did* (1) written-wrid[7]**writ*ed***

When Serena was given the same test item a year later, she still demonstrated some uncertainty over "wrote", but eventually produced it, saying "wr-wro-wrote".

Such variability has been shown to be characteristic of speech production in typically developing children (Dodd and Bradford, 2000; Forrest, Elbert and Dinnsen, 2000; Pinker, 1999; Stackhouse and Wells, 1997) and is

---

[6] It is interesting to note that such tense "agreement" between auxiliary and main verb did not occur with regular main verbs, that is, utterances such as "*Did* ya *liked* that?" and "I *did walked* in the park yesterday" were not heard. While Crystal (1997a) argues that forms such as "What *did* you *bought*?" give an indication of the complexity of learning how to use tense marking in question formation, data from the girls suggest that there is a more general issue to do with the combination of auxiliary and irregular main verbs in all sentence types. And, in fact, Crystal's own examples also involve irregular main verbs.

[7] Serena applied a trill rather than an approximant.

viewed by Crystal (1997a) as a sign of continuing acquisition of grammatical structure, a process which is still evident after the age of 9 according to Scott (1988). As Crystal states:

> "The study of errors is important, because they show children breaking fresh grammatical ground. They provide the main evidence of how children go about actively learning new constructions" (19971, p.245).

We may therefore take the above examples of idiosyncratic patterns in the utterances of Serena, Gabrielle and Ingrid as evidence that their linguistic development was continuing on the path towards adult competence. Indeed, many of the over-regularized verb forms that were heard once or twice early in the study were never found again in the data. Forms such as "drived", "hurted", "comed", "heared", "choosed", "brokened", and "thinked" were superseded by the "correct" past tense forms on later visits and "mice" was heard instead of "mouses" towards the end of the study. Sometimes, an over-regularized form appeared after a prolonged period of using the "correct" form exclusively. According to Pinker (1999):

> "A striking feature of children's past-tense errors is that they appear, sometimes suddenly, after long stretches in which the children use the past tense correctly when they use it at all" (p.193).

What is also clear from the above communicative episodes is that the girls are *aware of* anomalies of various kinds in linguistic patterning and are consciously attending to them in pursuit of a "correct" or "appropriate" form. Over time, and with more experience and practice, they appeared to be learning to straighten these anomalies out. Such instances of self-correction and experimentation imply that language learning is an active and, at least partially, conscious process. The mere act of self–correction also indicates a degree of metalinguistic awareness as to the existence of particular words and how they "should" sound (Menn and Stoel-Gammon 1995).

5.4.4 Past tense elicitation task

In addition to analyses of the girls' over-regularizations of irregular past tense verbs in spontaneous speech, their past tense formation was investigated using a past tense elicitation task adapted from Ullman (1993). This was administered to Ingrid at 12;2 and to Serena and Gabrielle at 14;8 and 13;0 respectively. The test items consisted of 16 existing regular verbs ("scowl", "tug", "flush", "mar", "chop", "flap", "stalk", "scour", "slam", "cross", "rush", "rob", "drop", "look", "stir", "soar"), 14 existing irregular verbs ("swim", "dig", "swing", "wring", "bend", "bite", "feed", "make", "give", "think", "stand", "keep", "drive", "send"), 12 novel non-rhyming verbs (i.e., nonsense words that do not rhyme with existing irregular verbs) ("spuff", "dotch", "stoff", "cug", "trab", "crog", "vask", "satch", "grush", "plam", "scur"), and 14 novel irregular rhyming verbs (i.e., nonsense words that rhyme with existing irregular verbs) ("strink", "frink", "strise", "crive", "shrell", "vurn", "steeze", "shrim", "cleed", "sheel", "blide", "prend", "shreep", "drite").

The same experimental method was used by Clahsen and Almazen (1998) who studied the elicited past tense responses of four participants with Williams syndrome and compared them with two subgroups of younger typically developing children whose chronological ages (5;4 to 5;7 and 7;1 to 7;6.) matched the "mental ages" of the children with Williams syndrome. A group of participants with specific language impairment (SLI) aged between 9;3 to 12;10 were also used for comparison with the help of data from van der Lely and Ullman (1996). We used the results of Clahsen and Almazen's (1998) study for comparison purposes with the test responses of Serena, Gabrielle and Ingrid. Specifically, we compared the girls' responses with those of one of the subgroups of control children (age 7;1 to 7;6) and with those of the participants with Williams syndrome and SLI on the same task. The results along with Clahsen and Almazan's (1998) data are summarized in Table 5.5. Note that the numbers indicate the percentage of "correct" responses given by each participant or group.

As can be seen, on the existing regular items (e.g., "scowl", "tug", "chop"), Serena and Ingrid applied the regular past tense marker on most occasions (75%) (the 16 existing regular verbs were not administered to Gabrielle.) The control children and the participants with Williams syndrome also mostly produced the "correct" past tense of regular verbs (WS = 90.6%, CTR = 95.6%). The children with SLI differed significantly from Serena and Ingrid and the other participants since they applied the regular marker to only 22.2% of the verbs, while 68.2% were left unmarked.

Ingrid produced the "correct" form in 85% of cases on the existing irregular items and only over-regularized two items ("wringed" and "sented"). Gabrielle responded "correctly"to only half of the items and applied the regular marker to the rest. Serena supplied the "correct" past irregular for only one item, "swam", and either over-regularized the rest

(50% of cases) or repeated the bare stem (42.8% of cases). The control group, in contrast to Serena and Gabrielle, produced irregular past tense forms most of the time (88.5%). The participants with Williams syndrome, like Gabrielle, applied irregular patterns about half the time. The responses of children with SLI to the existing irregular items were similar to those of Serena and Gabrielle: they very rarely supplied the "correct" irregular past forms and left the majority (71.5%) of the verbs unmarked. However, unlike Serena and Gabrielle, they did not over-regularize many verbs and only applied the regular marker to 7.9 % of the items.

Table 5.5 "Correct" responses on past tense elicitation task compared to controls and children with Williams syndrome and SLI (with data taken from Clahsen and Almazen, 1998.)

Verb type	Child's response (%)					
	S.	**G.**	**I.**	**SLI**	**WS**	**CTR**
Existing regulars						
Regular	75.0	N/A	75.0	22.2	90.6	95.6
Irregular	0		6.2	0	9	0
Bare stem	0		12.5	68.2	9.4	4.3
Existing irregulars						
Irregular	7.1	50	85.7	17.6	57.2	88.5
Regular	50	50	14.2	7.9	29.0	1.4
Bare stem	42.8	0	0	71.5	7.0	10.1
Novel rhymes						
Irregular	0	21.4	7.1	3.9	3.6	75.0
Regular	50	78.5	85.7	9.7	64.3	18.6
Bare stem	50	0	7.1	75.3	28.6	5.7
Non-rhymes						
Regular	50	83.3	100	6.8	100	94.2
Irregular	0	0	0	1.5	0	0
Bare stem	33.3	8.3	0	72.7	0	5.8

S. = Serena, G. = Gabrielle, I. = Ingrid, SLI = participants with Specific Language Impairment, chronological age 9;3 to 12;10, WS = participants with Williams syndrome, CTR = control group.

For the novel, non-rhyming verbs, Gabrielle applied the regular marker to most of the items (83.3%) while Ingrid applied it to all of them (100%). Serena, on the other hand, applied the regular marker only 50% of the time, leaving the remaining items unmarked. Like Gabrielle and Ingrid, the control group and participants with Williams syndrome appeared to have no difficulty in producing the regular past tense forms of most of the verbs. It was a different picture for the participants with SLI, who again left the majority (72.7%) of the verbs unmarked.

The clearest evidence that Serena, Gabrielle, and Ingrid tended to favour the regular marker was found in their responses to the novel rhyming irregular verbs where they applied it between 50% and 85% of the time, with Serena again leaving half of the items unmarked. In comparison, the control children produced irregular past forms of these verbs 75% of the time. The participants with Williams syndrome, like Serena, Gabrielle and Ingrid, showed an opposite pattern to the control children and only produced irregular past forms 3.6% of the time, while regularizing 64.3% of the other items. Similar to Serena, Gabrielle and Ingrid and the participants with Williams syndrome, the children with SLI appeared to have problems with applying irregular patterns to novel verbs and they did so only 3.9% of the time. However, unlike Serena, Gabrielle and Ingrid and the participants with Williams syndrome, the children with SLI applied the regular past tense marker in only 9.7% of cases. A similarity between Serena and the group with SLI (but not the group with Williams syndrome) was that they both left a high proportion of the novel irregular verb forms unmarked - 50% for Serena and 75.3% for the SLI group.

In sum, Serena, Gabrielle, Ingrid performed very well when the "correct" response was a regular past tense form. This was also the case for the control children and participants with Williams syndrome but not for the children with SLI. However, Serena and Gabrielle (but not Ingrid) and the group with SLI did less well than the control children and the participants with Williams syndrome in producing the conventional past tense forms of existing irregular verbs. When Serena, Gabrielle and Ingrid were required to produce the past tense of novel irregular verbs, they applied the regular marker on 50-85% of the items, unlike the control children and SLI group, but like the participants with Williams syndrome.

Overall, then, it is difficult to reach a conclusion about the girls' over-regularizing tendencies. The girls differed amongst themselves as to their use of particular strategies and, as a group, did not clearly fit the documented profiles of any of the comparison groups.

5.4.5 Over-regularizations: summary

In summary, the following observations concerning over-regularizations were made:

1. Serena, Gabrielle and Ingrid over-regularized regular patterns to irregular forms for all major word classes in spontaneous, conversational speech. Over-regularization rates of 4.5% or below were comparable to that obtained by Marcus et al. (1992).

2. The girls' production of over-regularizations was variable; they alternated between "correct" and over-regularized forms over extended periods occasionally during the same conversation or within the same turn. This picture of variability and of type and frequency of "errors" has been documented elsewhere (e.g., Pinker, 1999), suggesting that the linguistic development of the girls was taking a fairly typical course.

3. Although Serena, Gabrielle and Ingrid continued to produce over-regularizations throughout the duration of the study, they were clearly settling on the "correct" forms over time, suggesting that they were still actively learning English morphological patterns during the course of the study.

5.5 Over-regularization and innateness

Over-regularization has long been a bone of theoretical contention between supporters of connectionist or "associationist" theories of language acquisition (e.g. Plunkett, 1995; Rumelhart and McClelland, 1986) and supporters of rule-based models of language and cognition, most prominent amongst whom are the Chomskyan advocates of innate linguistic universals (e.g., Pinker, 1991). In fact, over-regularizations are frequently cited in the technical and popular literature as direct evidence in favour of linguistic nativism (e.g., Lenneberg, 1964; Trask, 1999). For these scholars, language is acquired via the workings of an innate rule-forming device in the child's mind and children's evident capacity to generalize structures such as the regular past tense is presented as confirmation of this view (Pinker, 1991, p. 485). Consistent with this position is the claim that all children indulge in over-regularization at around the same age with the rate of over-regularization thought to develop in a U-shaped curve (Marcus et al., 1992).

As the advocates of nativism have stressed, children's over-regularizations are a clear sign that language acquisition is no mere process of imitation since their parents do not say forms like "sayed" and "mices" (Pinker, 1989; Stromswold, 1995). Thus, children are creating language rather than repeating back what they have heard others say. Furthermore, the rule-like processes that underlie the production of over-regularizations are obviously acquired without explicit instruction. On those grounds, nativist scholars take over-regularization to mark a biologically determined stage of growth in the grammatical "module", working according to a fixed developmental schedule (Pinker, 1995). In Locke's critical period model (Chapter 1), the appearance of over-regularizations in the child's speech is "the most conspicuous form of internal evidence" that the "Grammatical Analysis Mechanism" (GAM) is at work (Locke, 1997, p.272). If first language acquisition begins after the close of the critical phase for GAM activation at around 3 years, the result will be permanent morphosyntactic impairment, with inflectional morphology particularly affected (Locke, 1997; Smith-Lock, 1993). Let us now consider this prediction against the evidence from the speech of Serena, Gabrielle and Ingrid.

As we have shown above, Serena, Gabrielle and Ingrid were producing over-regularizations of various types at a fairly typical rate within the respective age ranges of 10;2 to 13;2, 13;4 to 14;10 and 10;8 to 12;7 (see Table 5.4a). Ingrid, at 3;10, was possibly just at the outer limits of Locke's hypothetical critical period when she was adopted. However, she had had more or less no linguistic experience at all in her early years and zero experience of English morphology. She had little or no opportunity, therefore, to absorb any relevant linguistic material or formulaic phrases on which the GAM could go to work. Serena and Gabrielle, on the other hand, were adopted when they were older – at 7;5 and 6;3 respectively – and, therefore, well outside Locke's critical period (2-3 years or 20 to 37 months), Pinker's (1991) looser 4 year limit and the even later time limit of 5 years in Krashen (1973) and Krashen and Harshman (1972). The girls' production of over-regularizations is, therefore, problematic for all such critical period concepts. The fact that Serena, the oldest at adoption, had the highest rate of over-regularization of the three is also a clear challenge to any expectation that one might see a "slowing down" in grammar acquisition capability after the theoretical cut-off point of choice. The production and rate of over-regularizations in the speech of Serena, Gabrielle and Ingrid are, therefore, without explanation in terms of any of the critical period models considered and directly confound the predictions of Locke's model in particular.

5.6 The acquisition of morphology: conclusion

In this chapter we have shown that all three girls had reached Brown's (1973) Post Stage V, with a predicted chronological age of 47+ months, in their acquisition of English morphology when the study began. At this most advanced stage in Brown's framework, children are taken to have acquired the whole morphological system. This level of achievement in the morphosyntactic subtleties of English is a striking confirmation of the girls' intact language learning abilities despite years of extreme global deprivation.

Furthermore, a close examination of the spontaneous speech of Serena, Gabrielle and Ingrid demonstrated that they were exhibiting the same kind of grammatical creativity which has been claimed to be characteristic of the language of typically developing children. In particular, between the respective ages of 11;3 and 13;2. 13;1 and 14;10, 10;8 and 12;7, Serena, Gabrielle and Ingrid produced over-regularization "errors" that were qualitatively and quantitatively similar to those that are reported to be present in the speech output of young children.

Given the almost complete lack of meaningful linguistic interaction in the years they spent in orphanages, this means that the girls' ability to work out and apply regular morphological patterns was due to their later post-adoption experience. The linguistic development of Serena, Gabrielle and Ingrid, then, is altogether inconsistent with any general contention that there are early maturational constraints on first language learning. More specifically, the over-regularization findings would appear to contradict the claims of "modular" versions of the critical period concept according to which some grammatical rules develop "on a schedule not timed by environmental input" (Pinker, 1991, p.482). On the contrary, the girls' developmental histories and their different ages at adoption present a picture in which acquisition of grammatical rules is very much "timed by environmental input" and can occur much later in life than most critical period models would allow. Furthermore, the most time-restrictive critical period model of Locke (1997) appears to be dramatically disconfirmed. The evidence in fact shows that the Romanian orphans – well after the supposed cut off point of 3 years – demonstrated the *only* behaviour that Pinker (1991) cites as evidence of innate mechanisms and which Locke considers "the most conspicuous form of internal evidence" for the workings of the innate GAM.

Finally, one might be inclined to wonder why a phenomenon as slight as over-regularization has been made to bear such theoretical weight in debates over language acquisition. The reason for this has to do with the way in which nativist linguistic theory emerged in the early 1960s and differentiated itself in relation to the then prevailing behaviourism. Against an approach which taught that imitation of adult models followed by reinforcement was the basic learning mechanism, it was justifiable to starkly counterpose the fact that children produce forms that they have never heard. However, this fact did not constitute reasonable grounds for veering to the opposite extreme and dropping learning altogether in favour of innate grammatical knowledge and language "growth", although that is how many standard textbooks present the theoretical choices on offer (see Trask, 1999; Pinker, 1999). In a more enlightened theoretical landscape in which analogising, innovating and imitation are shorn of their behaviourist connotations and given their due as intelligent, creative skills, we no longer have to make such a choice. Tomasello (1999, 2003), for example, recognizes the role of analogical processes, including "over-regularization", in the child's construction of his or her language but argues that these are dependent on more general meaning-finding and pattern-recognition skills which one can see at work in all domains of life.

CHAPTER SIX

SPEAKING IN SENTENCES:
THE ACQUISITION OF SYNTAX

6. 1 Introduction

In this chapter we continue our examination of the structural linguistic features on display in the everyday conversational speech of Serena, Gabrielle and Ingrid. Here we will combine quantitative and qualitative methods of analysis to provide a detailed picture of the syntax of the girls' utterances, paying particular attention to their use of those complex sentences indicative of the more advanced levels of syntactic ability in later childhood and adolescence. This analysis of complex sentences will allow us a clearer insight into the girls' overall linguistic progress as well as allowing further consideration of possible critical period effects on their language learning.

We begin with an analysis of "true" complex sentences in the girls' spontaneous speech in relation to Paul's (1981) "stages" of complex sentence development. We then attempt to ascertain to what extent the girls used structures at the phrase and clause level which are found in the spontaneous speech of older children and adolescents. We will then illustrate the hierarchical complexity in evidence in the girls' utterances by giving a constituent structure analysis ("parsing") of selected sentences. Finally, we discuss the implications of their progress in syntax for the concept of a critical period for language acquisition.

6.2 Complex sentences in spontaneous speech

6.2.1 "True" complex sentences: quantitative analysis

Utterances from Serena, Gabrielle and Ingrid were examined in relation to the charts developed by Paul (1981) which "outline some milestones in development of complex sentence production" (p.36). "True" complex sentences are largely "characterized by the fact that they contain more than one main verb" (Paul, 1981, p.36).[1]

Paul's charts are based on the conversational data obtained from 59 typically developing children aged between 2;5 and 6;11 who were filmed interacting with their mothers during 15-minute free-play sessions. These conversations were transcribed and analysed, the children then being grouped according to MLU values, ranging from 3.00 to 5.01 and beyond. The charts can be used to place the complex sentence structures appearing in a child's speech at one of several developmental "stages".[2] These are summarized in Table 6.1, together with the MLU, predicted age range and ratio of "true" complex sentences (in a speech sample lasting 15 minutes) that would be expected for each stage.[3]

Table 6.1 Paul's (1981) stages of complex sentence development

Paul's Stage	Expected Mean Length of Utterance (MLU)	Age (Predicted)	Proportion of True Complex Sentences
Early IV	3.00-3.50	34-37 months	1-10%
Late IV to Early V	3.51-4.00	38–42 months	1-10%
Late V	4.01-4.50	43-46 months	10-20%
V+	4.51-5.00	47+ months	10-20%
V++	5.01 and above	47+ months	20% and above

[1] Sentences containing verb phrases with catenatives or semi-auxiliary forms such as *gonna, wanna, gotta* are not considered to be "true" complex sentences on the grounds that such forms are not independent main verbs (Paul, 1981, p.37). Thus, a sentence such as "I wanna go home" will be described as "simple" rather than "complex".

[2] Paul's (1981) categorization of complex sentence structures follows Brown's (1973) convention for placing children's morphological development into "stages" characterised by periods of "distinct developmental achievements" (Miller 1981, p. 25).

[3] In her developmental charts, Paul (1981) gives for each stage "the percentage of TRUE complex sentences" that would be expected in a child's 15-minute free speech sample.

The ratio of "true" complex sentences in utterances produced by Serena, Gabrielle and Ingrid was worked out using Paul's (1981) recommendations. Samples of spontaneous speech lasting roughly 15 minutes from the early and late stages of the study were selected and transcribed. Speech transcripts were organised into communication units or C-Units (Loban, 1976) since average MLUs for Serena, Gabrielle and Ingrid during the study exceeded 5.0 (following Miller, 1981).[4] The proportion of "true" complex sentences was calculated by dividing the number of complex sentences in the C-Unit sample by the overall number of C-Units. The percentage of complex sentences along with the MLU values for each C-Unit sample are presented in Table 6.2.

Table 6.2 Percentage of complex sentences for selected C-Unit samples along with MLU values.

	Date of C-Unit Sample	Age	Mean Length of Utterance	Percentage of Complex Sentences
Serena	07.10.98	11;7	6.78	31%
	20.05.00	13;2	5.68	21%
Gabrielle	07.10.98	13;3	5.18	21%
	16.10.99	14;4	5.60	27%
Ingrid	09.06.98	10;8	5.74	22%
	16.05.00	12;7	5.14	28%

According to Paul's developmental charts, the proportion of the girls' complex sentences at the commencement of and throughout the duration of the study was equivalent to, if not beyond, Stage V++, the latest stage in Paul's developmental charts. This is also what would be expected from their MLUs, since these were above 5.01. Based on the available data, it appears that the percentage of the girls' complex sentences in spontaneous speech was beyond the expected level for 4 year old children.

---

[4] The segmentation of discourse into C-Units, also known as T-Units (Loban, 1976), is a procedure employed in many studies of preadolescent and adolescent children's written and spoken language (e.g,. O'Donnell, Griffin and Norris, 1967; Scott, 1984b). A C-Unit consists of any utterance that can function as an independent unit of meaning. This might involve a main sentence and all the subordinate clauses and phrasal elements contained within, or a nonclausal one-word response such as "yes" in answer to a question.

The next step was to carry out a qualitative analysis of the girls' complex sentences in relation to Paul's developmental charts.

6.2.2 "True" complex sentences: qualitative analysis

6.2.2.1 Conjoined sentences

Paul (1981) describes two classes of complex sentences. The first consists of conjoined sentences which are composed of two or more main clauses often connected by a conjunction such as *and*, *but*, *or*. It is not until around 34 - 37 months of age (Brown's early IV Stage) that children recognizably conjoin two clauses within the same utterance using coordinating conjunctions (Brown, 1973; Miller, 1981). Paul's complex sentence development charts show that 50% to 90% of children in her lower MLU groups 3.00 - 3.50 produced conjoined sentences containing *and*. However, it was only in the higher MLU groups of 4.51 - 5.00+ that over 90% of the children produced these. This indicates that *and* in conjoined sentences is not used by most children until Paul's Stage V+ (predicted age 47+ months, MLU = 4.51 - 5.00).

Serena, Gabrielle and Ingrid produced conjoined sentences throughout the duration of the study:

and

Serena:	(04.06.98)	You mustn't break it (2) because you'll have to pay a lot of money for it *and* you 'aven't got much money for that, 'ave you?
	(24.04.99)	This is my right *and* this is my left.
	(20.05.00)	You said, "I want to play a game" *and* I said "I want doesn't get."
Gabrielle:	(22.07.98)	He'll have a pint *and* I'll have an orange juice.
	(24.04.99)	Your nails are too short *and* mine are as well.
	(20.05.00)	The boy is stirring *and* the other one's pouring the milk.

Ingrid:	(09.06.98)	One's called Black Beauty *and* one's called Maria.
	(13.04.99)	You put an arrow like that (1) *and* you just ignore that one.
	(16.05.00)	I've got erm five pounds *and* I'm so poor.

but

Serena:	(16.10.99)	I don't go out with him though *but* I just fancy him.
Gabrielle:	(16.10.99)	You'll 'ave to sit there *but* turn your back to me (2) so I can comb your hair properly, not.
Ingrid:	(17.12.99)	He used to say "Let's do that" *but* I didn't know what he said (2) because he went too fast.

These examples indicate that Serena, Gabrielle and Ingrid, throughout the duration of the study, were all beyond Brown's Stage IV (3 years old) (Brown, 1973; Miller, 1981) as well as beyond the highest stages of Paul's (1981) complex sentence development charts, (i.e., Stages V+ and V++), that is, above the level of most 4 year old children.

6.2.2.2 Embedded Sentences

The embedded sentence

> "contains a clause, that is, a sentence-like segment that contains a main verb, within a larger sentence. In embedded sentences, the clause is not independent, but serves as a constituent part of the main, or matrix, sentence" (Paul, 1981, p.36).

The clause may function as the subject (e.g., "*What I'm making* is a hat"), the direct object (e.g., "You can hear *what I'm saying*") or as an adverbial (e.g., "The woman used her umbrella *because it was raining*"). Paul describes 10 types of embedding, defined below followed by examples from the girls' spontaneous speech:

1   Simple infinitive clauses with equivalent subjects

"These include clauses marked by *to* in which the subject of the clause is the same as that of the main sentence. The subject of the clause does not usually appear, because it would be redundant. (This category does *not* include the catenative, or the semi-auxiliary forms gonna, gotta, wanna, hafta, or s'posedta, which appear to function as unanalysed wholes)" (Paul, 1981, p.37).

Serena:	(11.03.99)	[I got in] I wanted to ask the questions, didn't I?
Gabrielle:	(18.03.00)	Yep! But I don't-can't be bothered to show you.
Ingrid:	(09.06.98)	Are you allowed to get the guinea pigs out?

2   Full propositional complements

"These clauses contain a complete surface sentence. They usually follow a verb such as *know, wonder, guess, think, pretend, forget, say, mean, tell, remember,* or *wish*. The clause may or may not begin with *that*, but does not begin with a Wh-word" (Paul, 1981, p.37).

Serena:	(16.10.99)	I wish I could sleep again.
Gabrielle:	(24.04.99)	I think that my mum is here.
Ingrid:	(16.05.00)	I said we've got right bossy dinner ladies.

3   Simple non-infinitive WH-clauses

"These clauses begin with a Wh-word such as *when, what, where, why, how, if,* or *like*. They do not contain the infinitive marker *to*" (Paul, 1981, p.37).

Serena:	(20.05.00)	He known him when he was at lower school.
Gabrielle:	(24.04.99)	I don't know what you mean.
Ingrid:	(10.03.99)	It's only where I kept it.

4   Infinitive clauses with different subjects

"The subject of the infinitive clause is not the same as that of the main sentence. The subject of the clause usually does appear" (Paul, 1981, p.37).

Serena:	(18.03.00)	(She) carried the small boy to put-post the letter.
Gabrielle:	(16.10.99)	I don't want Serena to hear.
Ingrid:	(17.12.99)	He got this builder to pull it out.

5   Relative clauses

"These modify nouns. They can be marked by *which, who, that,* or *what* in child speech, but often do not contain any relative pronoun at all" (Paul, 1981, p.37).

Serena:	(1103.99)	Put the ones who haven't got glasses down?
Gabrielle:	(24.04.99)	That's the only girls I know.
Ingrid:	(19.10.99)	I know a friend who does athletics.

6   Gerund clauses (i.e. non-finite verb clauses)

"These contain –ing verbs. The –ing form must be part of a noun clause. The -ing adjectives, as in *Let's play with the stacking cups*, are not considered instances of gerund clauses for the purpose of this analysis" (Paul, 1981, p.37).

Serena:	(20.05.00)	I had one ticket for English for interrupting class.
Gabrielle:	(24.04.99)	That's like me playing basketball.
Ingrid:	(22.07.98)	Imagine me being on the water flume.

7   Unmarked infinitive clauses

"These do not contain *to* in the surface sentence and are usually headed by *make, help, watch* or *let*" (Paul, 1981, p.37).

Serena:	(20.05.00)	Let me work this out please, young lady.
Gabrielle:	(24.04.99)	You could let Serena play this game.
Ingrid:	(09.06.98)	Let me put it back on.

8   WH-infinitive clauses

"These are marked by both a *Wh-word* and *to*" (Paul, 1981, p.37).

Serena:	(16.10.99)	I don't know what to do.
Gabrielle:	(16.10.99)	I don't know how to make it.
Ingrid:	(17.12.99)	Don't know how to say that.

9   Double embeddings

"An embedded clause is contained within another embedded clause, which is in turn embedded in a matrix sentence. One of these clauses may include a catenative" (Paul, 1981, p.37).

Serena:	(20.05.00)	I know it'd be nice to see his friends and my friends.
Gabrielle:	(24.04.99)	I thought Serena said she was goin' outside.
Ingrid:	(17.12.99)	That's what I didn't know what she said.

10   Embedded and conjoined

Some complex sentence types contain both a conjoined and an embedded clause (Paul, 1981).

Serena:	(16.10.99)	I said I was gonna be a vet then I changed my mind.
Gabrielle:	(16.10.99)	Shall I tell you what sweets I had today and then you tell me what sweets you got, shall I?
Ingrid:	(10.03.99)	When I 'aven't got anyone to play with I always talk to myself and (2) people get a bit annoyed.

The above examples of all 10 types of complex sentences show that Serena, Gabrielle and Ingrid were capable of producing all of the structures that were used by 50 - 90% of the children in all of the MLU groupings of Paul's sample, that is, they produced constructions consistent with all of the developmental stages (Early IV, Late IV-Early V, Late V, V+ and V++) in Paul's charts. Serena, Gabrielle and Ingrid also produced sentences containing more than one embedding which do not reach consistent usage until late Stage V, and sentences with non-finite verb (or gerund -*ing*) clauses and with the conjunction *because* which do not emerge until Stage V+. Other late emerging structures produced were sentences containing the conjunction *if* and sentences containing both a conjoined and embedded clause. The use of these forms was reached by over 90% of children in the highest MLU group of 5.01 and above, corresponding to Stage V++. These more advanced structures are, according to Paul (1981), signs of continuing learning in syntax. Thus, while Serena, Gabrielle and Ingrid produced sentence structures corresponding to all Paul's stages, the types of sentence they produced, throughout the study, were most characteristic of Stage V++, corresponding to an MLU of 5.01 and above, with a predicted chronological age of 47+ months.

6.3 More advanced grammatical constructions

The next stage was to ascertain whether Serena Gabrielle or Ingrid used structures found in the spontaneous speech of children over the age of 7. There are particular aspects of language development, such as types of noun and verb phrase elaboration, that are reported to continue to develop throughout middle and late childhood (Scott, 1988; Karmiloff-Smith, 1979). Crystal (1997a) also notes that "more advanced grammatical constructions" continue to emerge throughout childhood:

> "A popular impression of grammatical learning is that it is complete by age 5; but recent studies have shown that the acquisition of several types of construction is still taking place as children approach 10 or 11" (p. 245).

6.3.1 Noun phrases

Between the ages of 9 and 19, the structure of the noun phrase undergoes significant elaboration according to Scott (1988):

> "noun phrase postmodification via prepositional phrases, relative clauses, non-finite clauses … and appositive constructions ... are particularly active growth areas" (p.63).

Prepositional phrases

An increase in the use of prepositional phrases to postmodify nouns continues until the age of 13 (O'Donnell, Griffin and Norris, 1967). Scott (1988 citing Scott, 1987) gives some examples of these constructions:

a)   "The leather made him think of a sail *on a ship*" (p. 64).
b)   "and they talked about the food chains *in the* desert" (p.64).

Postmodification through prepositional phrases was evident in the spontaneous speech of Serena, Gabrielle and Ingrid:

Serena:	(08.09.98)	Hello ladies and gentlemen, we're gonna have a race *to the bike.*
Gabrielle:	(24.04.99)	Looks a bit like me *in my summer top.*
Ingrid:	(13.04.99)	What's a elephant *up a tree*

Non-finite clauses

Non-finite clauses can also postmodify nouns and the use of these constructions also undergoes some development towards and during the early teen years (Scott, 1988; O'Donnell, Griffin and Norris, 1967). Scott (1988, p.64, citing Scott, 1987) gives the examples below:

a)   "The desert has one main tree *called the soursos.*"
b)   "and he had a machine *controlling his brain.*"

Following are examples from the girls' speech of noun phrase elaboration via non-finite clauses:

Serena:	(16.10.99)	He's got another girl friend *called Kelly Johnson.*
Gabrielle:	(18.03.00)	L: What's this? {*shows picture of man in a diving helmet}* G: A head *blowing a bubble.*
Ingrid:	(13.04.99)	I don't like people *copying me.*
Serena:	(07.10.98)	Yes so what's the point *of arguing*?
Gabrielle:	(07.10.98)	Just scribble on your work and forget the idea *of colouring.*
Ingrid:	(10.09.98)	My dad's got a really good map (2) *for walking.*

Appositive constructions

The use of apposition to postmodify noun phrases is, as Scott (1988, p.64) says, a sign of linguistic development during late childhood and the early teens. She gives the following examples (citing Scott, 1987):

a)   "it's about Jennifer *the girl* she starts a recycling project."

b)   "Mr Spoon, the village policeman he's not very pleased with
          them finding out."

Noun phrase postmodification in the speech of Serena, Gabrielle and
Ingrid also involved the use of appositive constructions as the following
examples illustrate:

Serena: (18.03.00)   S: I see Eleanor (2) just walking in
                                  the house.
                                  L: You've just seen who, sorry?
                                  S: Eleanor, *my sister*.
Gabrielle: (24.04.99)   That's a bit like me and my mum and
                                  Sally-Anne, *my sister*, having dinner.
Ingrid: (22.07.98)   Yeah, d'you know, we did a trick on
                                  Tom, *my friend*.

Scott (1988) reports that these three areas of postmodification continue to
develop during the preadolescent and adolescent years. According to
Perera (1984), the use of these structures in spoken language does not
reach an adult level of competence until the age of 15 or 16. Therefore, the
fact that Serena, Gabrielle and Ingrid were found to use all the forms in
question meant that considerable syntactic development had already taken
place in their speech and was possibly still ongoing.

6.3.2 Verb phrases

With regard to the verb phrase, the appearance or increase of several types
of construction are claimed to represent "syntactic growth" (Hunt, 1965;
Loban, 1976; Scott, 1988).

Non-finite verb forms

Loban (1976) suggested that non-finite verb forms that occur only in
subordinate clauses indicate syntactic progress between late childhood and
the early teen years. According to Scott (1988):

> "[Loban] argued that non-finite verbs allow for a more direct expression of
> subordinate thought because subjects are optionally deleted and auxiliary
> verbs carrying tense and number are always deleted" (p.66).

Serena, Gabrielle and Ingrid all produced non-finite verb forms within
subordinate adverbial clauses in their spontaneous speech:

Serena:	(16.10.99)	No, I was asleep *dreamin'* about my lovely boyfriend.
Gabrielle:	(24.04.99)	Actually it's a little bit silly *pretending being* a T.V. lady.
Ingrid:	(14.12.98)	And he got *fed up of going* on the (2) road.

Modal auxiliaries

Hunt (1965) found a significant increase in the use of modal auxiliaries such as "will", "shall", "should" and "might" in the language samples of North American children between eighth and twelfth grades (ages 13 to 17 years) (Scott, 1988). Similarly, Scott (1984b) reported the increased production of "could" and "would" in the spoken narratives of children between the ages of 8 and 12. Serena, Gabrielle and Ingrid used modal auxiliaries to "talk about the possibilities for action as well as the facts of action" in the same way that children from the age of 10 have been noted to do (Scott, 1988, p.66):

Serena:	(16.10.99)	I wish I *could* go out with him but I can't.
Gabrielle:	(20.05.00)	Well I *should* 'ave really 'ave worn my glasses really.
Ingrid:	(19.10.99)	I *would* hate to be chased by a horse.

Perfect tense (perfective aspect)

Use of the perfect tense form ("have" + past participle) with its "perfective aspect" (Crystal, 1997b) steadily increased between the fourth and twelfth grades (9 to 17 years) in Hunt's (1965) sample of children. The perfect tense is principally used to express an action or state of being continuing up to the present moment (Crystal, 1997b; Quirk et al., 1985). Thus there is a subtle semantic difference between the perfect tense, with its flavour of "current relevance", and the past tense (Crystal 1997b, p.96). According to Scott (1988), appreciation of the perfective aspect may be a later emerging skill. Serena, Gabrielle and Ingrid were all noted to use the perfective aspect:

| Serena: | (16.10.99) | You *haven't seen* Nicholas for a long time, have you? |
| Gabrielle: | (16.10.99) | What, *has* my hair *grown* long then? |

Ingrid: (21.09.98)   Some people *have had* their tooth
                                   tooken out in our school before.
                 (13.04.99)   I'*ve done* a bit of Spanish with Mrs
                                   Rogers.

6.4 Clause types in subordinate clauses

According to Scott (1988), a wide range of clause types are used by
children by the time they reach school age. These involve combinations of
the five basic sentence-building elements in English: subject, verb, object,
complement and adverbial. However, "only a few of these clauses occur
frequently" (p.68), including SVO, SVOA and SVA clause types
(O'Donnell, Griffin and Norris, 1967). Over 90% of subordinate clauses
spoken by a 9-year old will be one of the three main clause categories:
nominal, adverbial and relative (O'Donnell, Griffin and Norris, 1967;
Scott, 1988).

6.4.1 Nominal clauses

Nominal clauses, containing either non-finite or finite verbs, can fulfil the
grammatical functions of object, subject, or adverbial (Crystal, 1997b).
The majority of nominal clauses serve the role of direct object as in
propositional complements (Paul, 1981) or *that* or Wh-clauses such as "I
think that this is great" and *to*-infinitive clauses such as "She wanted to
drive home." These clause types are extremely frequent throughout
childhood and the adult years during spoken conversations when
statements or views are offered and during narrative activities (Scott,
1988). Nominal clauses functioning as direct objects frequently occurred
in the girls' speech:

to-infinitive

Serena: (07.10.98)   I don't really want *to do colouring.*
Gabrielle: (16.10.99)   You need *to do your hair again.*
Ingrid: (14.12.98)   You're not even allowed *to watch the
                                   play.*

that or Wh-clauses:

Serena: (20.05.00)   Some people say *that George is small.*

| Gabrielle: | (24.04.99) | She'll say that-*that jacket doesn't even look like fashion_ at all*. She'll say that's-*that's from Marks and Spencer's.* |
| Ingrid: | (10.03.99) | I don't know *what "weary" looks like.* |

Constructions with nominal clauses functioning as direct objects are very common in the spoken and written discourse of children and teenagers in the 9 to 19 age range (Scott, 1988) and were also very common in the speech of Serena, Gabrielle and Ingrid. However, nominal clauses as grammatical subjects are rare. Hunt (1965, cited by Scott, 1988) studied the written samples of 13-year olds and found that only 3.6% of the nominal clauses acted as subject elements. The use of subject nominal clauses was noted for Serena and Gabrielle:

Serena:	(07.10.98)	*Just because I'm doin' something* doesn't mean that you have to know.
	(24.04.99)	*Just because somebody was around our house* doesn't mean distraction.
Gabrielle:	(16.10.99)	*Whoever [duːz] the better* yeah [can 'ave the prize] can have a prize.

6.4.2 Adverbial clauses

Throughout later childhood and the teenage years (9 to 19), high-frequency adverbials such as those headed by the time adverb *when* and the reason adverb *because* make up around 75% of all adverbial clauses produced (Loban, 1976; Scott, 1988). These also frequently occurred in the talk of Serena, Gabrielle and Ingrid:

Because

Serena:	(08.09.98)	I don't like her, Mrs Jackson *because* she's winnin'.
Gabrielle:	(16.10.99)	Can I go outside then (2) *because* I need some fresh air?
Ingrid:	(09.06.98)	I don't know which branch *because* I don't know how it happened.

When

Serena:	(24.04.99)	Have you done this before *when* you was little?
Gabrielle:	(16.10.99)	*When* I'm older I'm gonna have my second holes done.
Ingrid:	(09.06.98)	I: Can you do handstands? L:[[I used to- I: [[*When* you used to be little, I mean?

Increases in the production of less frequently occurring adverbials such as the conditional *if* and purpose (*in order*) *to* reach a developmental peak by the elementary school years (Scott, 1988). Scott (1984b) studied the spoken narratives of children aged between 6-12 years and found that reason (*because*), time (*when*) and purpose (*to*) adverbial clauses comprised the majority of instances of adverbial subordination, while the conditional *if* was virtually absent. However, *if* clauses have been reported to increase in frequency when the discourse type involves children's written game instructions rather than spoken narratives (Perera, 1984; Scott, 1988). Adverbial clauses headed by *if* occurred comparatively often in the conversations of Serena, Gabrielle and Ingrid:

Serena:	(19.10.99)	Why am I-*If* I'm pointin' (at) the right one, why d'ya n- need to say that?
Gabrielle:	(07.10.98)	*If* you're gonna be nasty to me, I'll just tell my friends in the street (2) you're really ugly.
Ingrid:	(10.09.98)	*If* you want to know what I'm doing, I'm colouring this out.

A sign of linguistic maturity - and one often found in the speech of adolescents - is the use of *if* clauses to express hypothetical situations (Scott, 1988; Perera, 1984). Preschoolers commonly use *if* clauses to express real situations occurring in the immediate context such as "*If* I get dollie, we can play a game." However, it may take several years, usually up to preadolescence, before *if* is used to encode imaginary situations or those occurring outside the "here and now". As the following examples demonstrate, Serena, Gabrielle and Ingrid did use *if* adverbials to talk about hypothetical situations, suggesting that they possessed a facet of linguistic maturity typically reached by late childhood:

Serena:	(20.05.00)	*{Serena is shown a picture of a boy falling off a fence}* That's funny. Imagine *if* I fell off; I'd laugh.
Gabrielle:	(16.10.99)	*If* I went to a party with my boyfriend I('d) hit your boyfriend. That's what I'd do.
Ingrid:	(14.12.98)	*{Talks about telling a story on a bus}* I('d) laugh *if* we did it on a real, real bus.

Some of the most frequently occurring adverbial clauses in the girls' spoken language were headed by *if*, *when* and *because*. The production of high and mid-frequency adverbials such as *if* and *because*, however, may actually decrease during the preadolescent and adolescent years to be replaced by a greater diversity of adverbials. These may include some of the less common subordinating conjunctions such as the conditional adverbs *unless* and *although* (Scott, 1988), which were rare in the data for Serena, Gabrielle and Ingrid. The following is an example of Serena's use of *although*, which occurred early in the study:

| Serena: | (071.0.98) | That's s'posed to be white *although* I dunno. |

There is a range of adverbials that occur infrequently but whose presence is considered to be a sign of continuing linguistic development (Scott, 1988). Included in this group of low-frequency adverbials are concessional subordinators such as *even if*, *though*, adverbs of manner like *as*, some of the rarer conditional adverbs such as *unless, supposing* and *in case* and adverbs of time such as *since*, which has been noted to occur in the speech of 14 year olds. According to Scott (1988):

> "These particular adverbials tend to be used more often by high-ability groups than by low-ability groups of students (Loban, 1976), and therefore may be more sensitive indicators of syntactic development during the 9-through-19 age range than some of the more common adverbials" (p.71).

Some of these more sophisticated, later developing adverbials were used by Serena, Gabrielle and Ingrid at least once in the data:

| Serena: | (07.10.98) | Then don't shout just whisper *like* I'm talking. |

	(24.04.99)	D'you need the loo by the way, *in case* you do that?
	(20.05.00)	Take as long *as* you like.
Gabrielle:	(24.04.99)	*Even if* that's right, is that a problem?
Ingrid:	(22.07.98)	I've known him *since* I were little and he used to be naughty as well.
	(14.12.98)	*Even if* it were somebody else, I wouldn't believe everything.
	(13.04.99)	You always do keep-fit *though* outside we do something else.

Serena, Gabrielle and Ingrid also used a range of other subordinating conjunctions such as adverbials of time (*after*, *before*, *while*), preference (*better than*, *rather than*), comparison (*as if*), result (*so*, *so that*), and similarity (*like*). Note that the purpose adverbial *to*, which develops early, was also used. Examples of these adverbial clause types are presented below.

Serena:	(07.10.98)	What would you like to do *while* we colouring?
	(24.04.99)	I think that school is *better than* doing this.
	(18.03.00)	You sound *as if* you (.) gonna be stress.
Gabrielle:	(24.04.99)	Well me and Serena can play a game *while* N. [du:z] this.
	(16.10.99)	When can I meet him just *so that* I can be horrible to him, yeah?
	(16.10.99)	I want to know what sweets they are *before* I like 'em.
Igrid:	(22.07.98)	It's *like* turning a steering (.) really (.) wheel.
	(13.03.99)	Right and you just ignore that one and then you put an arrow on it (2) *to* show that it goes down or up.
	(19.10.99)	They're tryin' to knock your bone, aren't they, *to* see if you got any nerves or something?

Another subtle indicator of syntactic development may be non-finite verb forms in adverbial clauses (Scott, 1988; Perera, 1984). Following are examples of these later emerging types of adverbial clauses in the girls' spontaneous speech:

Serena:	(08.09.98)	Gabrielle looks happy (2) *playin' with Daniel.*
	(18.03.00)	I see 'Lizabeth (2) *just walking in the house.*
	(20.05.00)	I've got detention this Monday (2) *for not signing my diary.*
Gabrielle:	(07.10.98)	[It's for-] It's *for making a decoration (2) to do.*
	(18.03.00)	It's silly *going to school.*
	(20.05.00)	I'm no good *at reading at all today.*
Ingrid:	(02.12.98)	I went to see what sort of rides there were down there (3) and I went, right, and there weren't even enough *to choose from.*
	(16.05.00)	But it's not hygienic *to do that.*

Some of the adverbial forms (e.g. low frequency subordinators, and non-finite verb clauses) indicative of syntactic development (Scott, 1988) were already present in the girls' spoken language at the study's commencement. Serena had attained this level of syntactic maturity within 4;10 years, Gabrielle within 6;9 and Ingrid within 6;2 years of entry into their respective adoptive homes. Non-finite adverbial clauses occurred more often in the data corresponding to later visits than earlier ones, suggesting that further syntactic development had taken place over the course of the study itself. This was particularly marked in Serena's case. When her C-Unit sample for 07.10.98 was studied in detail, it was found that there were several adverbial clauses headed by the subordinating conjunctions *if*, *because* and *when* but that there were no adverbial clauses containing non-finite verb forms. However, 19 months later, Serena's C-Unit sample for 20.05.00 contained several incidences of non-finite adverbial clauses which, according to Scott (1988), indicate increasing syntactic maturity:

Serena:	(20.05.00)	I've got a detention this Monday (2) *for not signing my diary.*
	(20.05.00)	I had one tic-ticket for English *for interrupting class.*
	(20.05.00)	I know it'd be nice *to see his friends and my friends* (2) hm.

6.4.3 Relative clauses

Although relative clauses are less common than either nominal or adverbial clauses, their occurrence is significant with regard to syntactic development (Scott, 1988; Hunt, 1965; Loban, 1976). Loban (1976, cited by Scott, 1988) suggested that greater frequency of relative clauses in speech was associated with children with above average language ability, while Hunt (1965) found that the frequency of relative clauses in written samples steadily increased through to twelfth grade (17 years). In addition O'Donnell, Griffin and Norris (1967) established, through the study of third (8 years), fifth (10 years) and seventh grade (12 years) children's written and spoken language samples, that relative clause frequency increased with age (Scott, 1988, p.72).

According to some studies, the majority of relative clauses follow object, adverbial or complement nouns, that is they are right-embedded and are rarely centre-embedded, (i.e., postmodifying the subject). For example, Scott (1984b) found that centre-embedded relative clauses were rare in the spoken language of children in early adolescence. Citing the work of Romaine (1984), Scott (1988) states:

"Romaine found that some centre-embedded relatives appeared in spoken language by the age of 10 and suggested that by that age children have better control of true embedding operations as opposed to conjunction operations" (p.73).

The occurrence of this type of relative clause was noted in Serena's speech:

Serena: (10.03.99)   Mr Humphrey, *who*'s our Maths teacher, gave us all a sheet.

Relative clauses most frequently postmodify object nouns where the relative pronoun, *who(m)*, *whose*, *which*, *that*, or *what*, functions as the subject of the embedded clause (Scott, 1988) although there may be no relative pronoun at all (Crystal, 1997b; Paul, 1981). The majority of the girls' spoken relative clauses postmodified complement or object nouns and were sometimes marked by a relative pronoun (*that, what* or *who*) and sometimes not. *Who* was also used in direct or indirect questions or to mark nominal clauses functioning as direct objects such as "I know who my boyfriend is" (Gabrielle, 16.10.99). The pronouns *which* and *whose* made rare appearances but *whom* was entirely absent. The following are a selection of the relative clause-like structures (following the object or complement noun) in the girls' conversational speech:

Serena:	(08.09.98)	This is all cards *you gave me.*
	(16.10.99)	Is that the last one *you said?*
Gabrielle:	(17.09.98)	It's you *that's got to tell me about your holiday.*
	(16.10.99)	Well, I'm just doin' the things *I made up, okay?*
Ingrid:	(02.12.98)	Did they like my test (2) *who you showed?*
	(17.12.99)	That's another one *I found funny.*

Although the following examples are not all strictly relative clauses, they illustrate the girls' use of non-finite forms of the verb (in this case the *-ing* and *–ed* participles) in subject or object complement position:

Serena:	(08.09.98)	There's a person *standing there* (2) with that pointing at her.
	(08.09.98)	That's my sister *riding a bike.*
Gabrielle:	(17.09.98)	Did ya see them two *sittin' next together on Sunday?*
	(18.03.00)	There was a man *driving a bus.*
Ingrid:	(02.12.98)	I know a girl *called Carrie* and she's from Romania.

Another relative clause structure that emerges late is the non-restrictive type that follows the subject as in "Mr Jarvis, who is sitting at the back, has ordered" (Perera, 1984; Scott, 1988). According to Crystal (1997b), this relative clause type "provides optional, extra information which could be omitted without affecting the noun's identity" (p.142). Serena occasionally used a non-restrictive relative clause to postmodify a subject as in "Mr Humphrey, *who*'s our Maths teacher, gave us all a sheet" (11.03.99).

Frequency of relative clauses in speech

The frequency with which Serena, Gabrielle and Ingrid produced relative clauses compared to other syntactic structures (such as adverbial clauses) appeared to be comparatively low and this appears to be congruent with the language of typically developing children and adolescents (Scott,

1988). According to Scott (1988), citing the work of O'Donnell, Griffin and Norris (1967):

> "relative clause frequency increased from 1.0 to 3.4 per 100 T-Units in the written samples of third-, fifth-, and seventh-grade students; comparable figures for spoken language samples were 2.6, 3.3 and 3.9" (p.72).

The frequency of relative clauses per 100 C-Units was calculated for samples of language for Serena, Gabrielle and Ingrid. The results are summarized in Table 6.3.

Table 6.3 Percentage of relative clauses for selected C-Unit samples.

	Date of C-Unit Sample	Age	Relative Clauses Per 100 C-Units
Serena	07.10.98	11;7	4
	20.05.00	13;2	2
Gabrielle	07.10.98	13;3	0
	16.10.99	14;4	0
Ingrid	09.06.98	10;8	1
	16.05.00	12;7	0

It was found that for Serena, 4 relatives occurred in her C-Unit sample for October 1999 and 2 for May 2000, while for Gabrielle, there were no relative clauses found in either of her C-Unit samples for October 1999 or October 2000, although in the latter case a relative pronoun was used to introduce a nominal clause: "I know *who* my boy friend is, lovely and-lovely and handsome." Although relative clauses did not occur in Gabrielle's two C-Unit samples, they appeared elsewhere in her speech transcripts as in:

Gabrielle: (07.10.98)   L: So, who's Dana?
                                        G: O:hh. Sky Hall's friend *who goes to {name of school}*

In Ingrid's case, only one relative clause was present in her C-Unit sample for June 1998. Nearly 2 years later, Ingrid's C-Unit sample for May 2000 contained no relatives at all.

During the early part of the study, there were signs that Serena sometimes found relative clauses difficult to produce accurately. The following example indicates that, at 11;7, Serena occasionally stumbled over the construction of these complex sentence types:

Serena: (08.09.98)   *{Serena talking to her teacher Mrs Taylor, T., during a game of cards}*
                                     S: Ah, we're not doing very well are we?
                                     T: No, you're not concentrating.
                                     S: I a:m. You the not-you the no:t (.) one who concentrating *{laughs self-consciously}*

Similar difficulty with the production of negation in relative clauses was evident 6 months later in March 1999 when Serena was 12:

Serena: (11.03.99)   *{Serena and Lisa talking about a game}*
                                     L: D'you know how to play that then?
                                     S: Yeah, "Guess Who." Y'gotta try and answer questions say, "Have you got (1) erm glasses?" and they say, "No", then you get all (2) the ones who got glasses=The ones *not* got glasses on.

6.5 Conjunctive adverbs

Conjunctive adverbs (Semel, Wiig, and Secord, 1995), also referred to as "adverbial conjuncts" by Scott (1988), are a group of adverbials such as *anyway* and *so* whose purpose is to relate or join together independent segments of discourse, that is, they "cause the sentence sequence to 'cohere'" (Crystal, 1997b, p.119). Adverbial conjuncts convey a range of meanings and often are used as important links between the clauses and sentences of a conversation or narrative (Scott, 1988; Crystal, 1997b). An example of a sentence containing an adverbial conjunct is: "I can't remember how to play *though*." (Gabrielle, 24.04.99, 13;9). A study by Scott (1984a) showed that by the age of 10, children are using around 4 conjuncts per 100 utterances with only a narrow range of conjuncts such as *though* and *then* being expressed (Scott, 1988). A further finding was that children's use of adverbial conjuncts is more frequent during peer interaction than the dyadic context of adult-child interview. By the age of

12 the diversity of the adverbial conjuncts used increases slightly to include forms such as *instead, only* and *otherwise*. Scott's (1984a) study suggested that the use of adverbial conjuncts continues to progress beyond the age of 12 and is, therefore, another linguistic area that develops during the preadolescent and adolescent years.

As Table 6.4 indicates, the number of adverbial conjuncts that Serena, Gabrielle and Ingrid produced in conversational speech steadily increased during the study and was either roughly equivalent to or beyond that of 10-year-old children. They used several types of adverbial conjunct, which have been reported to occur in the speech of children aged 10 to 14 (Scott, 1988).

Table 6.4 Number and type of adverbial conjuncts per 100 utterances

	Date of Transcript	Age	No. of adverbial conjuncts per 100 utterances	Type of adverbial conjunct used
Serena	07.10.98	11;7	7	then, so, really, now, though
	16.10.99	12;7	5	really, though
	20.05.00	13;2	10	well, just, or something, then, so, at all
Gabrielle	07.10.98	13;3	12	then, well, so, by the way, actually, anyway
	16.10.99	14;4	20	though, anyway, then, well, actually, so, really
Ingrid	09.06.98	10;8	3	though, actually so, though, and
	17.12.99	12;2	9	everything, or something, and that

The following examples illustrate the way in which Serena, Gabrielle and Ingrid spontaneously used a small range of conjuncts which includes "inferential" *then,* and "concessive" *though,* and *anyway* (Scott, 1988, pp. 74-75):

Serena:	(24.04.99)	I can't remember how to play *anyway*.
	(16.10.99)	I don't go out with him *though* but I just fancy him.
	(16.10.99)	That wasn't a stripey one, uhuhh e:r er number two: Tsk! looked at the stripey one *instead*.
Gabrielle:	(24.04.99)	Can I go outside and then Serena plays the game *then*?
	(24.04.99)	I have no idea what game you're playing (2) *anyway*.
	(16.10.99)	L: Can you make yours like that? G: How ya s'posed to *though* with these-these bricks *then*?
Ingrid:	(10.09.98)	L: Does he do lots of walking then? I: No: I like walking *though*.
	(14.10.98)	Who'll be at home *then*?
	(19.10.99)	There's not a goblet on that (2) *so* how do I know?

There appeared to be a number of changes to the girls' use of adverbial conjuncts during their adolescent and preadolescent years. At the start of data collection, when Serena, Gabrielle and Ingrid were respectively aged 11;3, 13;1 and 10;8, they already used conjuncts in their spoken language. However, a small number of common adverbs including *though*, *then* and *so* as in, "How ya s'posed to *though* with these-these bricks *then*?" (Gabrielle, 16.10.99, 14;4) appeared to increase in frequency over time. Serena's use of *though* seemed to increase with later visits and was particularly noticeable on 16.10.99, when 12;7, as in: "It looks good *though*." During the same visit, the speech of Gabrielle (who was also present during this visit) contained a much higher proportion of adverbial conjuncts when compared to data collected during earlier visits. She used two types, *then* and *though*, often as in the following examples:

| Gabrielle: | (16.10.99) | What shall I do *then*, tip it out *then*? |
| | (16.10.99) | What, was I messin' about *then* or not *then*? |

Other types of adverbial conjunct that Serena, Gabrielle and Ingrid produced throughout the study were *anyway* noted for all three girls, *by the way* and *all of a sudden* noted for Gabrielle and *just as well* used only by Serena. Adverbial disjuncts such as *actually* and *really* also regularly occurred in the speech of all three children as the following examples show:

Serena:	(08.09.98)	This-This is like a spoon *really*.
	(24.04.99)	I did quite enjoy this game *actually*.
Gabrielle:	(24.04.99)	*Actually*, it is a little bit silly pretendin' bein' a T.V. lady.
	(16.10.99)	I-I think I'm playin' a nice little game here, *actually*.
Ingrid:	(22.07.98)	Sometimes, it's quite funny, *actually*.
	(13.04.99)	Ooh the date is (2) hm. What's the date? Thirteenth. No, it's not *really*.

The occurrence of *well* at the beginning of sentences as in, "*Well*, I-I'm gettin' that one this Monday" (Serena, 13;2, 20.05.00) increased towards the end of the study when the girls were in or approaching their early teens. Adverbial conjuncts that were noted to occur in later visits but not during earlier ones included *instead* and *at all*. Interestingly, one change that characterized the later use of conjuncts by Serena and Ingrid involved the emergence of colloquial (or dialectal) phrases at the end of sentences such as *and everything, or something* and *and that*, forms which are very common in teenage and adult informal spoken conversation (Crystal, 1997b). The examples below demonstrate use of these forms by Serena and Ingrid at the respective ages of 13;2 and 12;2:

Serena:	(20.05.00)	You said "I want to play a game" *or somethin'*.
Ingrid:	(17.12.99)	It was a blue game. You had-It had a folder *and that*.

The above examples should demonstrate the structural complexity of the spoken language of Serena, Gabrielle and Ingrid at the clause and phrase level. In order to illustrate the hierarchical complexity in evidence in the girls' utterances, we will now select particular sentences for constituent structure analysis (parsing).

6.6 Constituent structure analysis (parsing)

The following constituent structure diagrams (or "parse trees") are based on the system used in Perkins (1999).[2] Each of the example sentences contains a construction considered to be indicative of "syntactic growth" (Scott, 1988).

1   Same level subordination: several occurrences of subordination may occur at the same level of hierarchical depth. For example, the sentence "What I said was what I meant" is "basically only a three-part structure, comparable to *That is that*" (Crystal, 1997b, p. 195).

Serena: (07.10.98)   Just because I'm doing something doesn't mean you have to know.

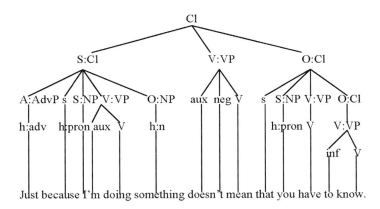

---

[2] Key to parse trees: Cl = clause, S:Cl = subject clause, O:Cl = object clause, V:VP = verb phrase, A:AdvP = adverbial phrase, S:NP = subject noun phrase, O:NP = object noun phrase, pre = preposition, aux = auxiliary, neg = negation, V = verb, s = subordinating conjunction, c = coordinating conjunction, m = modifier, q = qualifying, h:adv = head adverb, h:pron = head pronoun, h:n = head noun, inf = infinitive, d = determiner, int = intensifier.

2.   Double embedding: defined by Paul (1981, p.37) as "[a]n embedded clause ... contained within another embedded clause, which is in turn embedded in a matrix sentence."

Serena: (20.05.00)   I know it'd be nice to see his friends and my friends.

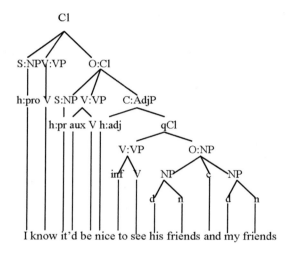

3.   Noun phrase postmodification via appositive clause.

Gabrielle: (07.10.98)   That's the way you do it.

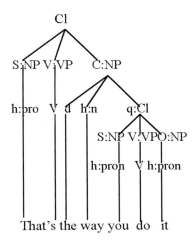

4.   Sentence containing Wh-adverbial clauses.

Gabrielle: (16.10.99)   It's where you put your toothpaste in
                                        when you sleep at your friend's house.

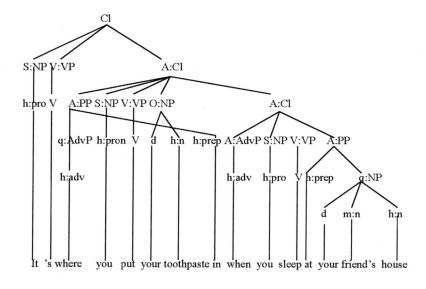

5.   Noun phrase elaboration via pre-modifying adjective phrase and postmodifying prepositional complement containing non-finite verb clause.

Ingrid: (10.09.98)   My dad's got a really good map for walking.

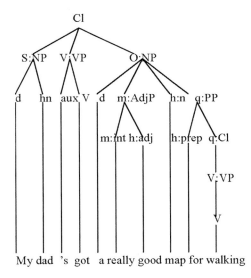

6.   Compound-complex sentence: containing both an embedded and
        coordinated clause.

Ingrid: (10.03.99)   When I haven't got anyone to play
                                     with I always talk to myself and
                                     people get annoyed.

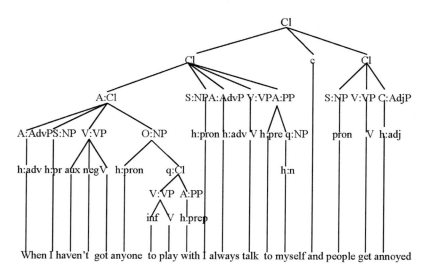

6.7 Syntactic competence and metalinguistic awareness

One factor possibly of wider significance in the study of post-deprivation
language development, if not language development generally, is that the
girls' spontaneous speech revealed a level of grammatical competence that
was not obvious from their performances on standardized language tests as
reported in Chapter 4. Indeed, the syntactic sophistication on display in the
girls' spontaneous complex sentences did not seem to be reflected in their
syntax scores, notably those from the Formulated Sentences subtest of
CELF-3. On this test, Serena, Gabrielle, and Ingrid produced "incorrect"
sentence types that they were capable of producing "accurately" in
spontaneous conversation. For example, Ingrid was marked down for her
one-clause utterance, "Because I cross on the zebra crossing." (16.05.00)
when asked to make a sentence using the reason adverbial *because*. Such
"incomplete" sentences are, of course, communicatively impeccable in
ordinary conversation, but the Formulated Sentences test scores them as

"ungrammatical" because it requires a "full" sentence with a main and dependent clause such as, "The cars stop *because* I cross on the zebra crossing." However, Ingrid's "I put them in the bin *because* it's all about maths", an utterance produced spontaneously on the same day as the test (16.05.00), shows that she was *able* to produce the required structure in a different context. Similarly, Gabrielle, when asked to make a sentence using the conditional subordinator *if*, gave the "ungrammatical" response: "If the boy was playing". Yet, Gabrielle had spontaneously used conditional *if* on previous visits in sentences such as "*If* I don't finish it at school (2) I'll probably get detention" (07.10.98).

Serena also had difficulty incorporating subordinating conjunctions into sentences when specifically asked to. For example, when Serena was asked to make a complex conditional sentence using the subordinator *if*, she said, "The girl and the boy was playing with the girl if (2) they was at home." While the response meets the structural criteria, since it consists of a main sentence with a dependent clause with *if*, the meaning of the sentence is unclear. However, during conversation, Serena produced sentences such as, "You need to use it carefully *if* you gonna use felt tips (2) not too hard" (07.10.98). Curtiss also drew attention to differences between Genie's responses to utterances in the test context (specifically WH-questions) and in spontaneous conversation:

> "In contrast to the formal test, Genie responds to WH-questions of the object almost 100% correctly in real life, as often and as consistently as with WH-questioning of the subject. She does not demonstrate any difficulty in understanding the transformed word order with *who, what, when, where, how,* or *why* questions" (Curtiss, 1977, p. 140).

Furthermore, Serena, Gabrielle and Ingrid seemed unable to spot the "ungrammaticality" of their "incorrect" responses when these were repeated back to them or when specifically asked. For example, Gabrielle, at 14;10, was asked to make a sentence using the correlative conjunction *or* to describe a picture of a market scene and said, "Or they're buying some apples." This was scored as "incorrect" according to test guidelines and repeated back to Gabrielle who appeared not to perceive anything unusual about it. In contrast, she produced sentences such as "'Ave I done one or 'ave I done two?" (20.05.00, 14;10) fluently in conversational settings. When Gabrielle was asked to use the correlative conjunction *either* in a sentence, she said, "The lady's either (2) helping them." Gabrielle was specifically asked, "Is this a sentence, Gabrielle?" to which she replied, "mm: Yeah." In response to one Formulated Sentences item

(20.05.00), Serena was asked to use the subordinating conjunction *whenever* and said, "Whenever I copy out the book I read the book." When the sentence was read back to Serena, she recognized that some aspect of this response sounded "strange", since she immediately said, "Sounds wrong really, doesn't it?" although it was not clear what she found "wrong" about it.

Why would a person be able to produce certain types of complex sentence in ordinary conversation but not as a response to a task in a test setting? The short answer is that the everyday conversational utterance and the test response are not the same kind of communicative action. The test tasks presuppose a form of metalinguistic awareness that is irrelevant to engagement in everyday conversation, namely familiarity with the term "sentence" and with particular criteria for evaluating sentencehood. Everyday conversation, of course, presupposes its own kind of metalinguistic awareness and intelligence, as discussed in Chapter 3. However, formal tests presuppose a particular kind of literacy-based metalinguistic awareness. The very idea of a "sentence", after all, is a product of literate practice and conventional literacy instruction and does not correspond to a functional unit of spontaneous speech (Halliday 1989), a point which is not usually taken into account in discussions of "syntactic well-formedness" (e.g., Bellugi et al, 1993). Thus, in terms of both the formulation of the communicative task (the goal of the test item) as well as the scoring of the response (a "full" sentence rather than "incomplete", but conversationally appropriate, utterance) we see the role of particular, literacy-based forms of metalinguistic awareness on the evaluation of children's linguistic competence.

In this regard, it is worth noting that Scott and Rush (1985, cited by Scott, 1988) reported that children aged around 9 years found it difficult to generate sentences incorporating conjunctive adverbs such as *however* and *otherwise* in a test situation. One 9 year old, when asked to produce a sentence containing *however*, said, "I can play today, however, today is Saturday". Scott and Rush (1985) also report that a 13 year old had much more success on the sentence generation task than younger children. This is certainly consistent with a view that the ability to create linguistic forms on demand in this way is a later developing skill associated with familiarity with written language and its norms (cf Crystal, 1997a).

The lesson to be learnt, then, is that standardized tests, particularly when used in isolation, may present a rather impoverished and distorted picture of children's linguistic competence and their use is bound to favour those children with a clearer sense of the literacy-based discourse of the test context.

6.8 Speaking in sentences: conclusion

Initial analysis of the syntactic complexity of the girls' utterances according to Paul's (1981) developmental charts put Serena, Gabrielle, and Ingrid at or beyond Stage V++, that is, beyond the expected level for 4-year-old children. Examination of syntactic structures present in the girls' spontaneous speech also revealed advanced hierarchical complexity at both the clause and phrase level. Analysis of complex (coordinated and embedded) sentences demonstrated the use of a variety of forms ranging from simple infinitives to double embeddings of the type and frequency that one would expect to find in the speech of 2 to 7 year olds (Paul, 1981). Serena, Gabrielle and Ingrid also used structures such as low frequency subordinating conjunctions (*even if, though, while*) marking adverbial clauses and non-finite verb forms and adverbial conjuncts (*then, so, anyway*) which are associated with continuing syntactic development in later childhood and the teenage years. Some frequently occurring forms, for example, nominal clauses functioning as objects (marked by *that* or the infinitive form of the verb) or adverbial clauses headed by mid-to-high frequency adverbials such as *if, because, when* and *to*, are also frequently found in the speech of typically developing older children and teenagers in the 9-19 age range (Scott 1988). Constituent structure analysis (parsing) of selected sentences demonstrated considerable complexity and many levels of hierarchical depth.

Some of the structures (e.g., low frequency subordinators, and non-finite verb clauses) considered to indicate syntactic development in later childhood (Scott, 1988) were already observable in the girls' speech at the study commencement. This suggests that a significant amount of syntactic development had already taken place over the 4;10-6;9 years since Serena, Gabrielle and Ingrid entered their respective adoptive homes. Furthermore, there were subtle indications that syntactic development was still taking place during the study: the use of conjunctive adverbs appeared to steadily increase (as is reported for typically developing children up to the age of 12 years and beyond) and, in Serena's case at least, non-finite adverbial clauses occurred more often in later visits than earlier ones. Also, all three girls appeared to be still in the process of developing some of the less common adverbial clause types (e.g,. with *although, unless, since*), whose presence is considered a linguistic mark of the preadolescent and adolescent years.

The overall impression, then, was that the linguistic competence of Serena, Gabrielle and Ingrid had developed along quite typical lines and at a quite typical rate since their adoption and that their language development was continuing on the path to adult competence. Extreme deprivation, even up until the age of 7 years (Serena's age when adopted), has not, therefore, resulted in an inability to develop spoken language to a level of sophistication which, in some respects, is indistinguishable from (or in advance of) that of typically developing older children.

As with the girls' progress in the acquisition of morphology, discussed in the previous chapter, the structural sophistication and hierarchical complexity of the girls' sentences appear to speak against any critical period effects operating on their language development. It is particularly difficult to see how such advanced achievements in syntax as illustrated above are compatible with critical period models such as in Locke (1997) and Pinker (1999) in which a 3-4 year deadline on linguistic input for "normal" development is proposed. Nor is there evidence from these findings for any "slow down" in syntactic development related to the age at which the children were adopted. On the contrary, the evidence shows that Serena, the oldest of the three on adoption (at 7;5), was still progressing syntactically in her teenage years, as were the other two girls. In short, the acquired syntactic abilities of all three girls constitute strong evidence against the critical period concept as applied to language.

CHAPTER SEVEN

THINKING WITHOUT WORDS:
PUTTING NONVERBAL COGNITION
TO THE TEST

7.1 Introduction

This chapter reports on the performances of Serena, Gabrielle and Ingrid on a selection of standardized tests designed to assess nonverbal cognitive skills. Our main objective is to give an overall picture of the girls' abilities in nonverbal thinking across a range of different tasks. Our second objective is to consider whether the girls' test performances lend any support to the idea of cognitive "dissociations" as argued for by nativist scholars (Fodor, 1983; Yamada, 1990) and as was argued for Genie specifically (Curtiss, 1981). To that end, we will compare the girls' performances with the reported test outcomes of children with Williams syndrome. We will then make qualitative comparisons between the girls' responses on some tasks with those of a group of younger, typically developing children. Finally, we will compare the girls' non language results with their language results as presented in Chapter 4.

7.2 Background

Prior to the administration of these tests, what could be said with some confidence about the development of the girls' nonverbal cognitive abilities? As we showed in Chapter 2, assessments of aspects of nonverbal cognition had been done at various times post adoption but there was no systematic testing procedure in place and, consequently, information about the girls' progress in these areas is inconsistent and sometimes anecdotal.

In Serena's case, there had been no professional evaluation by an educational psychologist since she was 7;8. Her visuospatial skills were discussed in an early school report (from 8;8) which mentioned that she had difficulty with matching exercises and jigsaw puzzles. At 11;8, Serena's learning support tutor informally estimated her intellectual level to be between 7-8 years. Her reading age at the time was put at 6-7, although no formal assessment had been carried out for that year.

Gabrielle, at 7;8 and 14;2, scored below the floor on the Block Design subtest of visuospatial cognition (WISC-III), with the clinical psychologist who administered the test reporting that Gabrielle had difficulty with spatial tasks in general. At 11;11, a second clinical psychologist had formally assessed her nonverbal cognitive level as being similar to a child aged 6-7 years.

Developmental reports for Serena and Gabrielle also indicated that their language and non-language abilities were at a similar level. The clinical psychologist's report for Gabrielle, then at 11;11, notes: "Gabrielle has a fairly consistent pattern of skills with no marked discrepancies between her verbal and nonverbal abilities." Similarly, Serena's most recent speech and language therapy report (for 11;7) concludes: "Serena's speech and language are commensurate with her general abilities."

In Ingrid's case, documentation was also sparse. At 7;1, an educational psychologist concluded that she was making rapid progress that was typical in sequence but from a "delayed starting point", and that her nonverbal functioning was similar to an "ordinary" child of 5-6 years. Later school reports (at 10;8) indicated that she was at the 7-8 year level if not beyond in terms of educational attainment. At 11;0, an educational psychologist confirmed that Ingrid still showed a "general developmental delay" but was making progress in learning nonverbal concepts including mathematical concepts.

7.3 Testing procedure

7.3.1 The tests

A number of standardized measures were administered to Serena, Gabrielle and Ingrid in order to assess spatial cognition, perceptual awareness and visual representation (drawing). As with the language test results reported in Chapter 4, we emphasise the caution to be exercised with the use of test age equivalents (Bishop, 1989a; Howlin and Cross, 1994; Meacham, 2006) and, therefore, also report percentile ranks and standard deviations from the mean where relevant.

1   The Block Design subtest of the Wechsler Intelligence Scale for Children – Third Edition, UK (WISC-III, Wechsler, 1992).

The Block Design test is one component of WISC-III, a widely used intelligence test for children between the ages of 6 and 16. The test involves the child manually arranging wooden blocks to replicate a series of geometric patterns within a strict time limit. It is designed to assess visuospatial skills, specifically the capacity to distinguish the properties of geometrical shapes such as triangle, cube, circle or pyramid and the spatial relationships among objects. There are nine test items altogether, involving two-, four- and nine-block patterns, for a maximum score of 69 points

2   Raven's Coloured Progressive Matrices (CPM, Raven, Court and Raven, 1978).

The CPM assesses nonverbal reasoning and perceptual skills and is standardized for children up to the age of 11 years. The test involves recognizing and completing coloured geometric patterns. The child is asked to identify the missing constituent that completes a pattern as items become more advanced. The CPM gives percentile ranks and assigns grades based on performance (RPM grades) ranging from V ("intellectually above average") to IV ("definitely below average in intellectual capacity"). The maximum raw score that can be obtained is 36.

3   Goodenough Draw-A-Man Test (Aston Index, Newton and Thomson, 1976).

The Goodenough Draw-A-Man test is a sub-scale of the Aston Index (1976) and assesses nonverbal cognition though drawing. The test involves drawing a picture of a person and from this a test age equivalent is derived by assigning numerical values to correctly represented features such as fingers, ears and legs. Points are also given for symmetry and proportion of facial and bodily features.

7.3.2 Behaviour during testing

On the Block Design test, Serena and Gabrielle appeared to have some difficulty with replicating the designs (beyond the trial items) using the wooden blocks. Sometimes they appeared uncertain as to whether their designs matched the picture or not or expressed a lack of confidence about being able to complete the test. Although Ingrid was easily able to complete the easier items, she, too, began to have problems copying the designs when the items became more difficult. On the CPM, the girls sometimes had to be encouraged to complete items because they said the task was too difficult. In contrast, they needed no encouragement to complete the Draw-A-Man test for which they displayed more confidence and which they found easier and more enjoyable to complete.

7.4 Performance on tests of nonverbal cognition

7.4.1 Test results

Test results for the girls are summarized in Table 7.1.

Table 7.1 Scores on tests of nonverbal cognition; chronological age (CA), time since adoption (TSA), test age equivalents (TAE), raw score (RS), percentile rank (PR), standard deviation (SD) from the mean or performance grade (RPM).

	Serena	Gabrielle	Ingrid
Block Design (WISC-III)			
CA	12;7	14;4	12;0
TSA	5;2	8;1	8;2
TAE	<6;2	<6;2	6;10
RS	6	9	19
PR	1	1	1
SD from the Mean	-3	-3	-2.3

Raven's Coloured Progressive Matrices			
CA	12;7	14;4	12;0
TSA	5;2	8;1	8;2
TAE	5;6	7;3	8;6
RS	15	19	24
PR	<5	<5	<10
RPM Grade	V, "intellectually impaired."	V, "intellectually impaired."	IV-, "definitely below average in intellectual capacity"
Goodenough Draw-A-Man Test			
CA	11;7	13;4	11;1, 11;6, 12;2
TSA	4;2	7;1	7;3,7;8, 8;4
TAE	6;6	8;0	9;0, 11;0, 10;0
RS	17	22	26, 35, 29

Let us first examine the results of each test separately.

1.   The Block Design subtest

The Block Design subtest was administered once to Serena (12;7), Gabrielle (14;2) and Ingrid (12;0). Their (raw) scores gave respective test age equivalents (6;2, 6;2, 6;10) which were similar to those that might be expected for children about half their age. The percentile ranks of 1 would suggest that 99% of children from the girls' chronological age groups would be expected to obtain higher scores. However, the inclusion of the time since adoption measure allows us to put such a wide divergence between chronological age and test age equivalent into perspective. Serena's time since adoption value, 5;2, is "ahead" of her test age equivalent of 6;2, while time since adoption values for Gabrielle, 8;1, and Ingrid, 8;2, are much closer to their respective test age equivalent scores of 6;2 and 6;10.

2.   Ravens Coloured Progressive Matrices (CPM)

The CPM was administered once to Serena (12;7), Gabrielle (14;2) and Ingrid (12;0). Performances on the CPM were comparable to those on the Block Design test. When the girls' (raw) scores were compared to the norms for typically developing children of 11;6 (range 11;3 to 11;8, the oldest age range the CPM is standardised for), the corresponding percentile ranks were between 5 and 10. In other words, between 90% and 95% of children of that age range would be expected to obtain scores higher than those of the girls. Scores for Serena and Gabrielle would be graded V ("intellectually impaired"), and Ingrid's would be graded IV ("definitely below average in intellectual capacity"). However, the girls' raw scores of 15, 19 and 24 fall within the 50th percentile, that is, the "intellectually average" range for much younger typically developing groups of children ranging in age from 5;3 to 8;8 (according to the CPM norms). As can be seen, the girls' respective time since adoption values of 5;6, 7;3 and 8;6 fall squarely within this range.

3.   Goodenough Draw-A-Man Test

The girls' drawings were compared to the Draw-A-Man Test scoring guidelines in order to obtain a rough idea of their test age equivalents. Serena's drawings were assessed at 11;7, Gabrielle's at 13;4 and Ingrid's at three points: 11;1, 11;6, and 12;2.[1] On this measure, Serena achieved a score of 17/50 points, indicating a 6;6 year test age equivalent; Gabrielle's score of 22/50 points indicated an 8-year test age equivalent; Ingrid's drawings attained scores of 26, 35, 29 indicating test age equivalents of 9;0, 11;0 and 10;0. As on the previous two tests, there is a disparity between chronological age and test age equivalents. Once again, however, there was a much closer fit between test age equivalent and time since adoption. Indeed, the girls' time since adoption values of 4;2 (Serena), 7;1 (Gabrielle), and 8;4 (Ingrid, final session) were all "ahead" of their respective test age equivalents.

The girls' drawings are presented in Figures 7.4 to 7.8.

---

[1] As Ingrid particularly liked drawing, an opportunity was taken to sample her drawings for comparison purposes over a longer time period.

Serena

As can be seen in Figure 7.4, Serena produced a figure with disproportionate head (drawn by using a roll of sellotape as a guide) attached to a trunk with bodily appendages such as arms, hands, legs and feet absent. However, facial features such as eyes, nose, nostrils, mouth, teeth, ears and hair are included. The ears and eyes are symmetrical and the facial features correctly aligned and well proportioned on the head.

Figure 7.4 Drawing by Serena at 11;7

Gabrielle

As shown in her self-portrait in Figure 7.5, Gabrielle produced a figure with disproportionate head and legs. Nearly all bodily features are included such as facial features, hair, ears, trunk, clothes, fingers, nails and even teeth. The feet are absent, but the ears and eyes are symmetrical and the facial features correctly aligned and well proportioned on the head.

Figure 7.5 Drawing by Gabrielle at 13;4

Ingrid

Figure 7.6 is Ingrid's drawing at 11;1. It is a self-portrait that shows a head with facial features and hair, trunk, arms and fingers, but no legs or feet. This drawing indicated a 9-year test age equivalent level. A picture drawn 4 months later (Figure 7.5) is more sophisticated, since it depicts a clothed figure with legs, feet and even shoes present. This picture indicated an 11-year test age equivalent level. Ingrid's most recent drawing (Figure 7.6) at 12;2 is a diminutive self-portrait. All major bodily features such as arms, hands, legs, head, hair and facial features are represented and correctly aligned and/or symmetrical. The drawing indicated a 10 year test age equivalent level suggesting that the Goodenough Draw-A-Man Test may not give reliably consistent measures over time.

Figure 7.6 Drawing by Ingrid at11;1

Figure 7.7 Drawing by Ingrid at 11;6

Figure 7.8 Drawing by Ingrid at 12;2

7.4.2.2 Tests of nonverbal cognition: general conclusion

Taken together, the results of all three tests of nonverbal cognition present a consistent picture of a wide divergence between test age equivalent and chronological age. The scores on some tests indicate a developmental level corresponding to children of about half the ages of the three girls. However, consideration of time since adoption allows a different perspective on these results. In each case, time since adoption values are much closer to, or indeed "ahead of", the corresponding test age equivalent. This may suggest that the time the girls spent in their adoptive homes is a more meaningful factor in understanding their developmental progress than their actual age. In fact, it suggests that the girls' nonverbal cognitive skills have developed along a course, and at a rate, that would be unexceptional for typically developing younger children. This finding is also consistent with the findings on the children's language tests, as presented in Chapter 4.

7.5 Comparisons with children with Williams syndrome

In this section we compare those test responses assessed as "inaccurate" by test criteria with those reported for children with Williams syndrome who are considered to display a "dissociation" between linguistic and non linguistic cognitive abilities (e.g., Bellugi et al., 1993; Bellugi, Lai, and Wang, 1997).

Block Design subtest of WISC-III

Bellugi and Wang (1996, p.2) described the performances of children with Williams syndrome as "markedly impaired", failing "to achieve the overall configuration of the blocks" and "characterized by selective attention to details of a configuration at the expense of the whole". In comparison to this description, the "inaccurate" Block Design responses by Serena, Gabrielle and Ingrid were arguably quite different. Figure 7.9 shows responses by Serena and Gabrielle on items 4 and 5 and Figure 7.10 shows all three girls' responses on items 6 and 7. It appears that the girls' responses tended to take into account the arrangement of the whole pattern rather than just focussing on selected parts.

Figure 7.9 Responses by Serena and Gabrielle on items 4 and 5 of Block Design

Item 4

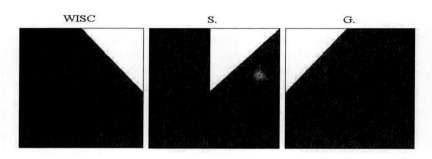

Item 5

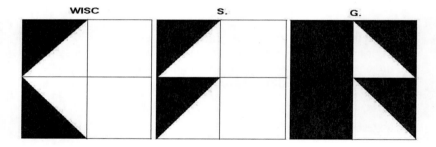

Figure 7.10 All three girls' responses compared for items 6 and 7 of Block Design.

Item 6

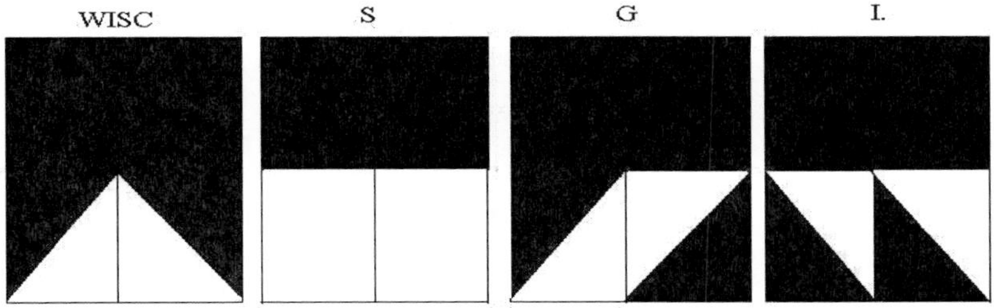

Item 7

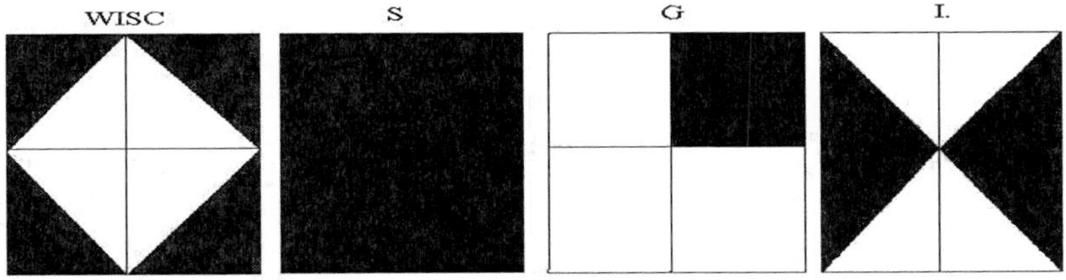

Goodenough Draw-A-Man Test

On drawing tasks, children with Williams syndrome are reported to "show specific attention to parts of an object, but parts may be placed on a page with no integration into a coherent whole" (Bellugi and Wang, 1996, p.3). In contrast, the drawings of Serena, Gabrielle and Ingrid were spaced symmetrically with attention paid to both internal detail and the organized whole of the figures, as Figures 7.4 to 7.8 have shown.

7.6 Comparison with younger children

With the aim of gaining a fuller insight into the progress of Serena, Gabrielle and Ingrid in nonverbal areas, we decided to compare their results on the tests with those of typically developing younger children attending a mainstream primary school. To that end, one boy (P.R.) aged 7;10 and one girl (L.H.) aged 7;1 were selected by the teacher to represent, respectively, the top ability range and mid-average ability range in the class. P.R. and L.H. were assessed on the CPM and Block Design tests in October, 1999. In addition, a group of 37 school children aged 7 to 8 years were asked to draw pictures for assessment on the Goodenough Draw-A-Man test.

7.6.1 Test results

Block design and CPM

Test results for P.R. and L.H. on the Block Design test and CPM are presented in Table 7.2.

Table 7.2 Scores of R.R and L.H on the CPM and Block Design subtest of WISC-III: chronological ages (CA), test age equivalents (TAE), raw scores (RS), scaled score (SS) percentile rank (PR) and standard deviation (SD) from the mean, or performance grade (RPM).

	P.R.	**L.H.**
Chronological Age	7.10.	7.1.
Block Design (WISC-III)		
TAE	10;10	7;2
RS	44	21
SS	15	10
SD from the Mean	+1.66	0
Ravens Coloured Progressive Matrices		
RS	32	23
PR	95	75+
RPM Grade	I, "intellectually superior"	II, "definitely above the average in intellectual capacity"

As we can see from the above, performances on the Block Design test corresponded to a test age equivalent for P.R of 10;10 years, +1.66 SDs above the mean of children in his chronological age group, and a test age equivalent of 7;2 for L.H, equivalent to the average range of children in her age group as indicated by a SD of 0. On the CPM, P.R. and L.H. obtained grades significantly above the average range of ability, since their total raw scores were at or above the 75th percentile for children in their age groups.

1.   Block Design

As P.R. got all the answers right, the "inaccurate" responses of Serena, Gabrielle and Ingrid on the Block Design test could only be compared to those of L.H as shown in Figures 7.11, 7.12, 7.13, and 7.14, below. There were clear similarities between the responses of Gabrielle and L.H on item 4 (Figure 7.11) and between those of Serena and L.H. on item 8 (Figure 7.12).

Figure 7.11 Gabrielle's block design compared to that of L.H. on item 4

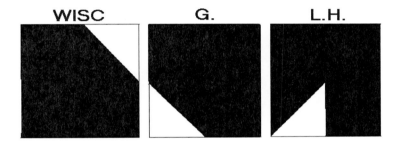

Figure 7.12 Serena's block design compared to that of L.H. on item 8

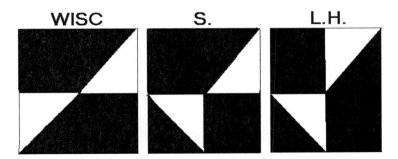

Serena and Gabrielle made exactly the same design as L.H. in response to one of the more difficult test items, item 9, as shown in Figure 7.13.

Figure 7.13 Block designs for Serena, Gabrielle and L.H. on item 9

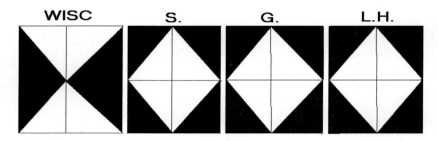

However, Ingrid's "inaccurate" responses on items 8 and 9 were *not* like those of L.H., as seen in Figure 7.13.

Figure 7.14 Ingrid's block designs compared to those of L.H. for items 8 and 9.

Item 8.

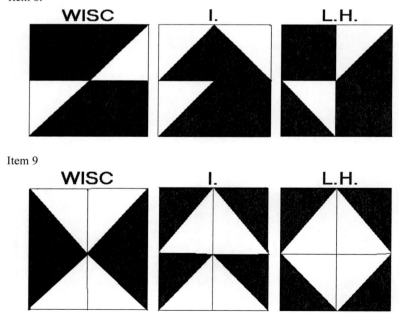

Item 9

2.   Goodenough Draw-A-Man Test

The drawings of Serena, Gabrielle, and Ingrid were compared with three randomly chosen pictures from the total set of 37 produced by the school children. According to test criteria, the test age equivalent levels for the three pictures were 7;6 (child E.) , 9;0 (child A.) and 10;9 (child C.). The artistic abilities of the school children varied quite widely, as can be seen from Figures 7.15 to 7.17. For example, the person represented in Figure 7.15 is quite rudimentary compared to that in Figure 7.17 and the disproportionately large head in Figure 7.16 is similar to Gabrielle's self-portrait (Figure 7.5). However, what the drawings of the younger children and Romanian adoptees have in common is that both the detail and the overall gestalt of the figures are depicted. In this respect, the visual representational abilities of Serena, Gabrielle and Ingrid appeared to be similar to that of typically developing younger children.

Figure 7.15 Drawing by child E., aged 8 years; test age equivalent: 7;6 years

Figure 7.16 Drawing by child A., aged 7 years; test age equivalent: 9;0 years

Figure 7.17 Drawing by child C., aged 7 years; test age equivalent: 10;9 years

7.6 Tests of language and nonverbal cognition

Finally, we compared the girls' nonverbal cognition results with their language test results as reported in Chapter 4 to see if there were any signs of a disparity between them of potential theoretical interest. We noted in Chapter 4 that caution needs to be exercised in the use and interpretation of tests with test age equivalents. Consequently, we decided to use percentile ranks in addition to test age equivalents as a basis for comparison. Percentile ranks are often used as markers of performance and help to give perspective to standardized test scores as regards the relationship between individual performance and performance of a larger group. To compare results more straightforwardly, we only report those tests that were standardized for the girls' chronological ages at the times they were assessed. Results are presented in Table 6.3.

Table 6.3 Results: Comparisons between latest scores on language tests and nonverbal cognition tests: time since adoption (TSA), test age equivalent (TAE), percentile ranks (PR) and standard deviation (SD) from the mean.

	Serena	Gabrielle	Ingrid
Block Design			
TSA	5;2	8;1	8;2
TAE	<6;2	<6;2	6;10
PR	1	1	1
SD from the Mean	-3	-3	-2.3
Raven's Coloured Progressive Matrices			
TSA	5;2	8;1	8;2
TAE	5;6	7;3	8;6
PR	<5	<5	<10
RDF(BAS)			
TSA	5;2	8;3	8;2
TAE	5;7	4;1	6;10
PR	2	1	14
CELF-3			
TSA	5;9	8;7	8;9
TAE	5;0	5;0	5;0
PR	1	1	1
SD from the Mean	-3	-3	-3

British Picture Vocabulary Scale			
TSA	5;2	8;1	8;2
TAE	8;3	10;2	8;11
PR	3	8	7
SD from the Mean	-1.93	-1.4	-1.46
Test For Reception of Grammar			
TSA	5;2	8;1	8;2
TAE	6;0	6;0	7;0
PR	1-5	1-5	1-5
SD from the Mean	-2.2	-2.2	-1.93

The overall pattern of results does not immediately seem to reveal any obvious disparity between performances on language and nonverbal tasks. Indeed, there seems to be a fair degree of consistency across these areas judging by percentile ranks which are mostly <10 (apart from Ingrid's PR of 14 on the RDF(BAS)) across Block Design, CELF-3 and TROG, although we should stress that nothing here can be said with complete confidence. But there is certainly no strong evidence here to suggest anything other than that the children's linguistic and nonlinguistic cognitive abilities are developing roughly in parallel.

7.7 Summary Discussion and Conclusion

Serena, Gabrielle and Ingrid obtained scores on psychometric assessments of visuospatial ability, perceptual awareness and visual representation (drawing) which were below those of children in the same chronological age groups. Percentile scores were below 10 and test age equivalents indicated the girls' performances were similar to those of younger children. However, looking at test performances with time since adoption rather than chronological age in mind helps to put such results into perspective since the girls' time since adoption values were much more in keeping with their test age equivalent scores. Qualitative comparison between the test responses of Serena, Gabrielle and Ingrid and typically developing children from the 7-8 year age group indicated some similarities. This appeared to confirm that the girls performed on these tasks in a way that might be considered consistent with their time since adoption values, suggesting perhaps that their cognitive development had followed a fairly "typical" course, albeit with a delayed start. Furthermore, the girls' test responses were markedly dissimilar to those of children with Williams syndrome for whom "dissociations" between language and other areas of cognition have been reported.

A further major finding is that, overall, the performances of Serena, Gabrielle and Ingrid on tests of non-verbal cognition paralleled their performances on conventional measures of language ability. On this basis, there is no hint of the selective impairments in visuospatial cognition relative to expressive language ability which have been reported for children who have Williams syndrome (Bellugi et al., 1993). Nor is there any indication of the "dissociations" between "computational" (i.e., grammatical and phonological) areas of linguistic ability and general cognitive capacity which have been reported for children with Down syndrome (Rondal, 1995; Fowler, 1988, 1990, Chapman, et al., 1998; Vicari, Caselli, and Tonucci, 2000).

These findings, therefore, offer no support in themselves for the nativist modularity position with its hypothetical "dissociations" between linguistic and nonlinguistic "modules" and between "modules" within the language system. They are, however, consistent with other theoretical positions outlined in Chapter 1 above, including the weak form of the Cognition Hypothesis, the Correlational Hypothesis and neuroconstructivism, which reject nativist assumptions about structural or narrow functional prespecification in linguistic and cognitive ability.

CHAPTER EIGHT

BRINGING BACK THE CHILD:
CONCLUSIONS AND IMPLICATIONS

8.1 Research questions

In this study of the language abilities of Serena, Gabrielle and Ingrid we set out to answer three questions:

Question 1

What progress have these children made overall in terms of their linguistic, communicative, cognitive and social development from backgrounds marked by extreme global deprivation during the first years of their lives?

Question 2

Does the linguistic development of these children provide evidence of a "critical period" for language generally or for "grammar" more specifically?

Question 3

Do these three cases provide evidence of cognitive "modularity" in the shape of "dissociations" between linguistic and non-linguistic competencies or between different aspects of linguistic competence?

Let us now try to answer these questions, drawing together the findings and observations from previous chapters.

8.2 Answers to research questions

8.2.1 Question 1

What progress have these children made overall in terms of their linguistic, communicative, cognitive and social development from backgrounds marked by extreme global deprivation during the first years of their lives?

Chapter 3 showed that the early orphanage experiences of Serena, Gabrielle, and Ingrid had deprived them of opportunities for physical, cognitive, social and linguistic growth, holding back their whole development as individuals. However, when the girls' environments changed for the better as a result of adoption, they engaged with the new opportunities for experiences and interaction and their behaviour on all fronts began to change and develop rapidly.

In terms of physical development, there were rapid gains in height and weight alongside dramatic developments in basic motor skills such as walking and chewing, although there were possibly longer-lasting effects on fine motor skills as in Ingrid's case. The girls were physically active and took up a range of hobbies, including sports like football. According to developmental reports, there was a typical onset of puberty in the cases of Serena and Ingrid.

In the case of nonlinguistic cognition, rapid development was generally also the rule. Serena, Gabrielle and Ingrid were all able to attend school and made good academic progress There were reports of continuing difficulties with abstract reasoning and visuospatial ability, although such reports rarely took time since adoption into account. Visuospatial skill, perceptual awareness and drawing ability were examined more closely in Chapter 7 with the aid of standardized tests of nonverbal cognition. The girls' scores were consistently well below those of their chronological age equivalents and according to the scoring guidelines, were comparable to those of much younger children. With time since adoption as baseline measure, however, we found that the girls' results appeared to indicate a rate and level of development of cognitive function that would be more in line with that of much younger, typically developing children. Further support for this view came from a comparison of the test performances of Serena, Gabrielle and Ingrid with those reported for children with a neurodevelopmental disorder (Williams syndrome) and with those of a group of typically developing younger children from a mainstream school. Finally we compared the girls' non verbal cognitive test results with their language results as reported in Chapter 4. The comparison appeared to show that the girls' scores in both areas were well "behind" their chronological ages, implying that their non verbal cognitive abilities were developing in parallel with their linguistic abilities. On this basis, a clinician's interpretation might be that Serena, Gabrielle and Ingrid had no particular difficulty with language, but rather a "global developmental delay" that affected language and non-language cognitive areas more or less equally. However, in the light of time since adoption, we might prefer to suggest a picture of acquired ability that parallels a quite "typical" developmental course, albeit with a later start.

Socio-emotional development perhaps presents a more complex picture. Serena, Gabrielle and Ingrid were certainly able to form positive social relationships with others, including with younger children, and successfully integrate into a variety of social contexts. On the other hand, "indiscriminate friendliness" (Chisholm, 1998; Wilson, 2003) and difficulty with expressing emotions were reported as subtle persistent issues even several years after adoption.

In terms of the development of communicative and linguistic abilities, Serena, Gabrielle and Ingrid appear to present a remarkable success story, as documented in a close study of their conversational skills (Chapter 3) and of the grammatical properties of their spontaneous utterances (Chapters 5 and 6). While the girls had entered their adoptive homes with virtually no productive language, at best a repertoire of less than twenty words, by the start of the study they had become sophisticated conversationalists. Indeed, from many points of view there was nothing particularly remarkable or unusual about how they conversed. Their talk was quite unlike that reported for children with disorders from the autism spectrum and exhibited none of the "quasi-autistic patterns" noted for other previously institutionalised children (Rutter et al., 2001, p.97). In short, Serena, Gabrielle and Ingrid displayed the skills one would expect of many older children or adolescents, including the ability to adapt their conversational style according to context and conversational partner. Conversational skills of this level of sophistication imply not only expertise in the structural regularities of adult English but also require the exquisite coordination in real time of complex linguistic, cognitive, social and motor resources. For that reason we suggested that the girls' conversational abilities offered the best and clearest evidence of their overall developmental progress as individuals since adoption.

Further close examination of their spontaneous speech (Chapters 5 and 6) demonstrated that they were well on the way to acquiring the whole adult morphological system of Standard English and were able to infer and apply word-formation patterns to produce "over-regularizations", a critical indicator for many theorists of genuine grammatical competence. The girls were also generally accomplished in sentence construction and could easily handle the forms of complex sentence considered to be characteristic of the speech of older children and adolescents. Furthermore, the girls' linguistic capacities in particular areas of morphology and syntax appeared to be still developing in their teenage years.

Chapter 4 reported on standardized assessments of the performances of Serena, Gabielle, and Ingrid on a variety of receptive and expressive language tasks. The girls did not obtain age equivalent scores on any of the tests: some scores were comparable to those of children aged 2-3 years below their actual ages while others were what would be expected for children about half their chronological age. These scores only slightly increased after a year. Such results, taken in isolation, might be interpreted as indicating clinical "delays" in language ability for their chronological ages with no marked difference between their receptive and expressive ability (Semel, Wiig and Secord, 1995). But taking time since adoption rather than actual age as a temporal baseline, it could be argued that the girls' linguistic progress looked more like that of younger children with a more "typical" developmental history. In the light of the findings of our analysis of the girls' naturalistic speech outside of the test setting, we also stressed that performance on standardized tests should always be evaluated cautiously in relation to the life histories of individual test participants and the communicative proficiencies which they are clearly capable of in different contexts. We also argued that such tests might, in any case, give a quite misleading picture of linguistic competence due to their implicit reliance on metalinguistic knowledge of a particular kind, a point to which we turn again below.

Question 1: conclusion

From an initial state of adaptation to an extremely impoverished and restricted daily routine, adoption by a nurturing family gave Serena, Gabrielle and Ingrid the chance to begin to make up for many lost years. Overall, our study indicates that, in many ways, their social, linguistic and non verbal cognitive development appear to have proceeded along a path and at a rate similar to that of a "typical" younger child without a history of extreme deprivation. In other words, if the girls had not "caught up" in all respects with same-age peers then they had made progress in language as well as in non verbal cognitive and social skills broadly commensurate with time spent in their adoptive homes. Consequently, the apparent "delays" in linguistic and cognitive development for the three girls, relative to their chronological ages, should not blind us to the remarkable congruence of developmental process and outcome between them and the "typical" younger child.

As a final exercise, in order to explore the possible significance of differences in age at adoption as a factor in overall progress, we may now combine the girls' scores from language and non-language tests, taking the median rather than mean test age equivalent scores (since the mean can be skewed by extreme scores either high or low). Table 8 allows these combined scores to be examined in relation to differences in ages at adoption.

Table 8 Median test age equivalents against age at adoption.

Child	Median test age equivalent (language and non-language combined)	Age at adoption
Serena	6;0	7;5
Gabrielle	5.9	6;3
Ingrid	7;0	3;10

Table 8 seems to show that the girls progressed equally well across the board at their different ages, offering no clear evidence of differences in outcome associated with the different ages at which they entered their adoptive homes.

As for language development specifically, we conclude that extreme global deprivation during the usual early language learning years is not a barrier to the subsequent development, with no apparent intrinsic upper limit, of sophisticated and grammatically advanced linguistic competence. This conclusion has clear implications for issues to do with language learning on which scholarly opinion is divided. To some, (e.g., Pinker, 1999) the most important structural aspects of linguistic ability are timed to develop within the early years so that children have basically learned the sentence structure of their language by the age of 4. For other scholars, however, (e.g., Crystal, 1997a) language learning continues well beyond the age of 5 into the teenage years. Our own study gives strong support to the latter position. Serena was 7;5, Gabrielle 5;9 and Ingrid 3;10 *when their language learning began* and they were continuing to acquire aspects of English sentence structure well into their teens.

8.2.2   Question 2

Does the linguistic development of these children provide evidence of a "critical period" for language generally or for "grammar" more specifically?

In Chapters 5 and 6 we considered the linguistic abilities of Serena, Gabrielle and Ingrid in relation to the predictions of different versions of the concept of a critical period for language acquisition, focussing in particular on the model proposed in developmental neurolinguistic theory (Locke, 1994, 1997). According to this model, an innate left-hemisphere grammatical analysis module (GAM) is timed to activate "only once in the life of an individual" between 20-37 months of age (Locke, 1997, p. 304). Creative "errors", or "over-regularizations", are considered to be the most obvious sign that the GAM is active (Locke, 1997, p. 274). Falsification of Locke's theory would "require evidence from a range of naturalistic behaviours and experimental tasks to indicate that analytical and computational capabilities are present" after the hypothetical GAM critical period deadline and "that utterance analyses are taking place in the vicinity of the left perisylvian area" (Locke, 1997, p.309).

Serena, Gabrielle and Ingrid represent a natural test of Locke's (1997) model because they were all linguistically deprived in the years up to and after the hypothetical critical period for GAM activation: they had built up no store of utterances during their first years of life and therefore had nothing for the putative GAM to work on. Furthermore, the girls' cases taken together allow us to see whether the age of the children when adopted was a factor in their subsequent progress in language learning.: Ingrid, adopted at 3;10, was not far beyond the GAM end point, while Serena, at 7;5, and Gabrielle, at 6.3 were much older.

Our in-depth study of "a range of naturalistic behaviours and experimental tasks" in Chapters 3-5 offered unambiguous evidence of the girls' advanced "analytical and computational abilities" in language. Serena,

Gabrielle and Ingrid all went on to acquire language without apparent difficulty to highly sophisticated levels, in both communicative and structural terms, within a timespan which looks fairly unexceptional when compared with younger, typically developing children from non-deprived backgrounds. Furthermore, between the respective ages of 11;3 and 13;2, 13;1 and 14;10, and 10;8 and 12;7, Serena, Gabrielle and Ingrid produced over-regularization "errors" that were qualitatively and quantitatively similar to those that are present in the speech output of children up to the age of 10. In addition, in terms of "experimental tasks", the girls' results on standardized language tests, while not as advanced in comparison with the evidence of their naturalistic talk, confirmed their acquisition of the full range of linguistic skills up to, at least, the level of a 4-5 year old child.

The bottom line here, then, is that all the girls, despite being linguistically deprived up to, or well beyond, the hypothetical cut-off point of the GAM at around 4 years, were able to acquire the most advanced grammatical structures and to display evidence of a continuing ability to learn and apply grammatical rules until well into adolescence. Serena's case, in particular, demonstrates that language learning is possible even if linguistic deprivation continues until the age of 7;5. In terms of the behavioural evidence, therefore, Locke's theory would seem to be straightforwardly disconfirmed by each of the cases of Serena, Gabrielle and Ingrid.

Is there, however, any evidence of differences between the girls' levels of linguistic (and nonlinguistic) achievement relating to the age at which they were adopted? The detailed qualitative analyses of morphological and syntactic structures in the utterances of Serena, Gabrielle and Ingrid in Chapters 5 and 6 showed all three to be functioning linguistically at equally advanced levels despite their different ages at adoption. Furthermore, there did not appear to be anything in the test results in Chapter 4 which gave any clear indication of a possible correlation between age at adoption and linguistic progress later in life. There was no appreciable evidence either of a "slowing down" in linguistic progress with a later age of adoption or of a more general "slowing down" with chronological age as would be consistent with critical period effects. In other words, the standardized test results appear to provide no evidence of critical period-related influences on language development.

If the documented facts of linguistic performance by Serena, Gabrielle and Ingrid appear to directly confound the predictions of such a temporally restrictive critical period concept as Locke's, they cannot, however, constitute a definitive disconfirmation. For one thing, theoretical goalposts can always be moved: one could argue that the GAM may lay "dormant" if no linguistic input is received early on, to kick in later if and when language is encountered. However, since the explanatory attractiveness of the critical period concept ultimately depends on an unambiguous empirical correlation between linguistic behaviour and a well circumscribed time period, such concessions inevitably weaken the hypothesis, perhaps even to the point of unfalsifiability. If, on the other hand, we simply extend the critical period to puberty, as in Lenneberg (1967), then we have different problems. First of all, cases of linguistic deprivation involving such an extreme time frame are vanishingly rare and necessarily fraught with manifold complexities and imponderables (as in the Genie case discussed in Chapter 1), making any specific claims about language development highly tendentious, as Lenneberg himself emphasized. Secondly, to posit a whole 9-10 year chunk of life as a "critical period" is perhaps taking too much of a theoretical liberty to begin with. If we cannot say that our findings provide solid evidence *against* the critical period concept in principle, then, they certainly do not provide any evidence *for* it and appear to directly contradict at least one of the more time-restrictive critical period models. If the critical period concept did not already exist, there would be no reason to invent it on this evidence. One might add that the larger-scale studies of language development in internationally adopted children, reviewed in Chapter 1, have also failed to provide any evidence for a critical period for language (or any other cognitive domain).

In relation to the nativist position more generally, however, the situation is more complex. In theory, the critical period concept could be dropped wholesale from nativist doctrine, along with the idea of "language areas of the brain" or the "language gene", without giving up one's nativist credo (Everett, 2012). The more substantial arguments for nativism were based on claims about the specificity and abstractness of the grammatical knowledge underlying linguistic performance although, as discussed in Chapter 1, these claims are no longer viewed as credible by many, perhaps most, linguists today. In the end, then, an advocate of linguistic nativism could just argue that a Language Acquisition Device or Grammatical Analysis Mechanism simply starts when it can and goes on until it is no longer needed. From that point of view, the doctrine of modularity, with its putative "dissociations", is perhaps more crucial to nativism than Lenneberg's now rather outdated speculations.

Finally, we should acknowledge that we have no evidence at all which bears on the second clause in Locke's condition for falsification of his hypothesis, namely "that utterance analyses are taking place in the vicinity of the left perisylvian area" (Locke, 1997, p. 309). However, it is difficult to see how this particular stipulation can be taken seriously as a criterion. After all, if a person is ostensibly able to acquire and use language with what the theory says is the "wrong" part of the brain, that is, the right hemisphere, then so much the worse for the theory. In the case of Serena, Gabrielle and Ingrid, then, if it turned out that any of them, or all three, had actually acquired their advanced linguistic (and conversational) competence using right hemisphere resources, it would be reasonable to conclude that the left hemisphere has no inbuilt specialisation for language learning and that the issue of lateralization is, as Deacon (1999) argues, a red herring.

Question 2: conclusion

A detailed examination of the spontaneous spoken language of Serena, Gabrielle and Ingrid provided no evidence to support any formulation of the critical period hypothesis for language generally or for grammar more narrowly. On the contrary, it would seem that children who experience extreme global deprivation up to the age of 4 years and beyond can go on to acquire language by all the strictest criteria applied by any theory. First language learning can even begin at 7 years, as in Serena's case, and continue during puberty with some aspects of morphosyntactic production still being perfected at this age. Of course, this conclusion needs to be tempered in light of the fact that the extent of the social and linguistic neglect that Serena, Gabrielle and Ingrid each experienced cannot be validated unequivocally. It is possible that the children *may* have received sufficient communicative stimulation from particular caregivers for some aspects of language development to have taken place before adoption. In such a case, the girls' linguistic development might more properly be considered as second, rather than first, language learning, or at least as "second first-language acquisition" (Chapter 1). Nevertheless, all available evidence strongly suggests that such linguistic stimulation did not take place and that the girls, as in Rutter et al. (2010, p. 15), were "nonverbal in the Romanian language" when adopted.

It is important, therefore, not to let the critical period concept inform or colour our entire perspective on human development. We may agree that the age at which opportunities for learning can be taken, and the period of time spent in such positive conditions, are crucial factors in the life experience and development of a child without having to believe in a biologically determined "critical period" for a particular skill or cognitive accomplishment. Studies of the development of post-institutionalised children certainly bear out the effects of early global deprivation on all aspects of children's bodies and minds. But they also bear witness to the importance of what happens next for these children, as emphasised by Clarke and Clarke (2000), and to their ability and determination to move on with their lives.

8.2.3 Question 3

Do these three cases provide evidence of cognitive "modularity" in the shape of "dissociations" between linguistic and non-linguistic competencies or between different aspects of linguistic competence?

In terms of the linguistic abilities of Serena, Gabrielle and Ingrid as observed in naturalistic contexts, it was not possible to discern any evident disparities between aspects of their linguistic competence (lexical, semantic, pragmatic, syntactic) although, as noted, phonological skills were not looked at specifically. Thus, if analysis of the conversational data of Chapter 3 demonstrated sophisticated abilities in the semantic and pragmatic areas, then the analyses of the syntax of the girls' spontaneous utterances in Chapter 6 showed advanced grammatical competence of a kind which would be expected in older children and adolescents. The language test results reported in Chapter 4 offered no evidence of a clear pattern of within-language disparities between vocabulary and syntax or between semantic abilities and syntax. The differences in scores on a vocabulary test (British Picture Vocabulary Scale) and a syntax test (Test for Reception of Grammar) turned out not to be statistically significant.

We also noted that the scores of Serena, Gabrielle and Ingrid on a standardized test of productive syntax (Formulated Sentences, CELF-3) did not seem to reflect the degree of syntactic sophistication in their spontaneous speech. However, on closer inspection such tests are perhaps better characterized as exercises in metalinguistic knowledge, having to do with the capacity to reflect on and talk about language. Of course, one might still argue that difficulty in exercising metalinguistic judgements is itself indicative of a limitation or immaturity in grammatical competence. On that basis, there might possibly be some grounds, albeit faint, on which to propose a "dissociation" between "conversational abilities" relying on pragmatic knowledge on the one side and a syntactic ability connected with "metalinguistic knowledge" of grammar on the other. Against such a position, we have argued that the forms of metalinguistic awareness and judgement which the testing context requires of the child are neither a simple reflection of, nor are they continuous with, their linguistic competence in naturalistic non-test situations. Serena, Gabrielle and Ingrid clearly demonstrate "metalinguistic awareness" by their participation in everyday conversation where successful turn-taking depends on lightning calculation and anticipation of the communicative functions of others' utterances, as well as explicit use of names of utterance types ("question", "answer", "apology", etc). As Taylor and Shanker (2003) have argued, this kind of linguistic reflexivity is part and parcel of ordinary language use and is evident early on in children's linguistic behaviour. By contrast, some types of metalinguistic awareness depend on experience with *written language* forms and norms, including that most fundamental construct we call the "sentence". Thus, performance in tests of so-called productive syntax may, in fact, presuppose long experience in literate ways of handling and talking about language as opposed to linguistic competence per se. A number of studies of internationally adopted children reviewed in Chapter 1 also drew attention to the role of school-based language and metalinguistic concepts in the assessment of older adopted children's linguistic abilities.

A comparison of standardized language test data with the non-language data in Chapter 7 similarly offered no evidence for a hypothetical "dissociation" between linguistic and non verbal cognitive abilities since the girls' test performances in both areas were roughly at the same level in relation to those of age-matched participants. To the contrary, a close association was found between the girls' performances on a measure of visuo-spatial cognition (the Block Design test, WISC-III) and on a measure of expressive language ability (Expressive Language Score, CELF-3) with all scores on both tests at -3 SDs from the mean of their chronological age groups. This is the converse of the marked dissociation between spatial cognition and expressive language ability which has been claimed for children with Williams syndrome (Bellugi et al., 1993) and Down syndrome (Bellugi and Wang, 1996).

Since our findings would not appear to support a "modular" interpretation, they appear much more consistent with some of the alternative theoretical positions discussed in Chapter 1, including the Cognition Hypothesis, the Correlational Hypothesis and Neuroconstructivism. While neither the Cognition Hypothesis nor the Correlational Hypothesis can countenance the independence of linguistic and non-linguistic cognition, along with attendant "dissociations", Neuroconstructivist theory has made a significant further contribution by showing how specialised abilities are best seen as *outcomes* of development rather than as initial cognitive prespecifications. As Karmiloff-Smith (1999) suggests:

> "The long period of human postnatal cortical development, and the considerable plasticity it displays suggest that progressive modularisation may arise simply as a consequence of the developmental process… there is no need to invoke innate knowledge or representations to account for resulting specialization" (p.560).

Finally, the more radical linguistic approaches (Conversation Analysis, Clark's "coordination" approach and integrationism), would no doubt discount the very possibility of "dissociations" between language and non-linguistic cognition on the grounds that language is simply not a cognitive system at all, let alone an independent one: linguistic interaction in context always involves a complex, intelligent real-time synthesis of different bodily and mental skills and resources.

Question 3: conclusion

In sum, our findings lend no support to the Chomskyan "modular" position according to which language is independent of or dissociable from other areas of cognition. Nor was any evidence found to support the autonomy of any narrow linguistic subdomain. Other theoretical models of child development which reject nativist premises offer a more plausible fit with our findings. Nevertheless, we cannot claim to have provided definitive disconfirmation of the "modular" perspective. The three participants, Serena, Gabrielle and Ingrid in our study are not, as we explained, representative of the different experiences of Romanian adoptees or of the outcomes and achievements of all postinstitutionalized children.

8.3 Overview and implications for future research

Living in, and adapting to, severely impoverished environments over long periods of time clearly has profound consequences for subsequent development in all areas of life. For Serena, Gabrielle and Ingrid their early experiences afforded little more than the minimal conditions for physical survival. On the other hand, stimulating environments afforded rapid developmental gains. Thus the effects of early global deprivation on social development are, in principle, neither permanent nor irreversible; learning abilities are not irrevocably impaired by early adversity.

The obvious implication of such a finding is that the quality of the environment is crucial in encouraging – or discouraging – physical, emotional, social, cognitive and linguistic growth. But it also suggests that "the environment" must be understood in terms of the chances for action and interaction which the child may find or create rather than a static backdrop or "input" condition to which the child may only react. Thus, the interactional potential of the orphanage environment was close to nonexistent but when opportunities for interaction were opened up by the appearance of the adoptive families and wider social network (parents, siblings, friends, schools), Serena, Gabrielle and Ingrid immediately seized them and made the most of them; all their abilities began to blossom. Improvements in diet lead to improvements in physical health and growth. The family context and encounters with peers brought experience of social contact and collaboration leading to increasing skills in the areas of social relatedness, conversation and play. Similarly, the repeated opportunities that the children had to share talk with others were the motivation and training ground for the development of all aspects of linguistic communication.

The account we have given of the girls' progress and levels of achievement in language contributes, we hope, to addressing the "gaping hole" (Scott, Roberts and Glennen, 2011) in our understanding of the developmental progress of older postinstitutionalized and globally deprived children. It is also consistent with the more general, and generally positive, picture emerging from large-scale studies of postinstitutionalized and internationally adopted children. This body of work, as we have shown, affirms the resilience of children, younger and older, in the face of prolonged early deprivation. While suggesting that length of early deprivation (up to 6 months) is an important factor in children's speedy and successful catch-up with children of the same age

(Rutter et al., 2010), it provides no support for a fatalistic or deterministic interpretation of this temporal dividing line, nor does it offer any clear support to the critical period concept for language or for modularity. This work also shows the great unexplained variability in children's development and achievements after deprivation.

We hope that the approach we have adopted demonstrates the value of combining a wide range of methods of observation and analysis in the study of children with unusual histories. There are implications here for the way that educational and clinical practitioners assess progress in socially deprived children. Finding exceptional ways to assess children with exceptional histories may better inform methods of intervention and remediation in such cases but may also have implications for what is understood or assumed to be a "typical" child or "typical" developmental history.

There are also theoretical implications. First of all, the in-depth, qualitative study of the unique learning experiences and achievements of older deprived children might lead us to question some of our most fundamental assumptions about linguistic, social and cognitive development. Secondly, we might note that much of the alleged evidence for cognitive and within-language "dissociations" rests on the comparatively reduced scores on standardized language tests of various populations of participants, e.g., those with acquired brain lesions (Caramazza, Berndt and Basili, 1983) and Williams syndrome (Bellugi, Wang, and Jernigan, 1994). What is presented as evidence for a grammatical "impairment" may, then, be nothing of the kind and in fact turn out to have more to do with a particular kind of literacy-based metalinguistic awareness, as argued above. If we are right, it may be that cognitive "dissociations" are simply an artefact of research assumptions and methodology.

In terms of general recommendations or suggestions for ongoing or future research into the language development of postinstitutionalized chldren, we would emphasise:

1. the need for naturalistic, qualitative studies of linguistic communication having regard, as far as possible, to the particular history as well as the personalities and motivations of the children whose language is being studied;
2. the need to avoid the implicit pathologizing of the language development of globally deprived children by a discourse of "delay",

"difficulty" or "impairment" in relation to same-age children; taking "time since adoption" as a baseline may help to give necessary perspective on children's linguistic and psychological progress;

3. the need to exercise caution with respect to the use and interpretation of standardized test procedures;

4. the need to appreciate what it is like for older previously deprived children (and their families) to grow up in these unusual circumstances and how their attempts to find their place in the world (expressed in "developmental outcomes") are affected by coming from so far behind;

5. the need to recognize that theoretical understanding of language and language acquisition has now moved beyond the narrow biological determinism of the Chomskyan paradigm to foreground the cultural and interactional foundations of children's language learning.

BIBLIOGRAPHY

Alajouanine, T.H. and Lhermitte, F. (1965) Acquired aphasia in children. *Brain* 88, 653-662.

Ambridge, B. and Lieven, E.V.M. (2011) *Child language acquisition. Contrasting theoretical approaches.* Cambridge: Cambridge University Press.

Ames, E. and Carter, M. (1992) Development of Romanian orphanage children adopted to Canada. *Canadian Psychology* 99 (6), 444-453.

Bakhurst, D. and Shanker, S.G. (Eds.) (2001) *Jerome Bruner: language, culture, self.* London: Sage.

Balason, D. and Dollaghan, C. (2002) Grammatical morpheme production in 4 year old children. *Journal of Speech and Hearing Research* 45 (5), 961-970.

Batchelor, J. (1999) Adaptation to prolonged separation and loss in institutionalised children: Influences on the psychological capacities of adults "orphaned" throughout childhood. *Dissertation Abstracts International Section A: Humanities and Social Sciences* 59, 3205.

Bates, E. (1979) Intentions, conventions, and symbols. In E.Bates (Ed.), *The emergence of symbols: Cognition and communication in infancy.* New York: Academic Press, 69-140.

Bates, E., Benigni, L., Bretherton, I., Camaioni, L., and Volterra, V. (1977) *Cognition and communication from 9-13 months: A correlational study program on cognitive and perceptual factors in human development (Report No. 12).* Institute for the Study of Intellectual Behaviour. Boulder: University of Colorado.

Bates, E. and Goodman, J.C. (1997) On the inseparability of grammar and the lexicon: Evidence from acquisition, aphasia, and real time processing. *Language and Cognitive Processes* 12, 507-584.

Bates, E, and MacWhinney, B. (1979) The functionalist approach to the study of grammar. In E. Ochs and B. Schieffelin (Eds.) *Developmental Pragmatics.* New York: Academic Press.

Bateson, P. (1979) How do sensitive periods arise and what are they for? *Animal Behaviour* 27, 470-486.

Bavin E.L. (Ed.) (2009) *The Cambridge handbook of language.* Cambridge: Cambridge University Press.

Beckett, C., Castle, J., Rutter, M., and Sonuga-Barke, E.J. (2010) Institutional deprivation, specific cognitive functions, and scholastic achievement: English and Romanian Adoptee (ERA) Study findings. *Monographs of the Society for Research in Child Development* 75 (1), 125-142.

Bellugi, U., Lai, Z. and Wang, P.P. (1997) Language, communication, and neural systems in Williams syndrome. *Mental Retardation and Developmental Disabilities Research Reviews* 3, 334-342.

Bellugi, U., Lichtenberger, L., Jones, W., Lai, Z. and St George, M. (2001) The neurocognitive profile of Williams syndrome: A complex pattern of strengths and weaknesses. In U. Bellugi and M. St George (Eds.), *Journey from cognition to brain to gene: perspectives from Williams syndrome*. Cambridge, MA.: MIT Press, 1-42.

Bellugi, U., Marks, S., Bihrle, A. and Sabo, H. (1993) Dissociation between language and cognitive functions in Williams Syndrome. In D. Bishop and K. Mogford (Eds.), *Language in exceptional circumstances*. Hove: Lawrence Erlbaum, 177-189.

Bellugi, U. and Wang, P.P. (1996) Brain and cognition. In G. Adelman and B. Smith (Eds.), *Encyclopedia of Neuroscience*. Amsterdam: Elsevier Science.

Bellugi, U., Wang, P.P. and Jernigan, T.L. (1994) Williams syndrome: An unusual neuropsychological profile. In S. Broman and J. Grafman (Eds.), *Atypical cognitive deficits in developmental disorders: Implications for brain function*. Hillsdale, NJ: Lawrence Erlbaum, 23-56.

Benzzaquen, A. S. (2001) Kamala of Midnapore and Arnold Gesell's Wolf Child and Human Child: Reconciling the extraordinary and the normal. *History of Psychology* 4 (1), 59-78.

Bettelheim, B. (1959) Feral children and autistic children. *American Journal of Sociology* 44, 455-467.

Bishop, D.V.M. (1989a) Quantitative aspects of specific developmental disorders. In T. Munsat (Ed.) *Quantification of neurological deficit*. UK: Butterworths.

—. (1989b) *TROG: Test for Reception of Grammar, 2nd edition*. Abingdon, Oxon, UK: Medical Research Council.

Bloom, L. (1970) *Language development: Form and function of emerging grammars*. Cambridge, MA: MIT Press.

—. (1973) *One word at a time*. The Hague: Mouton.

Boatman, D., Freeman, J., Vining, E., Pulsifer, M., Miglioretti, D., Minahan, R., Carson, B., Brandt, J. and McKhann, G. (1999) Language recovery after left hemispherectomy in children with late-onset seizures. *Annals of Neurology* 46, 579-586.

Boccia, M.L. and Pedersen, C. (2001) Animal models of critical and sensitive periods in social and emotional development. In D.B. Bailey Jnr., J.T. Bruer, F.J. Symons and J.W. Lichtman (Eds.), *Critical thinking about critical periods*. Baltimore, MD: Paul H. Brookes Publishing Co., 107-127.

Boehm, A. (1986) *The Boehm Test of Basic Concepts*. New York: The Psychological Corporation.

Bookbinder, G.E. (2000) *Salford Sentence Reading Test*. London: Hodder and Stoughton.

Bowerman, M. (1973) Structural relationships in children's utterances: Syntactic or semantic? In T. Moore (Ed.), *Cognitive development and the acquisition of language*. New York: Academic Press, 197-213.

—. (1974) Learning and the structure of causative verbs: A study in the relationship of cognitive, semantic and syntactic development. *Stanford University Committee on Linguistics: Papers and Reports on Child Language Development* 8, 142-178.

Bowlby, J. (1951) *Maternal care and mental health*. Geneva: World Health Organization.

—. (1969) *Attachment and loss: Vol. 1. Attachment*. New York: Basic Books.

Brown, L.J. (2003) The effects of severe global deprivation on language and cognition. PhD Dissertation, University of Sheffield.

—. (2006) Bringing back the child: the development of language after extreme deprivation. Paper presented at the Child Language Seminar, University of Newcastle upon Tyne, July.

Brown, L.J. and Jones, P.E. (2008) Bringing back the child: psychological development after extreme deprivation. Paper presented at the British Pediatric Neurology Association Conference, Leeds, January.

Brown, L.J., Locke, J.L. and Jones, P.E. (1999) The effects of severe social deprivation on language and cognition. Poster presentation at the British Psychological Society Cognitive Section, University of York, September.

Brown, L.J., Locke, J.L., Jones, P.E. and Whiteside, S. (1998) Language development after the "critical period": a case study. *Proceedings of the Fifth International Conference on spoken language processing (Sydney, Australia)* 6, 2695-2698.

Brown, R. (1973) *A first language: the early stages*. London: George Allen and Unwin.

Bruner, J. (1974) Organization of early skilled action. In M. Richards (Ed.), *The integration of a child into a social world.* London: Cambridge University Press, 167-184.

—. (1975a) From communication to language: A psychological perspective. *Cognition* 3, 255-287.

—. (1975b) The ontogenesis of speech acts. *Journal of Child Language* 2, 1-20.

—. (1977) Early social interaction and language acquisition. In H.R. Schaffer (Ed.), *Studies in mother-infant interaction.* New York: Academic Press, 271-289.

Candland, D. K. (1993) *Feral children and clever animals.* London: Oxford University Press.

Caramazza, A., Berndt, R.S. and Basili, A.G. (1983) The selective impairment of phonological processing: a case study. *Brain and Language* 18, 128-174.

Carlson, M. (1997) Psychological and neuroendocrinological sequelae of early social deprivation in institutionalized children in Romania. *Annals of the New York Academy of Sciences* 807, 419-428.

Carlson, M. and Felton, E. (2000) Social ecology and the development of stress regulation. In L.R. Bergman, R.B. Cairns, R-G Nilsson and L. Nystedt (Eds.) *Developmental science and the holistic approach.* Hillsdale, NJ: Lawrence Erlbaum Associates, 229-247,

Cazden, C. (1968) The acquisition of noun and verb inflections. *Child Development* 39, 433-448.

Chapman, R.S.(1981) Computing mean length of utterance in morphemes. In J.F. Miller (Ed.), *Assessing language production in children: Experimental procedures.* Baltimore: University Park Press.

Chapman, R.S., Seung, H.K., Schwartz, S.E. and Kay-Raining Bird, E. (1998) Language skills of children and adolescents with Down syndrome II: Production deficits. *Journal of Speech, Language, and Hearing Research* 41, 861-873.

Chiang, J.S. and Costello, J. R. (1983) The acquisition of syntax in first and second language learning. *International Review of Applied Linguistics in Language Teaching* 21(1).

Children's Health Care Collaborative Study Group (1992) Romanian health and social care system for children and families: future directions in health care reform. *British Medical Journal* 304, 556-559.

Children's Health Care Collaborative Study Group (1994) The causes of children's institutionalisation in Romania. *Child Care and Health Development* 20, 77-88.

Chisholm, K. (1998) A three year follow-up of attachment and indiscriminate friendliness in children adopted from Romanian orphanages. *Child Development* 69, 1092-1106.

—. (2000) Attachment in children adopted from Romanian orphanages: Two case studies. In P.M. Crittenden and A.H. Claussen (Eds.), *The organization of attachment relationships: Maturation, culture, and context.* New York: Cambridge University Press.

Chisholm, K., Carter, M. C., Ames, E. W. and Morrison, S. J. (1995) Attachment security and indiscriminately friendly behaviour in children adopted from Romanian orphanages. *Development and Psychopathology* 7, 283-294.

Chomsky, N. (1957) *Syntactic structures.* The Hague: Mouton.

—. (1959) A Review of B.F. Skinner's "Verbal Behavior." *Language* 3, 26-58.

—. (1965) *Aspects of the theory of syntax.* Cambridge, Mass: MIT. Press.

—. (1981) *Lectures on government and binding.* Dordrecht: Foris.

Chugani, H.T., Behen, M.E., Muzik, O., Juhasz, C., Nagy, F. and Chugani, D.C. (2001) Local brain functional activity following early deprivation: a study of postinstitutionalized Romanian orphans. *Neuroimage* 14, 1290-1301.

Clahsen, H. and Almazen, M. (1998) Syntax and morphology in Williams syndrome. *Cognition* 68, 167-198.

Clark, E.V. (2009) *First language acquisition* (2nd edition) Cambridge: Cambridge University Press.

Clark, H. H. (1996) *Using Language.* Cambridge University Press: Cambridge.

Clarke, A.M. and Clarke, A. D. B. (1976) *Early experience: myth and evidence.* London: Open Books Publishing.

Clarke, A.M. and Clarke, A.D.B. (2000) *Early experience and the life path.* Bristol, US: Jessica Kingsley Publishers.

Colombo, J. (1982) The critical period concept: Research, methodology, and theoretical issues. *Psychological Bulletin* 91, 260-275.

Comrie, B. (2000) From potential to realization: an episode in the origin of language. *Linguistics* 38, 989-1004.

Croft, C., O'Connor, T., Keaveney, L., Groothues, C. and Rutter, M. (2001) Longitudinal change in parenting associated with developmental delay and catch-up. *Journal of Child Psychology and Psychiatry and Allied Disciplines* 42, 649-659.

Cromer, R.F. (1974) The development of language and cognition: the cognitive hypothesis. In B. Foss (Ed.), *New perspectives in child development.* Harmondsworth: Penguin, 184-252.

—. (1976 The cognitive hypothesis of language acquisition and its implications for child language deficiency. In D.M. Morehead and A.E. Morehead (Eds.), *Normal and deficient child language.* Baltimore: University Park Press, 283-333.

—. (1988) The cognitive hypothesis revisited. In F.S. Kessel (Ed.), *The development of language and language researchers: essays in honour of Roger Brown.* Hillsdale, NJ: Lawrence Erlbaum Associates.

Crystal, D. (1987) *Clinical linguistics.* London: Edward Arnold Publishers.

—. (1997a) *The Cambridge encyclopaedia of language (2nd ed.)* Cambridge: Cambridge University Press.

—. (1997b) *Rediscover grammar.* Harlow, Essex: Addison Wesley Longman Limited.

Curtiss, S. (1977) *Genie: A psycholinguistic study of a modern-day "wild child".* New York: Academic Press.

—. (1981) Dissociations between language and cognition: Cases and implications. *Journal of Autism and Developmental Disorders* 11, 15-30.

—. (1988a) The special talent of grammar acquisition. In L.K. Obler and D. Fein (Eds.), *The exceptional brain: The neuropsychology of talent and special abilities.* New York: The Guildford Press, 364-386.

Curtiss, S. (1988b) Abnormal language acquisition and the modularity of language. In F.J.Newmeyer (Ed.), *Linguistic theory: Extensions and implications. Linguistics: The Cambridge survey, Vol. 2.* New York: Cambridge University Press, 96-116.

Curtiss, S., Fromkin, V. and Krashen, S. (1978) Language development in the mature (minor) right hemisphere. *Journal of Applied Linguistics* 39-40, 23-27.

Curtiss, S., Fromkin, V., Rigler, M., Rigler, D. and Krashen, S. (1975) An update on the linguistic development of Genie. In D. Dato (Ed.), *Developmental psycholinguistics: Theory and applications.* Washington D.C.: Georgetown University Press, 145-153.

Curtiss, S and Yamada, J. (1981) Selectively intact grammatical development in the retarded child. *UCLA Working Papers in Cognitive Linguistics* 3, 87-120.

Davis, K. (1940) Extreme social isolation of a child. *American Journal of Sociology* 45, 554-565.

—. (1947) Final note on a case of extreme isolation. *American Journal of Sociology* 52, 432-437.

Deacon, T. (1999) *The symbolic species: the co-evolution of language and the human brain.* London: Penguin.

Dennis, W. (1973) *Children of the creche.* New York: Appleton-Century-Crofts.

Desmarais, C., Roeber, B. J., Smith, M.E. and Pollak, S. D. (2012) Sentence comprehension in postinstitutionalized school-age children. *Journal of Speech, Language, and Hearing Research* 55, 45-54.

Dodd, B. and Bradford, A. (2000) A comparison of three therapy methods for children with different types of developmental phonological disorder. *International Journal of Language and Communication Disorders* 35, 189–209.

Dore, J. (1974) A pragmatic description of early language development. *Journal of Psycholinguistic Research* 4, 423-30.

Douglas, J.E. and Sutton, A. (1978) The development of speech and mental processes in a pair of twins: a case study. *Journal of Child Psychology and Psychiatry* 19, 49-56.

Dunn, L.M., Dunn, L.M., Whetton, C. and Pintillie, D. (1982) *British Picture Vocabulary Scale (BPVS)* Berkshire, England: NFER-Nelson.

Elliott, C.D. (1996) *The British Ability Scales, Second Edition.* Windsor, Berkshire: NFER-Nelson.

Eimas, P.D. (1985) The perception of speech in early infancy. *Scientific American* 252, 34-40.

Elsabbagh, M. and Karmiloff-Smith, A. (2006) Modularity of mind and language. In K. Brown (Ed.), *The Encyclopedia of Language and Linguistics, Vol. 8.* Oxford: Elsevier, 218-224.

Emmorey, K. (2001) *Language, cognition, and the brain: Insights from sign language research.* Mahwah, NJ: Lawrence Erlbaum Associates.

Everett, D. (2012) *Language: the cultural tool.* London: Profile Books.

Feral Child (2014) *Wikipedia,* http://en.wikipedia.org/wiki/Feral_child.

Fisher, L., Ames, E.W., Chisholm, K. and Savoie, L. (1997) Problems reported by parents of Romanian orphans adopted to British Columbia. *International Journal of Behavioural Development* 20, 67-82.

Flege, J.E. (1999) Age of learning and second language speech. In D. Birdsong (Ed.), *Second language acquisition and the Critical Period Hypothesis. Second language acquisition research.* Mahwah, NJ: Lawrence Erlbaum Associates, 101-132.

Flint, B. (1978) *New hope for deprived children.* Toronto: University of Toronto Press.

Fitch, J. L., Williams, T. F. and Etienne, J. E. (1982) A community based high register for hearing loss. *Journal of Speech and Hearing Disorders* 47, 373-5.

Fodor, J. (1983) *The modularity of mind.* Cambridge, MA: MIT Press.

Forrest, K., Elbert, M. and Dinnsen, D. (2000) The effect of substitution patterns on phonological treatment outcomes. *Clinical Linguistics and Phonetics* 14, 519-531.

Foster-Cohen, S.H. (1999) *An introduction to child language development.* London: Longman.

Fowler, A.E. (1988) Determinants or rate of language growth in children with Down syndrome. In Lynn Nadel (Ed.), *The psychobiology of Down syndrome.* Cambridge, MA: MIT Press, 217-245.

—. (1990) Language abilities in children with Down syndrome: evidence for a specific syntactic delay. In D. Cicchetti and M. Beeghly (Eds), *Children with Down syndrome: A developmental perspective.* Cambridge: Cambridge University Press, 302-328.

Fujinaga, T., Kasuga, T., Uchida, N. and Hasataka, S. (1990) Long-term follow-up study of children developmentally retarded by early environmental deprivation. *Genetic, Social and General Psychology Monographs* 116, 37-104.

Gathercole, S. and Baddeley, A. (1996) *The Children's Test of Nonword Repetition.* London: The Psychological Corporation/Harcourt Brace Jovanovich.

Genesee, F. (1981) A comparison of early and late second language learning. *Canadian Journal of Behavioural Science* 13, 115-128.

Genie (feral child) (2013) *Wikipedia,* http://en.wikipedia.org/wiki/Genie_(feral_child)

Geren, J., Snedeker, J. and Ax, L. (2005) Starting over: a preliminary study of early lexical and syntactic development in internationally adopted pre-schoolers. *Seminars in Speech and Language* 26 (1), 44-53.

Gindis, B. (2005) Cognitive, language, and educational issues of children adopted from overseas orphanages. *Journal of Cognitive Education and Psychology* 4 (3), 290-315.

Gleitman, H. (1995) *Psychology (4th ed.)* New York: W.W. Norton and Co, Inc.

Glennen, S. (2002) Language development and delay in international adoption: a review. *American Journal of Speech-Language Pathology* 11: 333-339.

—. (2007a) Predicting language outcomes for internationally adopted children. *Journal of Speech, Language, and Hearing Research* 50, 529-548.

—. (2007b) Language and the older adopted child: understanding second language learning. In J. Macleod and S. Macrae (Eds.) *Adoption parenting: creating a toolbox, building connections.* Warren, NJ: EMK Press, 106-109.

—. (2008) Speech and language "mythbusters" for internationally adopted children. *ASHA Leader*, December 16, 2008.

Glennen, S. and Masters, G. (2002) Typical and atypical language development in infants and toddlers adopted from Eastern Europe. *American Journal of Speech-Language Pathology* 11, 417-433.

Goldfarb, W. (1943) The effects of early institutional care on adolescent personality. *Journal of Experimental Education* 12, 106-129.

—. (1945) Effects of psychological deprivation in infancy and subsequent stimulation. *American Journal of Psychiatry* 102, 18-33.

—. (1947) Variations in adolescent adjustment of institutionally-reared children. *American Journal of Orthopsychiatry* 17, 449-457.

—. (1955) Emotional and intellectual consequences of psychological deprivation in infancy: A revaluation. In P. Hoch and J. Zubin (Eds.), *Psychopathology of childhood.* New York: Grune and Stratton, 105-119.

Goldfarb, W. and Klopfer, B. (1944) Rorschach characteristics of "institution children". *Rorschach Research Exchange* 8, 92-100.

Groza, V. and Ryan, S.D. (2002) Pre-adoption stress and its association with child behaviour in domestic special needs and international adoptions. *Psychoneuroendocrinology* 27, 181-197.

Groza, V. and Ileana, D. (1996) A follow-up study of adopted children from Romania. *Child and Adolescent Social Work Journal* 13, 541-565.

Gunnar, M.R., Morison, S.J., Chisholm, K. and Schuder, M. (2001) Salivary cortisol levels in children adopted from Romanian orphanages. *Development and Psychopathology* 13, 611-628.

Gutiérrez-Clellen, V.F. (1999) Language choice in intervention with bilingual children. *American Journal of Speech-Language Pathology* 8, 291-302.

Halliday, M.A.K. (1978) *Language as social semiotic.* London: Edward Arnold.

—. (1989) *Spoken and written language* (2nd ed). London: Oxford University Press.

Handlederry, M., Marcovitch, S., Godberg, S., McGregor, D., Gold, A., Washington, J. and Krekewich, K. (1995) Determinants of behaviour in internationally adopted Romanian children. *Journal of Developmental and Behavioural Paediatrics* 16, 300-301.

Harris, R. (1981) *The language myth.* London: Duckworth.

—. (1996) *Signs, language and communication.* London: Routledge.

Hess, C. W. and Thompson, C. F. (1996) Measuring linguistic development in a child adopted from Romania. *Perceptual and Motor Skills* 3, 944-946.

Hoff, E. (2001) *Language development* (2nd ed.). Belmont, CA: Wadsworth/Thomson Learning.

Howlin, P. and Cross, P. (1995) The variability of language test scores in 3 and 4 year old children of normal non-verbal intelligence: A brief research report. *European Journal of Disorders of Communication* 29, 279-288.

Hunt, K.W. (1965) *Grammatical structures written at three grade levels* (Research Report No. 3) Champaign, IL: National Council of Teachers of English.

Ioup, G., Boustagui, E., El Tigi, M. and Mosello, M. (1994) Re-examining the Critical Period Hypothesis: A case study of successful adult second language acquisition in a naturalistic environment. *Studies in Second Language Acquisition* 16-17, 73-96.

Johnson, A.K. and Groza, V. (1993) The orphaned and institutionalized children of Romania. *Journal of Emotional and Behavioural Problems* 2, 49-52.

Johnson, D.E. (2000) Medical and developmental sequelae of early childhood institutionalisation. In C.A. Nelson (Ed.), *The Minnesota symposia on child psychology, Vol 31: The effects of early adversity on neurobehavioural development*. Hillsdale, NJ: Lawrence Erlbaum, 113-162.

Johnson, D. E., Miller, L. C., Iverson, S., Thomas, W., Franchino, B., Dole, K., Kiernan, M.T., Georgieff, M. K. and Hostetter, M. K. (1992) The health of children adopted from Romania. *JAMA* 268, 3446-51.

Johnson, J. S. and Newport, E. L. (1989) Critical period effects in second language learning: The influence of maturational state on the acquisition of English as second language. *Cognitive Psychology* 21, 60-99.

Johnson, J. S., and Newport, E. L. (1991) Critical period effects on universal properties of language: The status of subjacency in the acquisition of a second language. *Cognition* 39, 215-258.

Johnson, J. S., and Newport, E. L. (1996) Critical period effects in second language learning: the influence of maturational state on the acquisition of English as a second language. In M.H. Johnson (Ed.), *Brain Development and Cognition: A Reader*. Oxford, UK: Blackwell Publishers Ltd.

Jones, P.E. (1995) Contradictions and unanswered questions in the Genie case: A fresh look at the linguistic evidence. *Language and Communication* 15, 261-280.

—. (2003) Critical realism and scientific method in Chomsky's linguistics. In J. Cruickshank (Ed.), *Critical Realism. The difference that it makes.* London: Routledge, 90-107.

Kaler, S. R. and Freeman, B. J. (1994) Analysis of environmental deprivation: Cognitive and social development of Romanian orphans. *Journal of Child Psychology and Psychiatry and Allied Disciplines* 35, 769-781.

Karmiloff-Smith, A. (1979) Language development after five. In P. Fletcher and M. Garman (Eds.), *Language Acquisition.* Cambridge: Cambridge University Press, 307-322.

—. (1992) *Beyond modularity: A developmental perspective on cognitive science.* Cambridge, MA: MIT Press/Bradford Books.

—. (1998) Development itself is the key to understanding developmental disorders. *Trends in Cognitive Sciences* 2, 389-398.

—. (1999) Modularity of mind. In R.A. Wilson and F. Keil (Eds.), *MIT Encyclopedia of cognitive sciences.* Cambridge, MA: MIT Press/ Bradford Books.

—. (2001) Why babies' brains are not Swiss Army knives. In H. Rose and S. Rose (Eds.), *Alas poor Darwin: Arguments against evolutionary psychology.* London: Vintage, 173-188.

Kinsbourne, M. and Smith, W.L. (Eds.) (1974) *Hemispheric disconnection and cerebral function.* Springfield, Ill: Charles C. Thomas.

Koluchova, J. (1972) Severe deprivation in twins: A case study. *Journal of Child Psychology and Psychiatry* 13, 107-114.

—. (1976) The further development of twins after severe and prolonged deprivation: A second report. *Journal of Child Psychology and Psychiatry* 17, 181-188.

—. (1979) An experience of deprivation: A follow-up study. In J.G. Howells (Ed.), *Modern perspectives in psychiatry of infancy.* New York: Brunner/Mazel, 112-116.

—. (1991) Severely deprived twins after 22 years of observation. *Studia Psychologica* 33, 23-28.

Krashen, S. (1973) Lateralization, language learning and the critical period: Some new evidence. *Language Learning* 23, 63-74.

Krashen, S. and Harshman, R. (1972) Lateralization and the critical period. *UCLA Working Papers in Phonetics* 23, 13-21.

Kreppner, J.M., Rutter, M., Beckett, C., Castle, J.,Colvert, E., Groothues, C., Hawkins, A., O'Connor, T.G., Stevens, S., and Sonuga-Barke, E.J.

(2007) Normality and impairment following profound early institutional deprivation: a longitudinal follow-up into early adolescence. *Developmental Psychology* 43, 4: 931-946.

Kuhl, P. K., Williams, K. A. and Lacerda, F. (1992) Linguistic experience alters phonetic perception in infants by 6 months of age. *Science* 255, 606-608.

Lane, H. (1976) *The wild boy of Aveyron.* Cambridge, Mass.: Harvard University Press.

Lenneberg, E. (1964) The capacity for language acquisition. In J.A. Fodor and J.J. Katz (Eds.), *The structure of language: readings in the philosophy of language.* Englewood Cliffs, NJ: Prentice-Hall, 579-603.

—. (1967) *Biological foundations of language.* New York: Wiley.

—. (1968) The effect of age on the outcome of central nervous system disease in children. In R. Isaacson (Ed.), *The neuropsychology of development.* New York: John Wiley and Sons.

Levinson, S.C. (1983) *Pragmatics.* Cambridge: Cambridge University Press.

Levinson, S.C. (Ed.) (2006) *Roots of human sociality: culture, cognition and interaction.* Oxford: Berg.

Loban, W. (1976) *Language development: Kindergarten through grade twelve.* (Research report No. 18) Champaign, IL: National Council of Teachers of English.

Locke, J.L. (1992a) Thirty years of research on developmental neurolinguistics. *Pediatric Neurology* 8, 245-50.

—. (1992b) Neural specialization for language: a developmental perspective. *Seminars in the Neurosciences* 4, 425-431.

—. (1993) *The child's path to spoken language.* Cambridge, MA: Harvard University Press.

—. (1994a) Gradual emergence of developmental language disorders. *Journal of Speech and Hearing Research* 37, 608-616.

—. (1994b) Phases in the child's development of language. *American Scientist* 82, 136-145.

—. (1995) Development of the capacity for spoken language. In P. Fletcher and B. MacWhinney (Eds.), *The handbook of child language.* Cambridge, MA: Basil Blackwell, 278-302.

—. (1997) A theory of neurolinguistic development. *Brain and Language* 58, 265-326.

—. (1999a) First communion: The emergence of vocal relationships. Paper prepared for the Conference on Emotion and Communication, Emory University, Atlanta, Georgia, March, 1999.

—. (1999b) Towards a biological science of language development. In M. Barrett (Ed.), *The development of language. Studies in developmental psychology*. Philadelphia: Psychology Press/Taylor and Francis.

Macavei, E. (1986) The consequences of the separation from the family on the child's psycho-social development. *Revista de Psihologie* 32, 44-53.

MacWhinney, B. and Snow, C.E. (1985) The Child Language Data Exchange System: An update. *Journal of Child Language* 17, 457-472.

MacWhinney, B. (1995) Computational analysis of interactions. In P. Fletcher and B. MacWhinney (Eds.), *The handbook of child language*. Oxford: Basil Blackwell, 152-178.

Malson, L. (1972) *Wolf children and the Wild Boy of Aveyron*. London: New Left Books.

Maratsos, M. and Chalkley, M.A. (1980) The internal language of children's syntax: the nature and ontogenesis of syntactic categories. In K. Nelson (Ed.), *Children's Language*. New York: Gardner, 127-214.

Marcus, G.F., Pinker, S., Ullman, M., Hollander, M., Rosen, T.J. and Xu F. (1992) Overregularization in language acquisition. *Monographs of the Society for Research in Child Development* 57.

Marcus, G.F. (1995) Children's overregularization of English plurals: A quantitative analysis. *Journal of Child Language* 22, 447-459.

Marcotte, A.C. and Morere, D.A. (1990) Speech lateralization in deaf populations: Evidence for a developmental critical period. *Brain and Language* 39, 134-152.

Mason, M.K. (1942) Learning to speak after six and one half years of silence. *Journal of Speech and Hearing Disorders* 7, 295-304.

Mayberry, R. I. (1993) First language acquisition after childhood differs from second-language acquisition: The case of American Sign Language. *Journal of Speech and Hearing Research* 36, 1258-1270.

McMullan, S. J., and Fisher, L. (1992) Developmental progress of Romanian orphanage children in Canada (Abstract) *Canadian Psychology* 33, 504.

McNeil, M. C., Polloway, E. A. and Smith, J. D. (1984) Feral and isolated children: Historical review and analysis. *Education and Training of the Mentally Retarded* 19, 70-79.

Meacham, A.N. (2006) Language learning and the internationally adopted child. *Early Childhood Education Journal* 34 (1), 73-79.

Menn, L. and Stoel-Gammon, C. (1995) Phonological development. In P. Fletcher and B. MacWhinney (Eds.), *The handbook of child language*. Oxford: Basil Blackwell, 335-360.

Merz, E.C. and McCall, R.B. (2010) Behavior problems in children adopted from psychosocially depriving institutions. *Journal of Abnormal Child Psychology* 38, 459–470.

Miller, J.F. (Ed.) (1981) *Assessing language production in children.* Baltimore: University Park Press.

Moltz, H. (1973) Some implications of the critical period hypothesis. *Annals of the New York Academy of Sciences* 223, 144-146.

Morrison, S.J., Ames, E.W., and Chisholm, K. (1995) The development of children adopted from Romanian orphanages. *Merrill Palmer Quarterly* 41, 411-430.

Nelson, K. (1996) *Language in cognitive development. Emergence of the mediated mind.* Cambridge: Cambridge University Press.

Neville, H.J., Mills, D.L. and Lawson, D.S. (1992) Fractionating language: Different neural subsystems with different sensitive periods. *Cerebral Cortex* 2, 244-258.

Newport, E.L. (1990) Maturational constraints on language learning. *Cognitive Science* 14, 11-28.

—. (1991) Contrasting concepts of the critical period for language. In S. Carey and R. Gelman (Eds.), *The epigenesis of mind: Essays on biology and cognition. The Jean Piaget Symposium Series.* Hillsdale, NJ: Lawrence Erlbaum Associates, 111-132.

Newton, M. and Thomson, M. (1976) *Aston Index.* Wisbech, Cambs: Learning Developmental Aids.

Nicole, S. (1979) Kaspar Hausar's recovery and autopsy: A perspective on neurological development and sociological requirements for language development. *Annual progress in Child Psychiatry and Child Development,* 215-224.

Obler, L.K. and Hannigan, S. (1996) Neurolinguistics of second language acquisition and use. In W. C. Ritchie and T. K. Bhatia (Eds.), *Handbook of second language acquisition.* San Diego: Academic Press, 509-523.

O'Connor, N. and Hermelin B. (1991) A specific linguistic ability. *American Journal on Mental Retardation* 95, 203-215.

O'Connor, T and Rutter, M. (2000) Attachment disorder behaviour following early severe deprivation: Extension and longitudinal follow-up. *Journal of the American Academy of Child and Adolescent Psychiatry* 39, 703-712.

O'Connor, T.G., Rutter, M., Beckett, C., Keaveney, L. and Kreppner, J.M. (2000) The effects of global severe privation on cognitive competence: Extension and longitudinal follow-up. *Child Development* 71, 376-390.

O'Donnell, R.C., Griffin W.J. and Norris, R.D. (1967) *Syntax of kindergarten and elementary school children: A transformational analysis.* (Research Report No. 8) Champaign, IL: National Council of Teachers of English.

Oyama, S. (1976) A sensitive period for the acquisition of a non-native phonological system. *Journal of Psycholinguistic Research* 5, 261-283.

—. (1979) The concept of the sensitive period in developmental studies. *Merrill-Palmer Quarterly* 25, 83-103.

Patkowski, M. S. (1980) The sensitive period for the acquisition of syntax in a second language. *Language Learning* 30, 449-472.

Paul, R. (1981) Analyzing complex sentence development. In J.F. Milller (Ed.), *Assessing language production in children.* Baltimore: University Park Press, 36-40.

Penfield, W. and Roberts, L.(1963) Speech and Brain Mechanisms. Princeton, New Jersey: Princeton University Press.

Perkins, M. (1999) *Syntax workbook.* Department of Human Communication Sciences, University of Sheffield, UK.

—. (2003) Negotiating repair in aphasic conversation: Interactional issues. In C. Goodwin (Ed.) *Conversation and brain damage.* New York: Oxford University Press, 147-162.

Perera, K. (1984) *Children's writing and reading.* London: Basil Blackwell.

Peters, A. (1995) Strategies in the acquisition of syntax. In P. Fletcher and B. MacWhinney (Eds.), *The handbook of child language.* Oxford: Basil Blackwell, 462-482.

Piaget, J. (1926) *The language and thought of the child.* New York: Harcourt Brace.

—. (1951) *Play, dreams, and imitation in childhood.* New York: Norton.

Pinker, S. (1984) *Language learnability and language development.* Cambridge, MA: Harvard University Press.

—. (1989) *Learnability and cognition: The acquisition of argument structure.* Cambridge, MA: MIT Press.

—. (1991) Rules of language. *Science* 253, 530-555.

—. (1994) *The language instinct.* Harmondsworth: Penguin.

—. (1995) Why the child holded the baby rabbits: A case study in language acquisition. In L. Gleitman, and M. Lieberman (Eds.), *Invitation to cognitive science, 2nd Edition. Volume 1: Language.* Cambridge, MA: MIT Press, 135-182.

—. (1999) *Words and rules: The ingredients of language.* London: Weidenfeld and Nicolson.

Plunkett, K. (1995) Connectionist approaches to language acquisition. In P. Fletcher and B. MacWhinney (Eds.), *The handbook of child language*. Oxford: Basil Blackwell, 36-72.

Prakash, P. (1984) Second language acquisition and the critical period hypothesis. *Psycho Lingua* 14, 13-17.

Provence, S. and Lipton, R.C. (1962) *Infants in institutions*. New York: International Universities Press.

Quirk, R., Greenbaum, S., Leech, G. and Svartik., J. (1985) *A comprehensive grammar of the English language*. London: Longman Publishers Ltd.

Raczaszek-Leonardi, J. and Cowley, S.J. (Eds.) (2012) *Language as social coordination: an evolutionary perspective*. Special Issue of *Interaction Studies*, 13 (1)

Ralph, M. (1994) Realising the rights of institutionalised Romanian children. *Educational and Child Psychology* 11, 35-44.

Raven, J.C., Court, J.H. and Raven, J. (1978) *Coloured Progressive Matrices (CPM)* London: UK: The Psychological Corporation.

Renfrew, C.E. (1988) *Action Picture Test* (2nd ed.). Oxford: C.E. Renfrew.

—. (1991) *Bus Story Test. A Test of Narrative Speech*. Oxford: Winslow Press Limited.

—. (1992) *The Word Finding Vocabulary Scale*. Oxford: C.E. Renfrew.

Richardson, B.L. and Wuillemin, D.B. (1981) Critical periods for the transmission of tactual information. *International Journal of Rehabilitation Research* 4, 175-179.

Romaine, S. (1984) *The language of children and adolescents*. Oxford: Basil Blackwell.

Rondal, J.A. (1995) *Exceptional language development in Down syndrome: Implications for the cognition-language relationship*. Cambridge: Cambridge University Press.

Rosenberg, D.R., Pajer, K. and Rancurello, M. (1992) Neuropsychiatric assessment of orphans in one Romanian orphanage for "unsalvageables". *JAMA* 268, 3489-90.

Ruben, R.J. (1997) A time frame of critical/sensitive periods of language development. *Acta Oto-Laryngologica* 117, 202-205.

Ruben, R.J. and Schwartz, R. (1999) Necessity versus sufficiency: the role of input in language acquisition. *International Journal of Pediatric Otorhinolaryngology* 47, 137-140.

Rumelhart, D.E. and McClelland, J.L. (1986) On learning the past tenses of English verbs. In J.L. McClelland, D.E. Rumelhart and the PDP Research Group (Eds.), *Parallel distributed processing: Explorations in the microstructure of cognition. Vol. 2. Psychological and biological models.* Cambridge, MA: Bradford Books/MIT Press, 216-271.

Rutter, M., Andersen-Wood, L., Beckett, C., Bredenkamp, D., Castle, J., Groothues, C., Kreppner, J., Keavney, L., Lord, C., O'Connor, T.G. and English and Romanian Adoptees study team. (1999) Quasi-autistic patterns following severe early global privation. *Journal of Child Psychology and Psychiatry and Allied Disciplines* 40, 537-549.

Rutter, M.L., Kreppner, J., O'Connor, T.G. and English and Romanian Adoptees (ERA) study team. (2001) Specificity and heterogeneity in children's responses to profound institutional privation. *British Journal of Psychiatry* 179, 97-103.

Rutter, M. and Sonuga-Barke, E.J. (2010) Conclusions: overview of findings from the ERA study, inferences, and research implications. *Monographs of the Society for Research in Child Development* 75 (1), 212-229.

Rutter, M., Sonuga-Barke, E.J., Beckett, C., Castle, J., Kreppner, J., Kumsta, R., Schlotz, W., Stevens, S., Bell, C.A. and Gunnar, M. (2010) Deprivation-specific psychological patterns: effects of institutional deprivation. *Monographs of the Society for Research in Child Development* 75 (1), 1-229.

Rutter, M., Sonuga-Barke, E.J. and Castle, J. (2010) Investigating the impact of early institutional deprivation on development: background. *Monographs of the Society for Research in Child Development* 75 (1), 1-20.

Rymer, R. (1993) *Genie: Escape from a silent childhood.* London: Michael Joseph.

Sacks, H., Schegloff, E.A. and Jefferson, G. (1974) A simplest systematics for the organization of turn-taking for conversation. *Language* 50 (4) 696-735.

Sanchez, M.M., Ladd, C. and Plotsky, P.M. (2001) Early adverse experience as a developmental risk factor for later psychopathology: Evidence from rodent and primate models. *Development and Psychopathology* 13, 419-449.

Schiff-Meyers, N. (1992) Considering arrested language development and language loss in the assessment of second language learners. *Language, Speech, and Hearing Services in Schools* 23, 28-33.

Schoenbrodt, L.A., Carran, D.T. and Preis, J. (2007) A study to evaluate the language development of post-institutionalized children adopted from Eastern European countries. *Language, Culture and Curriculum* 20 (1), 52-69.

Scott, C.M. (1984a) Adverbial connectivity in conversations of children 6 to 12. *Journal of Child Language* 11, 423-452.

—. (1984b) What happened in that: Structural characteristics of school children's narratives. Paper presented at the Annual Convention of the American Speech-Language-Hearing Association, San Francisco, CA.

—. (1987) Summarizing text: Context effects in language-disordered children. Paper presented at the First International Symposium, Specific Language Disorders in Children, University of Reading, England.

—. (1988) Spoken and written syntax. In M.A. Nippold (Ed.), *Later language development: Ages nine through nineteen.* Boston: College-Hill Press, 41-91.

Scott, C.M. and Rush, D. (1985) Teaching adverbial connectivity: Implications from current research. *Child Language Teaching and Therapy* 1, 264-280.

Scott, K.A., Roberts, J.A. and Glennen, S. (2011) How well do children who are internationally adopted acquire language? A meta-analysis. *Journal of Speech, Language, and Hearing Research* 54, 1153-1169.

Scovel, T. (1988) *A time to speak: A psycholinguistic inquiry into the critical period for human speech.* New York: Newbury House.

Semel, E., Wiig, E.H. and Secord, W.A. (1995) *Clinical Evaluation of Language Fundamentals* (3rd ed.). London: The Psychological Corporation/Harcourt Brace Jovanovich.

Serbetcioglu M.B. (2001) Critical learning period for speech acquisition and screening techniques in early detection of hearing impairment. *The Turkish Journal of Pediatrics* 43, 128-132.

Serbin, L.A. (1997) Research on international adoption: Implications for developmental theory and social policy. *International Journal of Behavioral Development* 20, 83-92.

Simon, N. (1979) Kaspar Hausar's recovery and autopsy: A perspective on neurological development and sociological requirements for language development. *Annual Progress in Child Psychiatry and Child Development,* 215-224.

Singh, J.A.L. and Zingg, R.M. (1939) *Wolf-children and feral man.* New York: Harper and Brothers.

Singh, O.P. (2001) Developmental quality analysis of the whole responses (W) among the Rorschach protocols of institutionalised children. *Journal of Personality and Clinical Studies* 17, 45-49.

Skeels, H.M. (1937) A cooperative orphanage research. *Journal of Educational Research* 30, 437-444.

—. (1945) A follow-up study of children in adoptive homes. *The Journal of Genetic Psychology* 66, 21-58.

—. (1965) Effects of adoption on children from institutions. *Children* 12, 33-34.

—. (1966) Adult status of children with constrasting early life experiences. *Monograph of the Society for Research in Child Development* 31.

Skeels, H.M. and Harms, I. (1948) Children with inferior social histories: their mental development in adoptive homes. *The Journal of Genetic Psychology* 72, 283-294.

Skodak, M. and Skeels, H.M. (1947) A follow-up study of the mental development of one hundred adopted children in Iowa. *The American Psychologist* 278.

Skodak, M. and Skeels, H.M. (1949) A final follow-up study of one hundred adopted children. *The Journal of Genetic Psychology* 75, 85-125.

Skuse, D. (1984a) Extreme deprivation in early childhood I. Diverse outcomes for three siblings from an extraordinary family. *Journal of Child Psychology and Psychiatry* 25, 523-541.

—. (1984b) Extreme deprivation in early childhood II. Theoretical issues and a comparative review. *Journal of Child Psychology and Psychiatry* 25, 543-572.

Smith-Lock, K.M. (1993) Morphological analysis and the acquisition of morphology and syntax in specifically-language-impaired children. *Haskins Laboratories Status Report on Speech Research,* SR-144, 113-138.

Snedeker, J., Geren, J., and Shafto, C.L. (2007) Starting over. International adoption as a natural experiment in language development. *Psychological Science* 18 (1), 79-87.

Snedeker, J., Geren, J., and Shafto, C.L. (2012) Disentangling the effects of cognitive development and linguistic expertise: A longitudinal study of the acquisition of English in internationally-adopted children. *Cognitive Psychology* 65, 39-76.

Snow, C.E. (1972) Mothers' speech to children learning language. *Child Development* 43, 549-565.

—. (1977) Mothers' speech research: from input to interaction. In C.E. Snow and C.A. Ferguson (Eds.), *Talking to children: language input and acquisition.* Cambridge: Cambridge University Press, 31-49.

Snow, C.E., and Hoefnagel-Hohle, M. (1978) The critical period for language acquisition: Evidence from second language learning. *Child Development* 49, 1114-1128.

Spitz, R.A. (1945) Hospitalism: An inquiry into the genesis of psychiatric conditions in early childhood. *The Psychoanalytic Study of the Child* 1, 53-73.

—. (1946) Hospitalism: A follow-up report on investigations described in volume I, 1945. *The Psychoanalytic Study of the Child* 2, 113-117.

St. James-Roberts, I. (1981) A reinterpretation of hemispherectomy data without functional plasticity of the brain: I. Intellectual function. *Brain and Language* 13, 31-53.

Stackhouse, J., and Wells, W. (1997) *Children's speech and literacy difficulties: A psycholinguistic framework.* London: Whurr.

Stromswold, K. (1995) The cognitive and neural bases of language acquisition. In M. Gazzaniga (Ed.), *The cognitive neurosciences.* Cambridge, MA: The MIT Press, 855-870.

Taylor, T.J. and Shanker, S.G. (2003) Rethinking language acquisition: what children learn. In H. Davis and T.J. Taylor (Eds.), *Rethinking linguistics.* London: Routledge, 151-170.

Thomas, M.S.C. and Karmiloff-Smith, A. (2002). Are developmental disorders like cases of adult brain damage? Implications for connectionist modelling. *Behavioural and Brain Sciences* 25, 727–788.

Thomspon, S.L. (2001) The social skills of previously institutionalised children adopted from Romania. *Dissertations Abstracts International: Section B: the Sciences and Engineering* 61, 3906.

Tomasello, M. (1999) *The cultural origins of human cognition.* Cambridge, MA: Harvard University Press.

—. (2003) *Constructing a language: a usage-based theory of language acquisition.* Cambridge, MA: Harvard University Press.

Trask, R.L. (1999) *Language: the basics.* (2nd ed.). London: Routledge.

Ullman, M.T. (1993) *The computation of inflectional morphology.* Cambridge, MA.: MIT Press.

van der Lely, H.K.J., Rosen, S. and McClelland, A. (1998) Evidence for a grammar specific deficit in children. *Current Biology* 8, 1253-1258.

van der Lely, H.K.J. and Ullman, M. (1996) The computation and representation of past tense morphology in specifically language impaired and normally developing children. In A. Stringfellow, D. Cahana-Amitay, E. Hughs and A. Zubowsiki (Eds.), *Proceedings of the Twentieth Annual Boston University Conference on Language Development.* Vol. 2. Somerville, MA: Cascadilla Press, 804-815.

Vargha-Khadem, P., Carr, L.J., Isaacs, E., Brett, E., Adams, C. and Mishkin, M. (1997) Onset of speech after left hemispherectomy in a nine-year-old boy. *Brain* 120, 159-182.

Vicari, S., Caselli, M.C. and Tonucci, F. (2000) Asynchrony of lexical and morphosyntactic development in children with Down Syndrome. *Neuropsychologia* 38, 634-644.

Vigilante, V. (1993) Caring for the Romanian orphans. *Rhode Island Medical Journal* 76 (3), 135-138.

Vygotsky, L.S. (1962) *Thought and language.* Cambridge, MA: MIT Press and Wiley.

Wada, J.A. and Davis, A.E. (1977) Fundamental nature of human infant's brain asymmetry. *The Canadian Journal of Neurological Sciences* 4, 203-207.

Wechsler, D. (1992) *Wechsler Intelligence Scale for Children* (3rd ed). Sidcup, Kent: Psychological Corporation.

Whitworth, A., Perkins, L. and Lesser, R. (1997) *Conversation Analysis profile for people with aphasia,* London: Whurr.

Wiig, E.H., Secord, W. and Semel, E. (1992) *Clinical Evaluation of Language Fundamentals-Preschool.* London: The Psychological Corporation/Harcourt Brace Jovanovich.

Wilson, S.L. (2003) Post-institutionalization: the effects of early deprivation on development of Romanian adoptees. *Child and Adolescent Social Work Journal* 20 (6), 473-483.

Wolf-Nelson, N. (1993) *Child language disorders in context: Infancy through adolescence* . New York: MacMillan.

Wuillemin, D., Richardson, B., and Lynch, J. (1994) Right hemisphere involvement in processing later-learned languages in multilinguals. *Brain and Language* 46, 620-636.

Yamada, J. and Curtiss, S. (1981) The relationship between language and cognition in a case of Turner's syndrome. *UCLA Working Papers in Cognitive Linguistics* 3, 93-115.

Yamada, J. (1990) *Laura: A case for the modularity of language.* Cambridge, MA: MIT Press.

Index of Names

SUBJECT INDEX